Advance Praise for
Stories at the Center

"Eric tells stories of love, pain, persistence, and joy like the true songwriter he is. Your heart, like mine, will be moved."

—John Oates, Rock & Roll Hall of Fame inductee, Songwriters Hall of Fame member, and author of *Change of Seasons: A Memoir*

"Eric's book is delightful. Fun, entertaining, and thoughtful. He has a gift for finding humor in life's most difficult challenges—and seeming to come out ahead. It's a journey through faith, family, and never losing sight of your dreams."

—Ray Stevens, two-time Grammy Award Winner, member of the Country Music Hall of Fame and Museum, and author of *Ray Stevens' Nashville*

"Eric Gnezda is one of those whose talents hinge in many directions, as a musician, storyteller, singer, entertainer, journalist, advocate, and more. In *Stories at the Center*, he brings every bit of that to bear witness to a life in search of purpose and meaning, always uplifting even in the low times and through loss and hardship, always in celebration of a world he finds constantly amazing."

—Ann Fisher, journalist and NPR host

"The author's poignant and often humorous telling of his tales, made up of masterfully chosen and rhythmically placed words, provides a portal into a human life. Cinematic episodes of a time, a place, and experiences very different from any of my own, but such a vivid and sensitive sharing of human thought and emotions, that I could've easily mistaken them for my own. In short, it's a literary Norman Rockwell painting, but with all the cracks of real life."

—Nellie Clay, songwriter, painter, and author of *A Passion Project: Crossing Paths with Inspiring Souls*

"Eric Gnezda has written a memoir that takes the reader through multiple journeys. From his early years living with a disabled father to a dynamic career as a performer and songwriter, the book is marked by tenderness, humor, and wisdom. As the poet James Wright would put it: This is a book by a grown man."

—Stephen Kuusisto, author of *Have Dog Will Travel: A Poet's Journey* and *New York Times* "Notable Book of the Year" *Planet of the Blind: A Memoir*

"Whether with Rock & Roll Hall-of-Famers, Grammy winners, or just an old friend like me, Eric tells inspiring stories with an artist's eye for compassion, nuance, and wit. I loved this book!"

—William Burtch, award-winning author of *Otherwise Wretched: Stories* and *W.G.: The Opium-addicted Pistol Toting Preacher Who Raised the First Federal African American Union Troops*

Stories at the Center

A Memoir of Miles, Music, and Meaning

Eric Gnezda

Mechanicsburg, PA USA

Published by Sunbury Press, Inc.
Mechanicsburg, PA USA

www.sunburypress.com

Copyright © 2025 by Eric Gnezda.
Cover Copyright © 2025 by Sunbury Press, Inc.

Sunbury Press supports copyright. Copyright fuels creativity, encourages diverse voices, promotes free speech, and creates a vibrant culture. Thank you for buying an authorized edition of this book and for complying with copyright laws. Except for the quotation of short passages for the purpose of criticism and review, no part of this publication may be reproduced, scanned, or distributed in any form without permission. You are supporting writers and allowing Sunbury Press to continue to publish books for every reader. For information contact Sunbury Press, Inc., Subsidiary Rights Dept., PO Box 548, Boiling Springs, PA 17007 USA or legal@sunburypress.com.

For information about special discounts for bulk purchases, please contact Sunbury Press Orders Dept. at (855) 338-8359 or orders@sunburypress.com.

To request one of our authors for speaking engagements or book signings, please contact Sunbury Press Publicity Dept. at publicity@sunburypress.com.

The epigraph is a quotation from *Further Fables for Our Time* by James Thurber Copyright © 1956. Reprinted by arrangement with Rosemary A. Thurber and The Barbara Hogenson Agency, Inc. All rights reserved. To learn more about James Thurber, visit JamesThurber.org and ThurberHouse.org.

Cover photo: Eric Gnezda at The Bluebird Cafe by Dan Mitchell, Mitchell Multimedia.

All Eric Gnezda music and lyrics © G-Ball Music (ASCAP).

FIRST SUNBURY PRESS EDITION: November 2025

Set in Adobe Garamond | Interior design by Crystal Devine | Cover by Lawrence Knorr | Edited by Sarah Peachey.

Publisher's Cataloging-in-Publication Data
Names: Gnezda, Eric, author.
Title: Stories at the center : a memoir of miles, music, and meaning / Eric Gnezda.
Description: First trade paperback edition. | Mechanicsburg, PA : Sunbury Press, 2025.
Summary: A memoir chronicling an unconventional path in the entertainment business. With a backdrop of his passions—running, songwriting, and service to others—Eric leads us on an adventure of joy and heartache that ultimately reveals life's true meaning. The story brings hope to anyone who longs for a world with renewed humanity and empathy.
Identifiers: ISBN : 979-8-88819-310-5 (softcover).
Subjects: BIOGRAPHY & AUTOBIOGRAPHY / Memoirs | BIOGRAPHY & AUTOBIOGRAPHY / Entertainment & Performing Arts | BIOGRAPHY & AUTOBIOGRAPHY / Music.

Designed in the USA
0 1 1 2 3 5 8 13 21 34 55

For the Love of Books!

To Dad, Gary, and Tony

"All men should strive to learn before they die what they are running from, and to, and why."

—James Thurber, *Further Fables for Our Time*, "The Shore and the Sea"

Contents

Acknowledgments *ix*

Introduction *1*

My Hometown *3*

My New House *10*

Martian Arts *16*

The Bullies *21*

Name-droppers *25*

Off to the Races *31*

Mom *35*

Visiting Lazarus *50*

Relief Pitcher *61*

Letter from Dad *68*

Sage Advice *75*

Losing Contact *85*

The Quitter *99*

Taking the Lead *116*

Prep Period *130*

Quality Time *136*

Resistance Running *141*

Olympic Dreams   *154*

Climbing the Ladder   *165*

Tony   *182*

Flippo   *200*

Running in Cottonwood   *210*

The Road Away   *215*

Songs at the Center   *226*

The Road Home   *249*

Dad's Death   *269*

About the Author   *276*

ACKNOWLEDGMENTS

WITH gratitude, I acknowledge the following people for their contributions to this work:

Stanley Rubin and his late wife, Judith Kitchen, the founders of the Rainier Writers Workshop MFA program at Pacific Lutheran University, who invested themselves personally into every one of their students. Faculty members, the late Sherry Simpson, Peggy Shumaker, my mentors, Brenda Miller, Gary Ferguson, Robin Hemley, and my nonfiction classmates, Bill Capossere, Julie Johnson Riddle, Barrie Jean Borich, Jaimie Kirby, and Theresa Bakker Smith.

My friend, original mentor, and author Stephen Kuusisto of Syracuse University and the Iowa Writers' Workshop, who encouraged me to write a memoir and engaged me with enthusiasm for new artistic directions.

Editors Gretchen Hirsch, Barbara Brannan, and Sarah Peachey, each of whom offered suggestions with grace, kindness, and knowledge, and Sunbury Press founder Lawrence Knorr for his faith in my work.

More friends than I can mention, but among them are those who read various versions of the work, Thomas Powel, Liz Streitz, Mark Wenden, Ted Barnes, Paul Reitter, Jacquie Farthing Galvin Ray, the late Bill Purpura, Gene Castelli, the late Chuck White, Pat Schmitt, Rebecca Wenden, Dan Girard, Amy Paulin, Bob Vance, Jerry Katz, David Duffett, Jim Paluch, Don Miller, Keith Larsen, and my niece Yvonne Smith.

My special friends, authors Donna Burtch and her brother William Burtch, with whom our weekly breakfast meetings were life changing. This book would not be published but for their patience and generosity.

The late Wendy Raphael, for whom there are never enough words to demonstrate my gratitude. Without her guidance, support, and commitment through the years, I might never have taken my artistic calling seriously.

My sisters Nicole Gnezda and Terry Gnezda for their lifelong love, for reading the manuscript, and, especially, for Terry's guidance and attention to detail in the final phases of the writing and publishing process.

My wife, Vicki, whose steady and reliable love frees me to pursue my muse, and my children, Caroline and Meredith, who inspire me in ways that I can only hope they'll one day understand.

My mother, Mary Gnezda Winter, for simply everything, especially for being the first to see—and nurture—the writer in me.

INTRODUCTION

AT age twenty-seven, I finally accepted my friend's invitation to visit his cabin in Maine. Coming from a family who didn't vacation—much less camp—I'd never seen much of nature outside of school field trips to a conservancy or two. His place was on Birch Island, less than twenty miles south of the Quebec border.

Awed by the region's unspoiled beauty, I stretched out alone on the dock one night to soak It all In. Sighs of cool air, harbingers of autumn arriving earlier than I was accustomed to in Ohio, fanned the scent of smoke from cabin fireplaces, the dock undulating to the mournful moans of the loons. Lying on my back, I looked up, my view flanked by silhouettes of the tall pines grown thick among the birch trees over the last century. At first, I saw nothing notable. Just the sky.

But then . . . Astonishment.

I saw it.

All in its unclouded splendor.

The Sky.

An inner-dialogue exploded between the enthusiastic grownup and the awestruck kid.

"Can you find the Big Dipper?"

"There it is!"

"The Little Dipper?"

"Yeah, right there!"

And the Milky Way. My God, the Milky Way. I finally understood how it got its name. Countless stars in a cluster, so concentrated they create an actual vast white *milky way*.

Somehow, among Ohio's interminable clouds, light pollution, and my own preoccupations and responsibilities, I'd missed it for twenty-seven years. But now I understood the ineffable wonder of astronomers, philosophers, poets, lovers, painters, theologians. They all had seen The Sky, the same one humankind had been peering at for millennia. The same one I had just discovered.

My mind opened in a time lapse. Fear peeled away, and I awakened to one of those profound paradoxes we so often find at the core of a truth. I'd never felt so tiny, yet never more significant. I realized I mattered, if only because I was part of this immense, sublime mystery.

I felt humbled, but empowered.

I was weightless. Full of gratitude. Free.

Alive.

I experienced what evolved people call "transcendence."

All those years ago, and the moment is still with me, leaving me to reflect on what I miss day to day. What sights? What sounds?

What have I lost?

What have I gained?

Universal questions, I know, but I'm now at an age where I look back on the many experiences and people I've loved, lost, and learned from, and I see a story. While the details on the outside provide intrigue, the real story is beneath, in the meaning I gained along the way.

My Hometown

I STILL live in the house I grew up in. I'm not agoraphobic—things just worked out that way. Three years after my father died, my mom called and asked me if I'd live in the house for three months until she sold it. Ultimately, she found the ideal buyer. Me.

Living in the same home through three generations has been a mixed blessing. I have deep roots and rock-solid friendships, but I can't get away from the memories. They are everywhere, like the layers of paint on a wall in the center of town. I see the latest colors, but can also recall the coats beneath, right down to the original surfaces of brick, wood, or stone. I wonder how many times I've rounded the corner of my street to finish up a run. Or a bike ride as a kid, or in my mom's car as a teenager, or in my SUV as a father. Sometimes I'll estimate the number of hours I've waited for a traffic light in town to change, or the number of miles I've walked behind my lawn mower, alternating each week among horizontal, vertical, and diagonal cutting lines in my nearly seventy-year-old yard.

My home is Worthington, Ohio, a suburb touching the north edge of Columbus. I went on a run before dawn the other day, the neighborhood still asleep, not yet burdened by the anxiety of a workday. Every house I passed reminded me of the untold mysteries within, each worthy of a book, a movie, or a song. *Or maybe a sitcom*, I thought, as I ran past a front door sitting deadpan between a pair of lights shining different shades of white.

What struck me at the moment was that, even with my breathing slightly elevated from exertion, I heard a midrange hum I'd never noticed before. Distant, persistent, like a wind that doesn't stop to catch its breath, the sound revealed itself to be freeway traffic a mile and a half away. What a contrast to the midnight train whistles that blow through the east and west ends of town. I find comfort in them, the familiar calls of kindred companions, reassuring me I'm not alone. Even as I sleep, trains bull their way through the darkness, delivering things I'll need in the metaphorical morning. The lonesome moans are lamentations of days gone by, when we placed more value on engaging with each other.

I've traveled on passenger trains a few times. I was amazed at how relaxed everyone was as inhibitions and social walls dissolved. I had easy conversations with strangers in the dining car. I was lulled to sleep by the 4/4 rock-'n'-roll beat of the rails... *one-and-TWO-and-three-and-FOUR-and*... I made friends with an African-American mother who placed her baby boy in my lap, and I cradled him through a stretch of Pennsylvania, free of self-consciousness, unafraid to reveal a hidden tenderness.

Trains connect us. Cars divide us. We drive in our own bubbles, with our own agendas, jockeying for an advantage on the way to disparate destinations where we'll compete again on the job, at the store, in the parking lot. Without even seeing each other's faces, we make demographic judgments, from the type of vehicle we drive, to the license plate, to the speed, to the way we change lanes. We have a horn to blare at the jerk who cuts us off, but no signal of gratitude for the kind soul who lets us over. The slightest current of highway traffic in the wee hours is unsettling, reminding me that, even when we are at rest, the rush continues, the game is still on. The world is relentlessly encroaching.

I know it's the same everywhere in America these days. Like other suburbs, Worthington sits on the cusp of more "progress." Major tech industries are relocating to Central Ohio, and high-density developers are nibbling on the edge of town like sharks circling dinner. Worthington, which *USA Today* recently named the third-best Historic Small Town in the Midwest, will always be the town I grew up in, with almost every experience that shaped me, from sports, to theater, to music, to writing, happening within a mile of my house.

The center of Worthington is The Village Green, a three-and-a-half-acre rectangle quartered by two major streets, still serving its original purpose, in limited fashion, as a gathering space. The town's original bell still hangs in the tower of an adjacent school. Years ago, my family joined many others in buying engraved bricks to help support the renovation of The Village Green.

Today, as you sit on a bench on the southwest quadrant and look down, you'll see ours:

The Gnezdas.

Worthington is a "New England village nestled in Ohio," some say, particularly realtors whose breathing accelerates whenever they catch wind of someone looking to list in the historic section of town, or "Old Worthington," as it's known. Sixteen square blocks of a New England coastal town without a coast.

Like nearly everyone else in my generation, I've seen locally owned stores sell out to corporations over the last fifty years. I find it hard to even set eyes upon the famous pizza chain now occupying what was once The Home Market, a family-owned grocery store where locally grown fruit and vegetables were displayed on homemade wooden racks out front, and where Mr. Bachelor gave me my first job at age fifteen. "I'm a stock and carryout engineer," I would lamely joke to anyone who would ask about my summer employment, a job that at the end of my first day made my legs throb with such pain I fell asleep with them elevated on sofa pillows.

I learned of another kind of ache as I was stocking the soap shelves. A bar of pink Camay brought back the unmistakable scent of my date to the spring dance, a "romance" she broke off a few weeks later in favor of an upperclassman. An introduction not only to the fragility of infatuations but also to the power of the senses, especially smell, to evoke a memory.

Through the years, neighborhood gas stations have been replaced by more pizza franchises, banks, and office buildings. Adams The Druggist, where kids gathered after school for penny candies and smokes, has long since been replaced by a CVS that dominates a nearby intersection. The Worthington Hardware Company, a town mainstay that employed many of my high school friends who wore their standard-issue blue vests with pride, has been sold and split respectively into a fitness center and pub.

Across the street, the ice cream shop, once Herm Beck Rambler, sits cater-corner to a French bakery and bistro that, at one time, for about fifteen minutes, was a Rolls Royce dealership. The barbershop is still a barbershop, and the former Worthington Savings Bank, having gone through several remodels, owners, and name changes, still stands where my mother took me when I was four to open my savings account with a deposit of ten dollars, her first step in granting me independence.

I see familiar faces from time to time, including the mayor, who, as a seventh-grader, taught my fifth-grade self to shoot a layup and is, no doubt, tired of me thanking him every time I see him.

As I grew up, my passions were many, and in adulthood, my career has been a process of merging them into creative endeavors. It's difficult to define my profession in a single word. Well-meaning people have told me, "Focus!" but depending upon how they know me, here are some job titles they've used: songwriter, singer, entertainer, speaker, journalist, author, comedian, satirist, entrepreneur, producer, interviewer, professor, advocate, artist, and media personality. Like tesserae in a mosaic, each pursuit complements another, and it can only be appreciated by stepping away and viewing it from a distance. While my career path has brought me myriad experiences, it's also worked against my ability to make money, as agents and managers have shied away from me because I don't fit in one of their convenient slots. "What the hell is he? A humorist? A songwriter? A speaker? A writer? A TV host?" One of my lifetime challenges has been reconciling the artist in me with the transactional world.

Sometimes I've succeeded.

My latest project is a public television series I created and host, *Songs at the Center*, an interview-performance series that showcases everyone from music royalty to emerging songwriters. Among our guests have been John Oates, Janis Ian, Bruce Cockburn, Suzy Bogguss, Ray Stevens, Molly Tuttle, Rodney Crowell, Mary Gauthier, Delbert McClinton, Jeff Daniels, Marc Cohn, Jim Brickman, and Tom Paxton, plus scores of other songwriters our audience "wants to know better." In our eleventh season coast to coast, the program features performers sharing the compelling stories behind their songs and lives. Often, episodes are recorded at the arts center within walking distance from my house. While the TV show is a joyful blend of my many passions, I also continue to write, perform, and pursue other ventures as a singer-songwriter, artist, and communicator.

Having watched the world evolve in the familiar surroundings of my hometown for a lifetime, I've been granted a unique perspective, seeing that our human needs don't fundamentally change. Only the faces and accessories. To live is to see paradoxes. While nothing changes, everything changes. When we're young, we move so furiously in the pursuit of our dreams and destinies that we don't notice the shifts we're creating in our wake. Only with time, as we age into reflection and observation, do we take in the wider landscape and see our path in hindsight, and how it came together and made sense. We also realize change travels in tandem with memory, each pulling in opposite directions. Memory draws us into the past, exchanging the real for relics, while change demands we leave the familiar for the future, which, often against our will, challenges our courage and faith. Through it all, we long for connection, love, identity, and meaning. My life has given me those in abundance, but not without years and years of doubt, conflict, and struggle.

One activity that has remained a constant in my life is distance running. Although I'm quite a bit slower and no longer interested in competing as I once did, running keeps me connected to my world in a way driving a car through town doesn't. Much like a walker, I get a close up view of life, seeing younger people as they pass through different stages, reminding me of my own development. Eight-year-old boys throwing footballs on the school grounds, teenagers zooming past in cars, and young parents walking their little ones in strollers. I see a family move into a "new" house, which, to me, is often the former home of a long-lost schoolmate, neighbor, teacher, or relative. At least three families have since moved into "the Bakers' house," but to me it will always be the Bakers' house.

When I run, my mind often ambles down memory lane like the crowd at our celebrated Saturday farmers markets in the center of town, stopping here and there to look at something catching my eye. Other times, the memories flash at me like the brass bands that march down High Street in our Memorial Day parade.

Years ago, my toes would pop off the surface with each stride. Now I run on my heels. I no longer care who might be sitting at a traffic light, on a bench, or at a table next to a flower box, watching this one-time galloper trudge by as if I were wearing iron Adidas. As I run past buildings and street corners I've known all my life, it's impossible not to relive events. I cross intersections, both literally and psychologically, for the millionth time. I recall triumphs and failures of the past. Gratitude, regrets, shame, and glory.

People, living and dead.

Memories, bittersweet. Sometimes amusing.

Old Worthington was "dry" until the mid-1990s, when the city finally permitted the sale of alcohol, which revitalized—or should I say vitalized—the center of town. When the first bar, The Old Bag of Nails Pub, opened, it was a pleasure to finally be able to walk the mile into Old Worthington with my wife, Vicki, and have a cold beer with a basket of the fish and chips that would soon become legendary in Central Ohio.

Not long after the appearance of the Old Bag of Nails, a strip club opened two miles north on the edge of town, which, of course, aroused the displeasure of some disgruntled residents, stimulating them to wave picket signs, take photos of license plates in the parking lot, and videotape the faces of patrons as they walked in, all of which only drew more clientele to a floundering business not long for this world anyway.

Meanwhile, I had been invited to a backyard cookout in celebration of a neighbor's high school graduation. I knew three generations of her family, including her grandmother, who was holding court with other female octogenarians on the screened porch behind the house. As I was passing through, the grandmother called out to me.

"So Eric, what do *you* think of the new bar in town?"

Just blowing through the room, I had no idea what they'd been discussing, so my mind went directly to the only "new bar" I could think of, the Old Bag of Nails, with the cold beer and delicious fish and chips.

"Oh, I *love* it!" I said. "It's a good thing I'm married, or I'd be living there!"

Padded porch swings creaked to a sudden halt.

Jaws dropped.

The air grew heavy with impending death. (My own.)

By Worthington, Ohio, standards, I'm a nonconformist, but not a degenerate. In a split second, that all changed. Until I realized I had misunderstood the question.

"Oh. *Oh!*" I said. "You mean the new *gentlemen's* club!"

Channeling a furrowed brow borrowed from the ghost of Richard Nixon, I continued, "Oh, it's terrible, just *terrible* for our community."

Rocking chairs squeaked back into action and breathing resumed. With my reputation resuscitated among the old guard, I slipped through the sliding glass door into the kitchen, where I went straight for another hot dog and more baked beans.

My New House

RUNNING south into the center of town takes me back to my freshman year in high school. With a swagger in my step, I worked out with the varsity team as the crowd assembled along High Street for the Memorial Day parade. We, of course, were engaged in unabashed teenage grandstanding, running more to be seen than for fitness, even causing an unsuspecting parade spectator here and there to dodge out of our way. Up ahead I spotted a familiar face, one I hadn't seen since my earliest days in school. She must have spotted me first, for she had stopped within the moving crowd, her eyes fixed on me, wide with surprise, her smile radiant with affection.

It was Mrs. Freeman, my first-grade teacher.

"My God," she communicated with every bit of her countenance, "look at the young man you've become!" With a singular focus, she watched me with expectation and receptivity as I came striding her way. Whatever admiration I could have wished for in my wildest dreams was right there, gleaming back at me.

But I was fifteen. With the older guys. And wearing photochromic lenses, the latest rage in 1970s eyewear, which turned dark in the sunlight, gave me a place to hide while scoping out my surroundings undetected. As much as I craved acceptance at that age, I was determined to not let anyone know. In my teenage mind, responding to Mrs. Freeman would have given myself away, so I denied my true feelings and blew right past her, my face locked in forward focus as if I were in a race. I sold my preoccupation well enough that, out of the corner of my eye, I could see her face didn't drop in disappointment. Still smiling, she seemed to be thinking I was too intent on running to notice her.

Such false preoccupation was an act I perfected until later years when I realized, through regret and pain, the importance of being able to accept a compliment and letting it sink in like water into my roots. First of all, to slough off someone's praise is to unintentionally invalidate them, and second, as an artist in today's world, it's necessary to be nurtured with as much affirmation as possible to balance out the vast amount of indifference and rejection that life sends our way.

Mrs. Freeman, by contrast, was a teacher who was free with her emotions. Passionate and tender, she was one of the first sensitive souls I'd ever known. She was of Portuguese origin, and word had it she'd been orphaned as a child, which might have explained why she was so kind. When her heart was touched, she wasn't afraid to cry. But she laughed even more. Her first name was Inez, Portuguese for "pure," "chaste," "holy." She had long, flowing black hair, gathered in a beehive, piled high and pinned with large, decorative combs or needles. Sometimes she wore her hair down, pulled loosely around the sides with a braid or two for artistic accent. I liked it best that way. We'd heard Mrs. Freeman was old. Forty-one! Older than any of our parents. But the only evidence was a couple of strands of silver hair around the temples of her youthful face, so warm, so receptive.

One day in her first-grade class, we had an all-school assembly. My classmates and I walked—nearly ran—two-by-two down the first flight of steps toward the basement auditorium. Holding a friend's hand, I let my other one skate along the brass rail over the terrazzo steps. Excited voices bounced off the walls, which, like the rest of the school, smelled like molding clay and the surrounding buckeye trees. We reached the hairpin turn at the top of the lower flight of steps, and suddenly, anticipation plunged into stunned silence. At the bottom of the stairwell, a man lay flat on the floor, his crutches strewn beside him.

While I watched in horror from the top of the steps, some of my friends came to his aid. Paul steadied his crutches, while Greg and a couple of others were trying to help him grab the handrail. As some of my classmates passed in curious reverence, others summoned Mrs. Freeman.

By the time I neared the bottom of the stairs, the man was standing and slipping his forearms back into the aluminum cuffs of his crutches, thanking the boys who had helped him. As I passed, I locked my eyes onto the double doors leading to the hallway and raced through them, hoping he wouldn't see me and no one would find out who he was.

My daddy.

At the age of six, my dad's disability was something I struggled to keep hidden from my classmates, my friends, and the world at large. I don't know exactly why I was embarrassed, but perhaps it had something to do with my belief that a father should be "strong." As a young boy, I could think of strength only in physical terms, so to have a dad who was lacking the ability to play sports, or especially work, made me and my family different, and it filled me with shame. For me as a first-grader, he was "weak" compared to the dads I saw on television and those who came into my classroom to pick up their kids.

Mrs. Freeman, however, partially made up for it, as she loved each of us as if we were her own children. She was less than five feet tall, and played an instrument complementing her sweetness—the dulcimer. Her voice, with a fragile vibrato, was as delicate as a hummingbird's. Eyes closed, Mrs. Freeman would sway to the words and music without inhibition, revealing a heart that, having endured suffering of its own, was unafraid to show its vulnerability.

She taught us songs of justice. Peace. Freedom.

Songs of conscience.

Songs of empathy.

If her class had an unspoken theme, it was "empathy." Whether singing a folk song or reading an Aesop fable, she was forever asking us to feel for the people in the stories. When we answered her questions, showing we finally understood the moral of a fable, her entire torso would join her head in swaying back and forth, as she said, "Yes! Yes!"

Just before spring break that year, I was sitting with my classmates on our sleeping mats, those bygone giant potholders with fringe at both ends. The mats offered little padding from the linoleum floor, making my ankles hurt as I sat with my legs crossed, a painful position for me as my body has always lacked flexibility. To relieve the pressure on my lower joints, I leaned back on my hands, elbows straight and wrists locked into right angles to support the rest of my body. The cool floor felt good on my palms, but the relief lasted only until my hands began to tingle. As I sat up, my red, wrinkled wrists ached as I released them from their cocked positions.

Normally when the class gathered, Mrs. Freeman would sit on a chair in the center of the semicircle, leaning forward as far as she could, her bright-colored, pleated dress flowing around her knees, her forearms propped on her lap. But this time she stood near the blackboard, as if about to give a lesson. She began an impromptu sharing session. From the floor, my classmates spouted off family plans for the upcoming spring vacation. Bruce, whose dad was a psychiatrist, was going to Carlsbad Caverns. Cheryl had just moved into a new home. Her dad, who sold swimming pools, was putting one in her backyard. She promised that when it got warm enough, she'd invite all of us over for a party.

"I'm moving into a new house, too!" I blurted out.

Mrs. Freeman, apparently surprised by my exuberance, focused her attention on me, bringing everyone else's eyes with her. Immediately I knew I'd made a big mistake. While I was excited about our new house, I certainly didn't want to talk about it. I withdrew my eyes from her, hoping she'd move on to someone else.

But she didn't.

Perhaps she mistook my impulsive burst of enthusiasm for a long-awaited cue, an opportunity to open up about the reason we were moving, in the company of empathic classmates.

"Eric," she continued with a measured tone, "would you like to tell the class why you're moving?"

My ears rang and my face heated up. My throat went dry. I wanted with all my heart to tell her no, but felt I no longer had the choice. My mother and Mrs. Freeman talked a lot, so surely she knew we were moving into a new house to accommodate my dad's disability. What Mrs. Freeman was not aware of, however, was how terrified I was to talk about him. Even I, until that moment, didn't know the depth of my own pain.

As I stood, Mrs. Freeman moved from the center of the room to the left, beside the door.

The room quieted.

"Well," I swallowed, my voice going hollow, "like Mrs. Freeman said, we're moving into a new house . . . and it's because . . . well . . . my dad . . . is . . . disabled."

Such a big word. *Disabled*.

I'd never dared say the word to myself, let alone in public.

Yet there, among my peers—center stage in my universe—the word tumbled from my mouth.

It was as if I'd been thrust into the driver's seat of a vehicle too big for me to handle. I'd never been behind the wheel before. My feet couldn't reach the pedals. I wasn't tall enough to see out the windshield. The immense, stiff-turning steering wheel needed the arms of a grownup, someone with muscle who could navigate this machine through such perilous emotional terrain.

But the speed only picked up, and soon I was driving other words too big for me.

"Disease."

"Multiple sclerosis."

"My dad's only on crutches now," I mumbled, lifting my eyes to the faces of my classmates, who appeared to be in deep reflection, "but the doctor said someday soon my dad won't be able to walk, and he'll need a wheel . . ."

As my lips wrapped around the first syllable, my stomach contracted, closing my windpipe as I was drowning in fear. I coughed up the rest of the word "chair," and in a split second lost all control, steering the oversized vehicle into oncoming traffic.

I was in tears.

My classmates stared in silence, witnesses at the accident scene.

I tagged my story as quickly as I could, "and that's why we're moving into a new house," and then I went back to my place on the floor, trembling, my arms pinned against my stomach.

I looked at Mrs. Freeman, expecting her typical rescue: open arms, reassuring words, and a hug. But for reasons I'll never fully understand, she was paralyzed. Though her eyes were fixed on me, she seemed strangely detached, thrusting me into further shame and convincing me to tamp down my feelings even more. I felt completely alone, getting the message more than ever that Dad's disability was something I needed to keep hidden. Even at home, my two older sisters were never embarrassed or shamed by Dad's disease. "Disability" flowed from their lips with ease in conversations with friends and strangers. As for my mother, Dad's MS was just another hardship in life she'd have to find a way to power through.

For me, however, the only boy in the family, it was a big deal. One that bored into my very identity.

The image of Mrs. Freeman frozen by the door has hung in my mind ever since. I look back and wonder what took hold of her. Perhaps she was in shock herself, absorbing the horror of underestimating my level of discomfort with Dad's disability. Or maybe she was stilled by the memory of her own childhood abandonment. Or maybe overcome by my extreme sadness.

Increasingly, as I reflect on the incident, it emerges as a reminder that human beings fail. Even the most compassionate and empathetic among us can miss an opportunity in an important moment. I can still see her standing at the door in a trance. Lost, helpless in the moment. She caught herself staring at me, then snapped out of it.

"Does anyone else have anything to share?" she asked the class.

No one raised a hand.

Sharing time was over.

Martian Arts

CRAIG White nearly convinced me he was a Martian. The television show *My Favorite Martian* was popular, and Craig's mind ran with it. I never became fully engaged with the series, which made me all the more susceptible to Craig's claim. Keep in mind I was a first-grader who thought you row, row, rowed your boat gently down the *street*, and I thought the human race was made up of human *beans*.

"Eric," Craig whispered during class, "watch that piece of chalk," pointing his finger toward the chalkboard tray just behind Mrs. Freeman. "See it move?" he asked, lifting his index finger, then dropping it.

"No," I said, torn between wanting to pay attention to him and not getting in trouble with Mrs. Freeman for talking in class.

"Watch this time."

He raised his finger, then lowered it again.

"See it?" he asked, as if the moving chalk would be obvious to anyone who was truly a Martian. And I wanted to be a Martian. More importantly, I wanted to be Craig's friend.

"Oh, yeah, I saw it this time!" I said, and to tell you the truth, I couldn't honestly say the chalk didn't wiggle on the surface of the chalkboard tray. It's possible that the movement was too slight for me to see, but to the eyes of a Martian with super-galactic vision, like Craig, that fragment jumped like a *Mercury* capsule off the launching pad.

Craig was the oldest kid in our class. He was the tallest. He was the fastest. He was by far the best athlete. And the best singer. A smooth, clear voice with a touch of rasp around the edges.

Nat King Cole at six.

Craig is still a master singer and guitarist, but even in the first grade, his imagination was overactive and daring. He played outdoors with reckless abandon. To join him was to take my life in my hands.

With his strong, athletic body, he seemed fearless. Craig's family had just moved into a new house in Rush Creek Village, a nearby development designed by a student of Frank Lloyd Wright. After school, his mom took me and Craig to their house for a playdate. The car had barely stopped in his driveway before Craig jumped out from the backseat. "Let's play Tarzan!" he said, running off into a wooded area behind his house that dipped into a ravine, split by a shallow creek. By the time I caught up to him, he was already swinging on a vine he'd found hanging from one of the thick trees on the banks of the creek. Gray, sinewy, braided by nature, his pendulum of dare had been polished by the repeated grip of his hands and feet.

"Aaah-yahi-yah-yiy-yah!" he hollered as he swung high above the creek bed of rocks and jagged shale. He was two-thirds of the way up the vine, which, from my viewpoint below, looked closer to the treetops than the ground. He seemed a hundred feet in the air, although it was probably only ten or twelve. Still, that was about seven feet higher than I was willing or able to go.

"C'mon, Eric! Swing!" he called from somewhere high on the bank when it was my turn. "Climb!" he commanded, as if every boy had the upper body strength, athleticism, and courage to swing from the treetops.

My feet barely left the ground, skimming the top of the creek.

Before long, Craig figured out it wasn't much fun to be the only one scaling the rare air, so we moved on to a different kind of dare.

"Hey, let's try out for the talent show!" he said as we walked through the school halls one day, and I found myself on another terrifying adventure with him: an audition. Standing outside Room 100, waiting for our names to be called, the acid in my stomach burned through my spine, which also absorbed the blow of each heartbeat that shot up to my ears. A fear I'd never felt before and one I swore I'd never put myself through again.

Ha!

We sang "This Land is Your Land" while his dad, seated behind us, accompanied us on guitar. Having survived the audition, my anxiety dissolved into euphoric relief, the next day swelling into celebration when we found out we'd not only made the show, but were the sole first-graders selected.

"We've got to dress alike!" Craig, the showbiz veteran, said, so we wore matching black pants and gray sweatshirts, which, of course, was his idea. "We're The TurtleNecks!" Craig proclaimed, thus naming our first band.

The TurtleNecks received a rabid ovation, and I learned one of the basic tenets of the entertainment business: The audition is always twice the ordeal of any performance.

Craig inherited his talent from his father, Chuck White, an accomplished folk singer in his day and a contemporary of the legendary Phil Ochs. Hired by WBNS-TV, the CBS affiliate in Columbus, Chuck was the first Black TV personality in Ohio and among the first in the country. Television was still young, with lots of local programming, so the industry needed versatile, creative people who could be utility players. One of the shows Chuck performed on was a daily morning program for kids that featured a menagerie of puppets, including Pierre Poodle, Horace the Horse, Mr. Tree, and the emotionally volatile, life-sized Dragon. Chuck was the voice and personality behind virtually all of the characters, so to sit upstage and play his guitar while Craig and I stood downstage and sang was an easy assignment for him.

Our school was experimental, seeking students of all races and economic means. Each grade was limited to twenty-five students, and in addition to the three Rs, we had music, art, and phys-ed classes every day. On the campus of The Ohio State University, the school stood atop what was once Ohio Field, the birthplace of Buckeye football. The building was designed by the architect of Ohio Stadium. Founded in 1932 on the progressive principles of educator John Dewey, the school served as a lab for the College of Education and was named, appropriately enough, University School, providing, among many other advantages, access to all of the university's facilities.

Even as first-graders, to study geology meant we'd take a stroll across OSU's iconic Oval and visit the museum at Orton Hall, where we'd examine everything from minerals to dinosaur skeletons. In phys-ed class, it was nothing to take a short trip to the university's indoor pools, and the first time I ran on a track was inside Ohio Stadium, the very grounds upon which legendary football coach Woody Hayes walked the sidelines in the fall, and where Jesse Owens had trained and competed on his way to making Olympic history with four gold medals in 1936.

Long before I was born, *Time* magazine called University School "America's Most Famous School." Of course, I didn't recognize any advantages at the time, only later appreciating what an extraordinary experience I had in elementary school, thanks to my parents, who, even though strapped for money, believed education was a top priority and managed to get us partial scholarships. I went to University School through fifth grade, until it was closed, ostensibly for budget reasons and concern that the progressive teaching styles were no longer relevant to the times. In fact, though, The Ohio State University president, along with the conservative Board of Trustees, wanted the school to be dissolved, so they formed a committee to "study" the school and "voted" unanimously to abolish it.

While University School was in existence, however, we were encouraged to discover our own passions. Our fine arts teacher, Miss Lloyd, was particularly good at helping two first-graders find our own way. She asked Craig and me what we wanted to make out of wood, and "A spaceship!" rocketed from Craig's mouth, as if a Martian would ever wish for anything else.

"Hmm," she paused. "What's your plan?"

Craig picked up an 8 x 2-inch piece of lumber and said, "We're going to soak this overnight in the sink, then bend it into shape."

Miss Lloyd looked at him as if his logic was from outer space. "Well, you can try," she said.

The next day we took the wood out of the sink and, as hard as we tried, our six-year-old arms couldn't make it bend, so we turned our attention back to the "music business," this time adding art and dance to our act. Miss Lloyd gave us each a gigantic cardboard shield as tall as we were, which we painted respectively in designs consistent with our concurrent studies of African culture. Craig and I decided that for the next talent show, with shields in hand, we were going to dance to a soundtrack. Halfway through the performance, Craig fell, but got right back up and in step. The audience either didn't notice or didn't care, because they rewarded us with wild cheers and applause.

"Hey," Craig exclaimed afterward, "they thought it was part of the show!"

A good lesson. For Martians and human beans alike.

The Bullies

THE first two summers in my new house were the best of my childhood. I rode my bike everywhere. I met new friends, discovered the Dairy Queen, and spent my days at the swimming pool. The world was wide open and welcoming—until the summer after fifth grade, with the arrival of those universal stealers of joy: The Bullies. No warning, they just showed up one day when I was getting out of the pool. With "Mony, Mony" blasting from the jukebox, a kid came up to me and, with hostility in his eyes, said, "You think you're bad, don't you, Gnezda?"

"*Bad?*"

It was a new term then, and I wasn't sure what it meant, but from his tone, I knew it was no compliment. He was three years older, I knew his name, but I had never had any interaction with him. This was the first time in my life I was aware he even knew I existed. I had no history with him. He caught me off guard. Why was he so angry with me? What had I done?

Surprised by his aggression, I didn't know how to react, so I ignored him. He waited for me until I left to go home, and then, with his small posse, he followed me. A hundred yards later, in front of the high school, the bully stopped me again.

"You think you're bad, don't you?" He took a swing, grazing my jaw. I was in deep trouble. Alone, with a group of older boys ready to beat the shit out of me. Out of nowhere, like an angel of mercy, a policeman drove up in his car, asked what was going on, told them to leave me alone and go home.

They did.

Later that summer I rode my bike to the pool, and as I left, the hoodlum and his gang were waiting for me. I took off like a Christian cat out of hell, outracing them as we passed the high school, then lost them by hiding in the front alcove of the adjacent elementary school, panting from fear and exhaustion.

"Where's the little prick?" one of them said as they rode circles in front of the school. They didn't spot me and, in time, gave up and rode off. Once the coast was clear, I pedaled home like my life depended on it—because I felt it did—checking every blind spot along the way.

For the next two years, The Bullies continued to keep their eyes on me, riding by my house on their bikes, one time spotting me helping my dad get out of the car into his wheelchair. I thought that perhaps seeing that might soften their hearts. It didn't. They kept chasing me.

A few weeks later, I felt a strong sense that I was again being protected by a larger hand. I was walking through my neighborhood when a couple of members of the gang spotted me and began their usual trouble. Before they could even let a punch fly, however, out of nowhere came a high school athlete, Jack Savage, an All-State baseball player.

"What's going on here?" was all he had to say. His presence alone was enough to make them scatter. Whether my rescuer knew me or not was a complete mystery, but he was in the right spot at the right time. My gratitude to him remains to this day.

I've also never forgotten The Bullies. The terror of leaving my house. Going to the pool. A basketball game. The park. When I was playing football in sixth grade, the adrenaline rushed into me as one of the gang members, a seventh-grader on an opposing team, came running straight at me with the ball. I got low, accelerated toward him, hit him in the thighs, wrapped him up, and dropped him on his back. The tackle was perfect and felt oh, so sweet.

"Great hit, Gnezda!" one of my coaches yelled.

"Look at him," another cheered, "he's limping back to the huddle!"

I won't lie. It felt damn good to nail him.

The Bullies

The bullying continued until the eighth grade, when the gang disappeared like a mysterious rash. In high school, I played sports with some of them, and as an adult I had some professional interactions. None of them ever mentioned a thing about those years of harassment, perhaps unwilling to remember, or hoping time had erased my memory.

The effects of being bullied, however, never dissolved, especially when the tormentors didn't own up to it and never apologized. Even now, I suspect that their menacing plays a role in my occasional lapses of confidence in personal situations. Their unprovoked threats, still ringing in my ears, contribute to my internal battle to rise above the suspicion that every stranger will find some reason to dislike me just because I exist. My anger intensifies just thinking of those guys, for they provided further hurdles in dealing with the primal insecurities in those awkward, vulnerable years between childhood and adulthood.

Yet, just like the tackle I made on the field that day, being the target of bullies has also helped me either to focus my anger on the person who deserves it or ultimately conserve it to create something beautiful.

In these days of social media, it's easy to look people up. What are these guys doing now? I found out that one is a billionaire, one a corporate attorney, one a retired marketing company owner, one a doctor. The leader of the group, who declared himself a "Man of God" on his Facebook profile, has since died. In his obituary, he is remembered for saying he "learned that the best feeling in life comes from giving to others."

Hmm. Maybe his was an authentic transformation. Maybe not. Yet he and his posse left an everlasting impression on me, one I'm not sure any of them would be proud to carry. As adults, I suspect The Bullies and I share the hope that no one judges us on our youthful indiscretions, but as we all learn, it's never too late to apologize.

One of the gifts from this experience is that it taught me how to deal with anger and bitterness. I often feel a kinship with others who display their tempers because it tells me they care about life and take it seriously. In previous years, I brought my own touch to a ritual many people use to overcome hostility. Every New Year's Eve, I type out a list of people who I feel have hurt me, done me wrong, or for some reason or another just pissed me off. I say a prayer asking to find it in myself to forgive them over the coming year, put the list in my tapered votive holder, burn it, then bury the minuscule ashes in the front yard by my bushes. When I interact with one of the people on my list, or they cross my mind, I don't feel as much anger because whatever was left of the bitterness has been buried. The method seems to be working. Hardly anyone ever made my list twice. This past year, I had no list at all.

Name-droppers

HARD Road is aptly named, for it rises from Olentangy River Road on a hill that has always been a bitch to run. I was introduced to it in high school when my friend Tom Short suggested we go for an easy jog on a Sunday afternoon.

About three miles northwest of my house, Hard Road used to be in the middle of nowhere. Once a rural two-lane highway dividing farmland, it is now a four-lane boulevard with a tree-lined median, two high schools, a middle school, a strip shopping center, an underpass, and a new library. By "new," of course, I mean that it's been built since I graduated from high school. Another way I'm turning into my dad. My sisters and I would find it hilarious whenever Dad would say, "up until a few years ago . . ." and it would be twenty-five years. Well, now twenty-five years ago *is* a few years ago.

I met Tom in the sixth grade. We hit it off immediately. For a variety of reasons. We'd been placed on the same football team, the orange and black of State Savings. We both loved basketball and running, and he was funny. Just one problem. He was a Republican. But he knew his stuff, or at least his side of the story, so we'd argue politics, which was something you could do in those days and still remain close friends.

We were sixth-grade pundits, debating between ourselves and, once, in front of the entire school, during the 1968 presidential election. He endorsed Nixon, using some erudite technique, such as Aristotle's Three

Modes of Persuasion. I beat the drum for Humphrey. Literally. I brought in my silver Ludwig snare and banged out a cadence. "Humphrey's great . . . in '68!"

What I lacked in Tom's ethos, pathos, and logos, I made up for in flams and paradiddles. Everyone shouted along. "Everyone" being the five or six kids in Worthington whose parents were Democrats in that era.

Tom came by his political interests honestly. His dad, Haskell Short, was the bureau chief for Scripps-Howard, which owned our now-defunct morning newspaper, *The Columbus Citizen-Journal*. The summer before school began, Mr. Short had taken Tom to the Republican National Convention. "I went there liking Rockefeller," Tom said with sixth-grade conviction, "but after I heard Nixon speak—Eric, if only you could've been there to hear what I heard—there was no doubt Nixon was the best man."

"The best man." It was a phrase Tom and his parents used frequently.

"What makes you think we're Republicans?" his mother teased me in the kitchen as Mr. Short sipped his Saturday morning coffee. "We just vote for the best man."

"Of course they do," Dad chuckled when I recounted the conversation to him. "It just so happens that 'the best man' always turns out to be a Republican."

Our parents seemed to get a charge out of the intensity with which Tom and I sparred, and soon we became the go-betweens for good-natured ribbing between our parents. Mom and Dad were thrilled the day Mr. and Mrs. Short accepted their invitation to come over for drinks.

"It was an honor," Mom said afterward, "that that man ever set foot in our house."

The Shorts seemed to enjoy Dad's sense of humor and, like most of the other neighbors, marveled at how much he kept up with the news.

After their first visit, Mr. and Mrs. Short came by every now and then, which meant the world to Dad. Even more to Mom. "Your father is just so starved for company and to feel that he matters."

I liked Tom's mom and dad, too. Mr. Short wasn't home much, but when he was, he took a genuine interest in what I was doing, asking me about my life beyond school. Mrs. Short was funny, her humor a blend

Name-droppers

of oblique observation and wry amusement. Like my mother, she did all the driving, which was odd, since Mr. Short was perfectly able to get behind the wheel himself, as he did, presumably, to go to work every day in downtown Columbus.

With Mr. Short in the passenger seat, and Tom and me in the back, she drove us in a white Mustang to the Ohio State Fair. That evening's show featured Bob Hope, Doc Severinsen, Boots Randolph, and Jethro Burns. "I thought this was a good show to take the boys to," Mrs. Short told Mom. "Everybody loves Bob Hope, of course, and with Tommy playing the sax, I want him to see Boots Randolph." On the days Tom had concert band, he'd walk to school smiling, his black sax case bouncing against the outside of his right knee.

Because of Mr. Short's connections, we got the VIP treatment at the fair. When we exited I-71 at Seventeenth Avenue, I entered a world I'd never seen before—the back entrance to the Ohio State Fair, where VIPs with parking passes were waved into a special lot, then directed toward the grandstand by friendly, almost deferential, off-duty police officers.

Quite a contrast to my annual trips to the fair with Mom and my sisters. We'd spend an inordinate amount of time circling the surrounding neighborhood in search of a free spot to park along the cracked curbs. Then we'd walk forever to the Eleventh Avenue entrance gate—a gigantic, red O-H-I-O with ticket booths at the base of each letter. Along the way we'd step over, around, or through streams and piles of what Mom, always euphemistic in scatological matters, called "animal mess." Forever vigilant in trying to mitigate life's unpleasantness for us, Mom would reach into her purse for tissues, dab them at the mouth of a perfume bottle, and hand them to us. "There, hold this to your nose so you won't smell the BM."

Entering the fairgrounds with the Shorts, however, didn't require a makeshift nosegay. We were ushered through a special gate and funneled past the grandstand directly onto the harness-racing track, where thousands of wooden, church-style folding chairs were planted like rows of corn.

Five years earlier, Mom had given in to our pleading and taken my sisters and me to see Herman's Hermits at the fair. Since she had no interest in the stage shows and thought the rides were unsafe, Herman's

Hermits was a departure from her habit of taking us solely to the animal exhibits and art show. Arriving before noon for the concert, we baked in the grandstand's unshaded general admission seats, waiting for the show that didn't start until 4 p.m. By the time Herman's Hermits hit the stage, we were restless and exhausted.

That was hardly the case with the Shorts. Dusk loomed as I walked with Tom and his parents down a center aisle, my eyes growing bigger with each row we passed toward the front: 20 . . . 12 . . . 7 . . . 4 . . . The stage, looking so ordinary from the grandstand, now towered over us like the imposing deck of an aircraft carrier. Stage lights splashed onto the first few rows. We stepped into the amber wash and found our seats. As we sat, I could feel myself dismissing the horde behind me as a common gray mass in the grandstand, vibrating in a low hum of anticipation, so distant, so removed. I had been ushered into the world of privilege, a place for boys whose dads were Somebody.

Boots Randolph came on first and introduced his guest, Jethro Burns, who was now a solo act since losing his comedic partner, Homer Haynes, a year earlier. Boots played "Yakety Sax," Jethro picked his mandolin, and the two of them bantered. Jethro sang a parody about being on a baseball team he and Homer had recorded based upon the Carl Perkins song, "Daddy Sang Bass." The song mentions beating the sox off the Red Sox and the legs off the Redlegs. But the day they played the Astros, it rained.

For some reason, I remembered that comedic bit all these years. As an early teenager, I thought it was funny and daring, maybe because it was the first time I'd heard anything approaching, at least by the standards of those days, a "dirty" joke in public.

It wasn't until Boots and Jethro were done and Doc Severinsen was well into his set that I realized night had fallen, the air still thick with late-summer humidity, the covered stage a glowing box in the dark. I'd never been particularly drawn to Doc as the sidekick bandleader on *The Tonight Show Starring Johnny Carson*, but on his own, he was unrestrained, driven, reveling under the spotlight. His sequins spit beads of light. Saliva dripped from the bell of his trumpet. Droplets of sweat flew into the crowd. There in 3-D, spewing bodily fluids and sometimes catching his breath, Doc Severinsen had become electric. And I became energized. I've loved him as a performer ever since.

Bob Hope, who grew up in Ohio, was as much a fixture at the fair as the golf club he took with him onstage. The crowd received him like a famous uncle making his annual visit to the family reunion, appreciating him more for his presence than for his jokes. His appearances also had a lot to do with our perennial governor, Jim Rhodes. They were friends. So, too, were Governor Rhodes and Tom Short, at least according to Tom Short. In school, Tom and I had argued over whether Rhodes was a crook. I repeated what the news had been saying, that Rhodes had ties to a mobster, although in truth I didn't fully understand the accusations. Tom said his dad and others had looked into the story and found it wasn't true. "Besides," Tom said, "if you knew Governor Rhodes like I do, you'd know that he couldn't be a crook. He's too nice of a guy."

"Well, I do know him," I said, pushed into stretching the truth further than any politician would dare. Fact was, I'd crossed paths with the governor only once the previous summer. Mom, my sisters, and I were walking between exhibit halls when Mom spotted him. "Hello, Governor," she said. Smiling, he nodded and asked us how we liked the fair, stopping long enough to be polite. Mom, unassuming but no doubt wanting us to have the chance to meet him, introduced each of us. He shook my hand, looked me in the eye and said, "Glad to meet you, Eric."

Within seconds Governor Rhodes walked on, but I felt like we'd known each other forever.

I didn't share the details of the encounter with Tom, of course, hoping he'd just believe I knew the governor and drop the subject. Yet he persisted.

"Ever been to his office?"

"No, b—"

"Well, I've been to his office a bunch of times with my dad."

That was a statement I could never compete with.

"Has the governor ever called your house?"

I shook my head.

"Well, he calls our house every night, right around ten o'clock."

"No, he doesn't. For what?"

"Just to chat with my dad, see how things are going."

Then Tom went on about how his dad had taken him to Wapakoneta for the homecoming parade in honor of Neil Armstrong. Governor

Rhodes was there with Bob Hope. "It was getting late, and Dad still had a story to write before deadline, so the governor said, 'You know, Tom seems kind of tired, so why don't I just take him home with me on the plane,' and I flew back to Columbus with him. The pilot dropped the governor off at Port Columbus, then flew me to Don Scott, where they park the plane."

Tom paused, poised for checkmate. "So if you ran into the governor," he asked, "would he call you by your first name?"

"He did the last time I saw him."

Off to the Races

I STILL see Tom Short every now and then. He grew up to be an evangelist, speaker, and author, running a national campus ministry and doing mission work around the world. To this day we agree on absolutely nothing when it comes to religion or politics, but, like our parents, we sure enjoy each other's company.

He happened to stop by last week. Vicki and I were sitting in our Coleman camping chairs on our driveway, our usual perch on warm evenings, when Tom, riding his bike, saw us, and came up the drive, the very site where he and I tangled in countless one-on-one basketball games so many decades ago.

As usual, there were plenty of laughs about those days.

He was a good basketball player, his greatest advantage being his intelligence. His soft shot was tricky to defend. Holding the ball loosely, he seemed to rise in slow motion, enticing me to go for the block, then, just as I'd lunge for the ball, he'd release it at an odd angle just out of reach, leaving me to swipe the thin air like a batter whiffing on a change-up. I'd return to my feet, just as the ball slipped through the bottom of the net.

I remember a game on his driveway during the spring of sixth grade. We were playing two-on-two with his older brother and a friend from across the street, both of them in high school. Usual rules. Best of three, one point per bucket, game to eleven, had to win by two and call your own fouls, which were plentiful in the tight confines of Tom's driveway, the basket suspended from the roof of the two-car garage.

Tom's brother got hit right between the legs. "Per-son-al foul!" he screamed, bending over holding his jewels. Just the fact that he could speak signaled the injury wasn't serious, and soon we were all laughing, Tom and his brother especially.

The ball was back in play when Mrs. Short came out through the front door. "Eric, your mom just called. She wants you to go home."

"What's the matter?" I asked, letting Tom go around me for another bucket.

"Students are rioting at Ohio State, and the highway patrol's been called in."

The game came to a dead stop.

Tilted heads. Quizzical looks.

Tom bounced the ball a couple times with both hands and threw up a shot, laughing. "She afraid you're going to get tear-gassed?"

Mrs. Short suppressed a smile as she headed back into the house.

As embarrassed as I felt, I was grateful Mom hadn't insisted on coming to get me. At least she'd let me ride my bike home.

"Thank God you're here," Mom exhaled as I walked into the kitchen through the garage, where I'd slipped my bike between the car and the wall. "You know they're rioting on the Oval."

"Mom, campus is ten miles away."

"You never know what could happen at a time like this."

"Even Mrs. Short thinks you're crazy."

"I don't care what Eileen or anyone else thinks. You're my son and it's just best that you're home. Besides, honey," she softened, "you need your rest for Field Day tomorrow."

Mom couldn't care less about Field Day, but she had a way of making her overprotectiveness sound like it was being done in my best interest. Even though I *could* use the rest, her summons to come home had everything to do with her anxiety and nothing to do with Field Day. For me, though, the next day was a big deal. The final race of the 660-yard run—"long distance" for a kid my age—and since the first day of school I'd made it my goal to prove that I was the best sixth-grade runner in all of Worthington.

This was especially important since I'd been humiliated over the winter in a wrestling match. Our gym class had participated in the Presidential Physical Fitness Awards, and I had been the only boy in my grade to win gold. For some reason, my gym teacher equated a gold fitness badge with being good at wrestling, a sport I'd never tried, never wanted to try, and knew nothing about. He was friends with a gym teacher at a competing elementary school, and the two of them decided to put on a wrestling meet, complete with trophies. With much ballyhoo, my gym teacher pitted me against their best wrestler, a boy named Kevin Foley, who'd one day be a state champion. Strong from the waist up and with elbows and knees that seemed double-jointed, Foley shook my hand in the middle of the mat, then pulled my feet from under me before I could inhale. A few seconds later I was pinned—with the whole school there to watch, not to mention Foley's older brother and *his* friends.

When it came to running, however, it was a different story. In a preliminary of the 660-yard run the week before Field Day, I'd beaten Brad Fallon, which was a big deal because he had an older brother who was a star on the high school track team. I stayed right on Fallon's tail, watching the brown soles of his black Converse All Stars alternate like rubber paddles, then I sprinted past him on the final straightaway to win the race and shock everyone. The victory qualified me to race against the best remaining runner in the school district, Ted Barnes, who had *two* brothers who were stars on the high school track team. Word was that he was going to be better than both of them—and he already owned a pair of spikes, although he wouldn't be allowed to wear them on Field Day.

The morning of the race, we found out the gym teachers had asked a couple of guys from the high school track team to help run the meet. The high schoolers led us across the football field to the starting line on the far side of the track. They didn't know me, but they knew Ted through his older brothers, even chatting with him as they lined us up. As the underdog, my fear deepened at their familiarity.

This is some serious shit, I thought.

I wanted the race to get started. I wanted the race to get canceled. One of the high schoolers took out a starter's pistol, a first for me, called us to our marks, raised his right arm, paused a count, then shot the gun. I fell in right behind Ted and ran on his shoulder. His stride was shorter than Fallon's but had more bounce. His feet popped off the track, his heels snapping up to his butt. He ran with finesse.

"Go, Ted, go!" the high schoolers yelled as we ran along the backstretch. My body hurt beyond what I'd ever experienced, yet I was determined to stay on Ted's heels, especially now that the high schoolers had been cheering him on. Coming off the final turn, my gasps for air cut into my windpipe like never before. I reached for my last bit of gas. With a final push, I pulled up on Ted and passed him as we crossed the finish line. The kids from my school went crazy.

The high school guys didn't say a word.

Mom

"I just hate being late," Mom huffed from the driver's seat as our LeSabre went airborne over speed bumps in the church parking lot, passing by rows of compliant cars long since kneeling in their spaces. "Everyone will know the Gnezdas are late again this week!"

That is, every Gnezda but Dad, whom we left home to nod off during the televised Mass and the Sunday news shows.

For the rest of the Gnezdas, however, if the draft of air we created from the swinging sanctuary door in the rear of the church didn't rustle a few napes, being led down the center aisle by the usher exhumed plenty of heads from their Sunday missals. The inevitable stir of dislodging a family or, worse yet, an elderly couple, from their places in the pew evoked derisive glares from judgmental onlookers, silently admonishing us for having just earned an extra three minutes in purgatory. Even so, the weekly public humiliations were never sufficient motivation for any of us, except Mom, to hustle a bit more on Sunday morning to get to church on time.

Mom's introduction to Catholicism came through her immigrant father, who took his family to Mass at St. John the Baptist Catholic Church every Sunday in his truck, her parents with the youngest child in the cab, and the rest of them in the open bed of the pickup. Although he was distrustful of the institutional Catholic Church, including priests and the Pope, his belief and faith in God was strong. It's impossible to speak of my mother without mentioning her father's pervasive influence. Like her father, Mom's faith is sturdy but not confined or defined solely by the doctrines and dictates of any church. She's spent her life searching, seeking, observing, reflecting, and studying, as she's taught me to do.

Mom told me recently that her father lit a votive candle every Sunday. I must have inherited the "candle gene," for long before I learned of his practice, I became enamored of candles. I light them on my desk every day. I've lit them at all kinds of churches, from St. Patrick's Cathedral in New York, to Mexico City Metropolitan Cathedral, to The Cathedral Basilica of St. Francis of Assisi in Santa Fe, and in any number of churches in small towns I've traveled through over the years. Candles also play an important role in my prayer time. In keeping with her father's influence, Mom taught me early that Catholic rituals are merely symbols for greater mysteries we cannot explain. We can't expect the rituals to do the work for us.

Mom was born on September 5, 1926, at her grandparents' home in Columbus. She was the oldest of seven children, five of them boys. Her father, Fortunato, or Grandpa Fort to us, was born among the high winding, narrow roads of Santa Lucia del Mela, Sicily, in 1893, and immigrated to the United States in 1912, at age nineteen, on the *Principe di Piemonte*, entering through Ellis Island. A risk taker who didn't like working for someone else, primarily because his standards of quality reached beyond others, Grandpa Fort started his own landscaping business on a bicycle. His clients found him charming, appreciated his detailed work and his sense of humor. As his business grew into a successful enterprise, he attracted a lot of wealthy clients.

By nature, he was persistent, but also a perfectionist and expected other's work to be flawless, too. Nothing made him madder than a half-assed job. "Even if you're a ditch digger," he'd say, "do the best job you can." When Mom cleaned her home as a child, Grandpa Fort inspected the window sills and baseboards to see if she had dusted the corners, a commitment to detail he planted in her. He brought to America a belief in hard, honest work as the core of life, and the endurance of suffering as a normal part of living. He commonly merged Sicilian and English words, which would later be coined "Siculish." One such word he used often was "coromensable," Siculish for "responsibility."

Despite being a force of nature, Grandpa Fort was diminutive in stature. Five-foot-two-inches tall and one-hundred-thirty pounds, he was thin, agile, and strong, inside and out, still climbing trees to trim them at age eighty-five. He wore size six-and-a-half cap toe boots, made from kangaroo skin, and would strike wood matches on the leather sole to light his Toscano cigars. Intelligent and intense, he had a Mount Etna-like personality. Similar to the Sicilian volcano, Europe's largest and still eruptive, his temperament could escalate from serenity to rage in a split second. His steadfast faith in God didn't keep Grandpa from cussing out a priest who tried to tell him how to plant a tree at the church, or biting the head of a goat that had browsed over to chew on a plant in his landscape inventory.

That godda-damma goat-ah!

When I was thirteen, I towered over Grandpa Fort as he cornered me in his kitchen one Sunday afternoon after church and hollered at me for half an hour in broken English. I had no idea why he was yelling at me or what he was saying.

"He was telling you to go to Sicily and buy land because it's cheap," Mom said from the driver's seat on our way home.

"Hell," Dad said from the passenger side, "for fifteen grand you could buy the whole island!"

Mom's mother, Assunta, or Grandma Susie, was born in Columbus in 1908, the daughter of immigrants from southern Italy. She was joined with Grandpa Fort through an arranged marriage when she was sixteen and he was thirty-two. Like Grandpa Fort, she was barely educated. She lived life instinctively, without sophistication or pretense, and showed an innate, tenacious love for her children, another virtue passed along to my mother. Because Grandma Susie could barely read, she learned with her kids, an example of devotion Mom still talks about. Grandma Susie loved to be with people and would dance with anyone. Men, women, children—it didn't matter. While Grandpa Fort also loved to dance—the polka, mazurka, and tarantella—I saw the two of them dance together only once, at their fiftieth wedding anniversary.

Although there wasn't much music in their house, when Grandpa Fort was in a good mood, he sang strains of "La Donna e Mobile" from Rigoletto, or "Vesti La Giubba" from Pagliacci. He admired Enrico

Caruso, and on Saturday afternoons he listened to Milton Cross and the Metropolitan Opera on the radio, which might explain how Mom learned to love opera. Grandma Susie, on the other hand, preferred the songs she'd learned in school, like "Oh, Susanna," and "Up on the Housetop." Their lives were a long, difficult labor simply to survive, which put an enduring strain on Mom and the rest of the family, physically and emotionally.

Mom's youngest years were spent in a working-poor immigrant neighborhood, where internal and social conflicts took hold. It was always hard for her to distinguish if the emotional hurt of discrimination and feelings of inferiority came from the shame of poverty, of being Italian-American, or of being Italian-Sicilian, or all three. The condescending attitudes she felt from non-Sicilian Italians were as hurtful in some ways as those from Americans. Even among Italian-Americans, Sicilians were discriminated against, viewed at the bottom of Italy's cultural and racial hierarchy. Historically, Sicilians were farmers and manual laborers—the working poor.

"Sicilians were viewed as uneducated, indigent, and dark-skinned," Mom said often.

Nevertheless, education was a top priority in her family. "No one can ever take away something you learn," was one of Grandpa Fort's personal proverbs, which Mom quoted all through my childhood, adding another of his: "Everything you learn will be useful sometime in your life."

From the beginning, Mom loved public school, which she still supports with a passion, because it became an equalizer for her, a path to assimilate into American culture, and the key to a deeper understanding of her heritage. In the first grade, she was the first student in class to learn all the words on giant flash cards and thus was awarded a book and her own seat at a big round reading table. Always a good student, she had many teachers who saw her potential and reached out to support her. In junior high school, Miss Nixon, a small, frail woman with immaculately styled short gray hair and a neck deformity that kept her from turning her head, singled Mom out and asked her to help in the school library. "Miss Nixon taught me so much about books," Mom said. "How to care for and repair them, how to Dewey Decimal them, shelve them, card catalog them, check them in and out, and most importantly how to respect them."

"I learned that being around books made me want to read." It also gave Mom a lifetime love of the humanities.

Miss Nixon also taught Mom about etiquette, proper English, tasteful dress, and American food. She took her to downtown restaurants and bought Mom her first wool skirt, navy blue with pleats, and a light blue sweater. "She believed in me, she thought I was smart, and she urged me to have the courage to do what I wanted to do, to go to college and broaden my horizons."

Once Mom reached high school, she was hired to work in the library, on a recommendation from Miss Nixon, and was paid thirty-five cents an hour in a New Deal program the Roosevelt Administration set up during the Great Depression.

Taking no part in high school social life, Mom was not allowed to date. Boys would come to her home, but Grandpa Fort wouldn't let them speak to her and told them to leave. Even Italian boys, for the record, were given no preference. One of her female friends, with whom she regularly ate lunch in the cafeteria, told Mom she could no longer eat with her because her high school sorority didn't approve of their friendship.

Mom's family lived in various houses, only one with indoor plumbing and electricity. Kerosene lamps emitted black carbon deposits on the glass globes and left an odor on everything—house, clothing, hair—that Mom claims she can still smell.

"I remember how hard it was to do schoolwork by that light," she said.

During the Depression, the bank foreclosed on Grandpa Fort's property and he lost everything, including his emerging business and his home, which was particularly devastating to him, for in his native Sicily, owning land was a symbol of security. Meanwhile, Grandma Susie went to relief agencies to get help for her family, taking all of her children with her no matter where she went. "We walked and walked, two to three miles to the bus line," Mom would tell us.

While walking home from school, and on weekends, Mom and her brothers gathered broken glass, and Coke and milk bottles strewn along the streets and alleys to sell at the nearby junkyard for a few cents. Grandpa Fort picked up stale cake and bread for free from the Wonder Bakery, next to the Catholic church. What the family could not use was peddled to people across the creek.

"It's terrible to be hungry," Mom would recall often. "You just can't concentrate on anything else."

In Mom's senior year in high school, after a minor illness, she was invited to live at the home of Dr. Oelgoetz, their family doctor who had delivered her. Before World War II, the Oelgoetzes had visited Sicily, where they were appalled at the abject poverty and substandard way the people lived. They saw animals and people living together in the same buildings. Mom suspects they believed they could guide her into a better lifestyle than the one she was born into. The day she left for the Oelgoetzes, Grandpa Fort told her, "Remember, you can't pick an orange with someone else's hand."

With her high grade point average and the support of teachers, especially those who were Ohio Wesleyan University alumni, Mom was awarded four-year tuition to OWU. Mrs. Oelgoetz, however, told her not to take the scholarship and, instead, enroll in secretary school. "OWU is for wealthy kids," she said. "You won't fit in. You'll always be on the outside looking in."

A few months later, with Mom ignoring Mrs. Oelgoetz's advice, Grandpa Fort scrambled together fifty bucks and the steamer trunk he'd brought with him from the old country in 1912 to move Mom and her belongings into Ohio Wesleyan. Although it would be viewed as a valuable antique these days, the trunk was the only "vintage" baggage on her floor, which embarrassed her. Still needing to pay for board, Mom worked as a waitress in the dorm and took various part-time jobs at a local department store, the OWU cashier's office, and the English Department, where she typed manuscripts for the noted professor and author Dr. Benjamin Spencer. She sold tickets to the university's lecture series so that, in return, she could attend the events.

"Every dime meant something," Mom said. Fifty years later, at a college reunion, a former classmate told her, "I remember you as the poorest girl I'd ever known."

The year after she graduated from college, Mom returned to OWU to serve as a resident counselor and complete courses for a teaching certification. When Dad told Grandpa Fort that he was going to marry his daughter, Grandpa Fort said, "If you two can't make it, nobody can," because, in those days, especially to an uneducated immigrant, what else would be expected of two college graduates who loved each other?

Of course, Mom had no way of knowing what would be asked of her in the coming years, but perhaps she could not have been better groomed for a life that traveled uphill all the way. "I never had time to learn how to play," Mom told us throughout her life. "From the time I was five I had to work."

The only thing she ever flunked was a phys-ed segment in college on relaxation. Even with the small things in life, her very existence seemed to be a deterrent to fun. The few times she attempted to enjoy herself, the world seemed to work against her.

Among her ill-fated attempts to indulge herself was the time she drove me and my sisters home from school, and we stopped at Isaly's ice cream store for an afternoon cone. Completely out of character, Mom ordered one for herself, too. While Niki, Terry, and I walked out, licking the sides of our double scoops, Mom carried her ice cream cone to the car. I stood next to her, waiting to get in the back seat on the driver's side. With too much on her mind and trying to keep her purse intact, she turned the key to unlock the car door and . . . *splat* . . . her scoop of ice cream plopped into the street, leaving her holding an empty sugar cone.

"Everything I do turns to shit!"

Funny words from a dear woman with a touch of Victorian in her, at least until our college years, when she'd been unable to convince us to curb our language, and, finally, gave in to a swear word now and then herself.

Because of Dad's illness and other demands, Mom didn't have much time to neighbor, although she became good friends with two women, Chris Baker and Jean Puglisi.

Chris knocked on our door to welcome us the first week we moved in. She came with her three kids, and Mom joked about how she'd been trying to get me to finish my piano lesson. Her comment embarrassed me, and I went into my closet and hid. I missed most of the visit. I soon learned Chris was from West Virginia and was a woman you never had to ask for help. "She saw the need and was always there," Mom said. "She was without pretense. Chris was one of those people who called it as she saw it."

When Chris died decades later, her son Dan told my mother that one of the reasons Chris loved her so much was because she never looked down on her.

"We shared similar, although different, backgrounds," Mom explained. "We both grew up in poverty, she with her Appalachian roots in West Virginia and me with my Italian roots in Columbus."

Like my mother, Chris was a superb cook, and many Fourth of Julys our families would get together for a lobster bake, with her husband, Darrell, driving me and Dad in the morning to pick up lobsters at the airport that were flown in from Maine.

Mom's other close friend was Jean Puglisi, a hairdresser she met when she took my sisters to get Barbra Streisand-like pebble cuts, a popular style in the late sixties. Jean looked at Mom, wearing a bun with the onset of gray roots, and said, "I would like to style your hair."

At first, Mom declined, then Jean said, "just let me touch up your roots," and a couple hours later Mom walked out of the shop with a state-of-the-art brunette bouffant all her own, along with the beginning of a long, caring friendship. Living a life in which Mom was always caring for someone else, Jean's nurturing was foreign to her. But she and Jean had much in common. Both had Italian ancestry, they loved to cook, their lives centered on their families, and they enjoyed people.

In time, I visited Jean, too, to get the latest-style haircuts throughout high school. "Your mother's very sad," she told me as I sat in her chair. "She knows your dad is dying."

It was the first time I'd heard those words. Mom had even told me she had talked to our family doctor and asked him *how* MS would take Dad, and what his last years would be like. But to hear, "Your dad is dying," especially from someone outside the family, hit me like the corner of a door in a dark hallway.

Although Mom told us many times that she wanted our lives to be as "normal" as possible under the circumstances, Dad's sickness affected Terry, Niki, and me every single day. Mom, trying to shield us from the inescapable pain, took on more of it than she should have.

"Sometimes I was so overwhelmed I screamed and cried," Mom said. "I regret those times. I was no saint."

But even saints have their moments of despair.

One day when I was in elementary school, Mom came into the family room, where I was sitting alone. She was in tears. "Eric, I don't know what I have to look forward to. Your dad's sick. I don't know where the money's going to come from. I've got to take care of you and your sisters. It's all on my shoulders. What am I going to do?"

I looked at her and replied, "Mommy, you just have to have faith."

Days later, she came back to me and said, "Do you have any idea how powerful your words were?"

As a child, I couldn't understand how my statement had such an impact on her, but as I think about it now, I know exactly where the words came from—Mom herself, as another example of her faith, which she has passed on to me.

I always knew I was loved, and her family was her top priority. "My family is my core, and nothing is more important to me than you," she'd say to us often. Through the years, she has always been available to me and my sisters—on the phone, at home, or in her office. Even today at age ninety-nine, she insists on cooking at family gatherings, where she takes no shortcuts. Every meal is prepared from her own recipes, be it homemade spaghetti and meatballs, ravioli, braciole, prime rib, or turkey. From her I've learned that cooking a meal is an art and an act of love and grace.

Perhaps her approach to life is best expressed in the quotation on the prayer card from St. Augustine that is still framed in her kitchen and words she's lived by for nearly one hundred years. "There are no labors too great for loving hearts."

Mom is morally conservative but politically progressive, and accepts social change easily, even though she might not understand it.

When I was six, she got tickets to see Robert Frost, who was scheduled to speak at Mershon Auditorium at Ohio State. "I just think you should see him," she said. But in the interim, he died and his daughter stepped in to speak for him.

Three years later, she came home from a political event and asked, "How'd you like to shake the hand that shook Robert Kennedy's?" And she gave me a program signed by the New York senator two years before he was assassinated. When I was in the eighth grade, she took me to see a live theater production of the musical, *Hair*, a show that, at the time, was outrageously controversial, primarily because the cast members took off all their clothes.

She has an affinity for the arts, still takes writing and painting classes, and has become a wonderful writer and watercolor artist. Always encouraging my creativity, she'd sit next to me with a typewriter when I was a child while I made up stories and plays and dictated them to her. When I was a freshman in high school, Mom worried about my penchant for procrastination. She would listen to my presentations the night before speech class until they were polished. Then, every night, as I went to bed around eleven o'clock, she'd just be sitting down in the den, her typewriter by a stack of books on her card table, working on her PhD dissertation. No matter what she had to do, we came first.

"Take one thing at a time," she'd advise, as she earned her doctorate at age forty-six while taking care of us all. As loving as she was, she had fears of failure, or at least of being unprepared. Her commitment to love and faith seems contrary to her vulnerability to fear. When I understand her past, however, it makes sense. I believe that is one reason she and my dad, who was more easygoing, were attracted to one another.

As Niki said about the days she'd call home from college, "Mom would always ask about my classes and Dad would say, 'Having any fun?'"

In studying for her own exams during graduate school, Mom would be absolutely beside herself with fear. "Oh, God, Walt," she fretted as she rushed by Dad on the way to an exam, "how am I going to do?"

"You're going to flunk, of course," he joked from his bed.

His comment didn't abate her panic, but a couple of days later she came home from class flashing a big smile and carrying a bouquet of flowers. The professor had promised the class that the student who got the highest grade on the exam would be awarded a bouquet of flowers from his garden.

"I feel like a blooming idiot," she told her classmates when the professor gave her the flowers, repeating the words to Dad when she arrived home.

Today her acute anxieties persist, everything from snow, to dogs, to highway travel, to roundabouts, to "staying out of the night air" to avoid sickness, and not flying at night to prevent what my brother-in-law lampooned as, "What, so you want to see the mountain before you hit it?"

And then there are her idiosyncrasies that approach fear but are actually a strict adherence to her excessive conscientiousness, which, granted, also contribute to her unrivaled competency.

I've fought my entire life to ward off my mother's fears so they don't become my own.

But they mess me up anyway.

As a basketball player, I was so scared of making mistakes I tensed up when I needed to relax. In eighth grade I choked on a last-second layup that would have won the game against our rivals.

During my college orientation, I called home to check in the day before classes began.

"After your classes tomorrow morning," she warned, "you'd better make a beeline to the bookstore!"

She made me afraid the textbooks would sell out, so, taking her comment to heart, I drove to class the next day in such a fury that I locked my keys in my car. An upperclassman came by to "help" me, breaking the glass out of my vent window. My first Saturday at college was spent thirty miles away at an auto glass store.

When her fears don't spook me, her need for control can be intimidating and often enrage me. When I was in college, she sent my sister Terry as an envoy when she was worried I wasn't taking my classes seriously enough. Until my mid-thirties, the fights with Mom were nearly constant over my "career choice," as she pushed graduate school or a "real job" that would bring me security. All things that worked for her, but none of which felt right to me. What was particularly ironic—and maddening—is that even though she encouraged me to live a creative life, being an artist was not something she intended for her son.

"Art is something to enrich your life," she said, "but you don't have to do it for a living."

As if being an artist were my choice. It chose me. Besides, I've learned again and again that the only true security in life is believing in yourself.

We'd get into many screaming matches, one of which happened the night I brought Vicki over to meet the family. Vicki and I arrived at Niki's house, and before I even had a chance to introduce Vicki to anyone, Mom and I got into an argument on the front porch. Vicki, coming from a soft-spoken family that never used profanity, wondered, "What have I gotten myself into?" To my good fortune, Vicki stayed with me, and today she and Mom couldn't be closer.

Despite my mother's persistent doubts about my career, I persisted on my path one step at a time, making mistakes, committing terrible misjudgments, trusting the wrong people, not listening to the right ones, and executing all the missteps that most human beings manage to make during their lives. Today, however, I am at peace with the road I traveled, and my mother is by far my most loyal supporter, never missing a gig or the taping of my TV show, when either is local. She stays up late every Saturday night to watch my TV show, and always sends me a supportive text about it the next morning.

With all the challenges my mom faced, she admitted that the one thing that would have put her over the edge was if any of us had gotten into trouble. On some level, Niki, Terry, and I understood that about her, and, consequently, never acted out our teenage angst by shedding responsibility for the sake of youthful pleasure. Our foregoing a period of reckless abandon was partly due to Mom's bequeathed fears, but mostly out of empathy and compassion for her and Dad. My buddies would run off to Colorado for the summer, to Florida for spring break, or to the mountains for a weekend skiing trip. I never felt I had that choice. Even if Mom said I could go, I still knew she preferred I stay home, if only to give her one less thing to worry about.

When it came time to pick a college, I didn't feel I had the freedom to go too far away. The family might need me. Even when I'd go out in the evening, I could never leave my thoughts behind. I went to a disco during college and saw some drunken guy puking in the sink. Nothing odd about that. But as I watched him, it occurred to me how much we take our lives and our health for granted.

Here's this guy who drank so much he's puking in the sink, and Dad's at home wishing he could drive himself out somewhere for a beer.

Heavy thoughts. Not exactly conducive to cutting loose. Or an appropriate topic of conversation while dancing with a girl to "Stayin' Alive."

Even those few times I did let myself go, if only for a moment, life would lower the boom. Mom would be frantic. Dad would be back in the hospital.

As much as I might have gained in learning responsibility at a young age, a rebel still remains poised for launch underneath, ready to lash out, wake people up, and cause chaos, even though decades have passed since such behavior would have been understood or forgiven. While I fantasize about having such memories to embrace, I'm too far down the line to deal with the consequences. So, it remains a "missed stage of development," which, to my regret, is lost forever.

For whatever I missed out on along the way, I suspect Mom is pleased with my restrained decisions, for her life gave her a similar perspective, including the sense of integrity she learned from her parents. During my youth, she and Dad told me about their college "friend" who offered to pay her to write term papers for an Ohio State football star. She declined, of course, and admonished him for choosing an unwise path. Decades later, after the man had gone on the straight and narrow and become a wealthy businessman, he sought Mom out to credit her for putting him on the right track.

An honest life is mostly free of unnecessary complications.

Growing up in a family with patriarchal values and old-world superstitions prepared Mom to survive in a man's world. When she was young, she was forbidden to handle the grapes in her father's cellar winery, or to help can fruits or vegetables, because she might be menstruating and would "contaminate" the contents. Later in life, she had little choice but to pioneer a professional career at a time when women were routinely belittled, discriminated against, and left uninvited to the tables of power. Years after Dad's diagnosis, it was still illegal for women to sign a mortgage or have a credit card in their own name. Even the concept of sexual harassment or the "Me Too" movement were decades away. In the 1960s, the idea of a woman in a PhD program was so foreign that when a professor in one of her Master's degree classes asked facetiously, "Can you imagine being married to a woman with a PhD?" the entire roomful of men guffawed. Mom, typically keeping to herself, sat silent, the laughter lapping around her like the cubs she'd one day corral.

When she applied for the doctoral program with an almost-perfect record, only one professor, all of whom were male, supported her application. Once accepted into the program, she put up with men on the make, most of them professors. One of them was persistent for years, and he even called Mom and asked her for a date three weeks after Dad died.

"I told him I wasn't interested then—or ever."

As fate would have it, Terry later had the same professor for a graduate school class, and he said to her, "You know, your mother is a real lady."

Respect finally won.

Although it's hard for me to imagine all my mother endured in the academic environment, after she finished her PhD, she was hired by Ohio State's College of Dentistry, and within two years became the assistant dean. She was one of only two women administrators in the college, and in time, became president of The Ohio State Association of Staff and Faculty Women. Although she didn't have a dental degree, the college recognized they needed an expert educator to improve the learning atmosphere for students and guide the teaching skills of the dentists.

Recognizing that Mom was more than holding her own in a man's world, her staff cut out a then-current Edward Frascino cartoon from *The New Yorker* picturing six men sitting around a conference table with a woman at the head clearly in charge, announcing with a confident air that she now feels fully self-actualized. On the torso of each man, her staff etched the name of a dentist she oversaw, penned in their corresponding sideburns and such, and colored the woman's hair jet black to resemble Mom's.

She kept it in her office forever.

Considering that women made up merely ten percent of the dental classes at that time, today I cheer inside when I visit my dentist, a young woman, who, now two generations later, can not only take her place for granted, but is also part of an emerging majority in the profession. Many women along the way have expressed admiration and gratitude for Mom. A middle-aged dermatologist said to Mom, a patient, "I should be applauding you. You were a trailblazer for me and so many other women in medicine."

I've witnessed countless people tell her what a difference she made in their lives, not the least of which was my dad, when he summed her up perfectly. "I certainly wouldn't want to work against her!"

Even so, many doctors accused Mom of having a "martyr complex" because she kept Dad home all those years instead of putting him in a facility where he would have received substandard care.

Through the weight of duties and lifetime responsibilities, Mom still manages to sustain her poise, optimism, and beauty, all expressed in her radiant smile. To this day, people think she is twenty years younger than she is, living testimony to what she always has always professed: "Real beauty shines from within." Through it all, she did more than just "keep things together" under unimaginable pressure; she raised a family that was strengthened rather than fractured by the misfortune of illness and disability.

Most of all, Mom gave me the gift of her authenticity. Every word, every laugh, every moment of despair, every flash of anger, every demonstration of love, is real. I always know where I stand with her, and, as a result, she gives me permission, for better or for worse, to be authentic myself.

For that, for everything, I love her more than you can imagine.

Visiting Lazarus

RUNNING through Old Worthington can be like jogging through Grover's Corner, especially during the holidays, when the town looks most like a New England village. The tree trunks in Old Worthington are covered in white lights. The shops are decorated, street lamps display wreaths with three candles, a replica manger scene sits in front of the Methodist church. The lights on the giant evergreens on each corner of the Village Green shine in celebration, and the Worthington Inn looks fittingly grand with its seasonal bulbs showcasing the snow that's been falling on the December grounds since it opened in 1831. While Worthington has its share of charm during the holidays, the standard for local Christmas decorations will always be the former F&R Lazarus & Company department store in downtown Columbus.

Dad had started using a wheelchair, which made family travel more challenging, but Lazarus at Christmastime was "one of those experiences" Mom insisted we share as a family. The five of us packed into our white Buick and made the half-hour drive to the corner of Town and High. For most people, the trip from Worthington to the heart of Columbus ran only twenty minutes, but with Mom's fear of highways, we typically traveled city streets at law-breaking speeds, stopping and starting at each traffic light, our torsos tossed like bull riders.

Carsickness aside, my anticipation flared as we hit Broad Street, where, beyond the top of the Statehouse, the tips of Lazarus's signature decorations glistened against the gray sky. Two gigantic trees of white lights, each crowned by a star. One tree on the roof surrounded the store's water tower like an angel's skirt, the other scaled the building's six-story facade.

The entrance to Lazarus, at South High and West Town streets, was center stage, with the store's Christmas window drawing the customary, captivated crowd, while Santa's elves played with toy trains, fairy-tale characters danced, and a local radio personality broadcast live. Mom and Dad remained at the curb while my sisters and I wedged our way up to the storefront to look at the miniature hobbyhorse and white-flocked trees in their Christmas window.

A few minutes later, with Mom pushing Dad, we made it to the entrance of the store, which welcomed us with a wave of warm air rising through the smooth silver grates of the mammoth threshold, the hard rubber wheels of Dad's chair rolling over them with a muffled rumble.

"You kids'll stay together?" Mom said as we convened inside the store. "Girls, you'll keep an eye on Eric? And help him with his shopping?"

"Of course," they said almost in unison.

"We'll meet for lunch in a half-hour in The Chintz Room on the fifth floor."

And my sisters and I were off to the Secret Gift Shop, a maze created just for the Christmas season where kids, guided by Lazarus employees in holiday outfits, could select gifts and charge them to their parent's accounts.

Niki and Terry, five and four years my senior, weren't crazy about going to the gift shop because they were too grown up for such things. But since I liked it and going there gave us a few minutes of independence, they were willing to put up with being led around by Lazarus employees not much older than them to look at ties, scarves, perfumes, and toys. A few years earlier, Terry had bought me a flat, spongy duck for the bathtub. Yellow with a red beak, it lasted a bath or two before the head tore from the body. Still, I thought the gift shop was the best thing going, especially because the boxes were made just for kids, with built-in handles so I could carry the gifts all by myself.

Heading to the gift shop under the close care of my sisters, I stepped onto the escalator, the steel steps rising. I looked down and caught sight of my parents below. Dad, his head slightly bowed, his bent knees propped awkwardly against each other, his elbows on the armrests of his green Everest & Jennings wheelchair, his hands dangling over his lap like washcloths hung out to dry.

Mom pressed her body into the back of his chair to begin the push, her head upright, her focus forward, her black purse rocking on the right rear handle of his chair as they made their way into the aisle.

Thirty minutes later, my sisters and I arrived at The Chintz Room. Mom and Dad were waiting at the entrance, a shopping bag now hanging on the rear handgrip of his wheelchair, Dad's right knee bobbing up and down in its usual tremor. I stood by, proud of my purchase, clutching the box handles like an oversized carton of animal crackers.

"There're five of us," Mom said to the hostess.

The hostess glanced down at Dad.

"We'll need a table with some extra room," Mom said with her brand of polite efficiency. "His chair won't fit otherwise."

The hostess scanned the dining room, then led us toward the back.

Why couldn't we sit against a wall so not as many people would see us?

My sisters fell in behind the hostess, amusing themselves along the way with their budding French.

"*Table ronde,*" Niki said.

"*Ronde!*" Terry repeated with mock affectation, extending her open hands like a diva.

"*Pour cinq!*"

"*Oui, oui!*"

Niki laughed, an involuntary "tee-hee-hee" kind of burst—her nose crinkling into the bridge of her eyeglasses, her head dipping to hide the full force of her emotions.

Their delight was my discomfort, as they were only bringing more attention to our family.

Mom, with her purple and orange crepe scarf dangling from the right pocket of her black, knee-length overcoat, pushed Dad. She maneuvered the wheelchair deliberately, cautiously, pausing frequently to adjust its course through the narrow channel of tables. The shopping bag scraped against the wheel like a belt of sandpaper. Diners, settled comfortably into conversation, were interrupted—a few had to scoot their chairs to make way for Dad. The hostess signaled for someone to remove a chair from our table so the wheelchair could slide in.

Our wake rolled to the banks of the room. Grownup heads were still turning. A parent told her kid not to stare "at the man in the wheelchair."

Once seated, I insulated myself by pretending to be engrossed in my immediate surroundings. The folds of the napkin. The short stem of the water glass. The flower in the slender vase at the edge of the table.

The server brought the menus.

Mom reached into her purse. A brief forage produced a white tissue, wadded and partially torn.

"Kids," Mom asked, "what do you want to drink?"

She pinched her nose firmly with the tissue, dabbed twice and stuffed it back into her purse without even a look. I often wondered how many tissues she actually had in there. She never seemed to have a clean one for herself, but was somehow able to pull out a brand-new tissue for me every time, which was good because Dad's handkerchiefs, though seldom dirty, were rough on my nose.

"A man uses a handkerchief," Dad would say, "not a Kleenex."

I imagined I'd be a man when I started carrying a handkerchief for things besides wiping my nose—like applying pressure to cuts and opening jars for Mom.

"Can I have a Coke?" I asked.

"Coke?" Terry said. "Not chocolate milk?"

"You may have a Coke," Mom said, her grammar always perfect.

"I swear the kid lives on chocolate milk," Terry said.

"And peanut butter," Niki added.

Terry extended her hand, cupped my forearm, and looked straight into me, her deep brown eyes, inherited from our Sicilian mother, growing wide with affection. "My little brother!" she said. "He's growing up!"

I felt both flattered and belittled.

But I said nothing. Besides, I knew my sisters were right. I *was* living on peanut butter and chocolate milk, and I was terribly self-conscious about it. But Mom had long ago given up on bringing white milk into my diet. Better to compromise the kid's calcium with chocolate, she must have rationalized, than for him to get no calcium at all. Plus, her plate was full with bigger concerns, so she saw to it that each week began with a quart of Meadow Gold chocolate milk in the refrigerator, delivered by the milkman with the funniest name I'd ever heard, Eddie Jaconetti, a delightful Italian guy who went to St. John's Church and always stopped during his route to spend time with Dad. Within a day or two after delivery, I'd finish off the chocolate milk, leaving me to dip into the reserve, a carton of white milk with a can of Hershey's syrup, its brown and silver wrapper sticky as flypaper from drops drizzled down the side.

The server brought our drinks.

Dad had ordered coffee. The cup wobbled in his loose grasp, sending a splash onto his right hand.

"Oh, Walt, let me help you with that," Mom said.

"I got it," he said.

In reflex, she placed her cloth napkin at the base of his saucer and dabbed the overflow.

"Godd—" he cut himself off, exhaling through clenched teeth, the corners of his mouth pulling taut. It was the same tone he used when his mother, Grandma Nez, called him "Wally"—or "Volley," actually, with her Slovenian accent. A nickname he detested.

"You know," Dad said to Mom, "there *are* a few things I can still do."

"I'm sorry, Walt, I was just trying to . . . kids, have you decided?"

Fortunately, the children's menu had one of the two things I'd order in a restaurant: grilled cheese. When it arrived, it came "garnished" with two round pickle slices, cut with ridges and nested in the cheesy gully between the sandwich's two triangle halves. I wanted to complain, but knew I was getting to the age when I couldn't in front of Dad, so I settled on, "Yuck, pickles."

"Oh, did I forget to tell them no pickles?" Mom said, more concerned about having created work for herself than giving in to my manipulation. I slid my plate toward her, she put the pickles on her bread plate, then returned my sandwich to me. But removing the pickles had not resolved the problem. In the spot where the pickles had nestled themselves, the cheese had turned pale and the bread soggy, casting the faintest shade of green. I took a bite over the discolored blotch, drew some Coke through my straw, and sent it all down in a single, awkward gulp.

Dad had ordered an oyster sandwich. Growing up near Lake Erie might have accounted for him loving just about any food coming from the water. Being a kid, I couldn't stand the thought. Our family "vacation" every August was to drive five hours to his hometown of Gowanda, New York, a village south of Buffalo, where a large number of Slovenians settled in the early twentieth century. Our trips would often coincide with the annual Slovenian Club picnic, where, between egg tosses—water balloons for kids—the beer cans floated amid tubs of clams.

The Slovenians clamored, if you will, to crack open the shells, and pile on the horseradish, a condiment way beyond my comprehension.

"Oh, you don't know what's *good*!" Dad would say, and he'd go on to explain that no horseradish was as delicious as Pa's, which is what he called his father, also a Slovenian immigrant. "Pa grew his own, you know," Dad said. "Everybody from the Old Country did. And he'd pile it on. His face would get all red, his eyes would water, then he'd slam his fist on the table and gasp for air like he was on fire. After it was all over, he'd go, 'Ahhhh . . . that was good!'"

I couldn't imagine anyone putting themselves through such misery, particularly when all it took was a pickle to ruin a sandwich.

My eyes moved from my grilled cheese to Dad's face. From the shoulders up, he looked healthy. Fit. His curly hairline had barely receded from his Navy portrait of twenty years earlier, in which he was smiling with his perfect teeth, his green eyes alive with youthful, masculine charm.

Mom and Dad had recently shown me another photo, a black-and-white snapshot taken when he was slightly older than I. Straddling a bike, striking a broad smile at the camera, he was full of optimism, hope, and enthusiasm for the future.

Except for his baggy pants and suspenders, the boy in the photo could have been me. Looking up at Dad as he sat next to me in The Chintz Room, I felt my heart swell, almost tickle, as I reveled in a bond my sisters and my mother couldn't share. Dad and I, father and son, were joined by blood *and* gender. I imagined someday, like him, I'd be shaving every morning. "Don't wish for it too soon," he'd tell me. "It'll be the last thing you'll want to do." Nevertheless, I'd get excited thinking about how my whiskers might be copper brown, too. I'd learn to tie a tie, and my voice would resonate with deep tones. My hands would grow large, with fingers thick enough to wear a big college ring like his.

Most of all, I would forever carry his name. *Gnezda*. A Slovenian name meaning "nest." Symbolism there, I long ago realized. My home was a nest—one that, at least physically, I've never left. Our home was sturdy but with abrasive edges and somewhat out of sync with the times, for Dad was confined to the nest while Mom foraged to provide for us.

Now, as I sat at the table with my family, I watched Dad stare at the oyster sandwich, which had been sitting in front of him for a while. He placed his right hand on top of it, unable to get his thumb underneath to grip it. He went through the motion again with his left hand, as if to demonstrate that, for all his effort, he just would not be able to get the job done himself.

A silent, reluctant call for help.

Mom, apparently hesitant to offer aid after the incident with the spilled coffee, had been waiting for her cue.

"I just . . . can't . . ." His consonants hissed with frustration. His right hand returned to his plate, this time knocking off the top of the roll as he tried too hard to grip it with fingers and a thumb, no longer having the dexterity to clutch such an unwieldy sandwich.

Mom leaned over and sliced it into sections, each of which was only slightly bigger than what I would later learn would be called finger sandwiches.

She picked up an end piece and held it vertically on his plate, awaiting his instruction. He responded by putting his partially open hand next to the slice, which Mom guided into his grasp. He swung his forearm like the boom of a construction crane, directing his sandwich slice toward his face—dropping an oyster along the way—and putting the whole piece in his mouth. His jaw quivered as it extended to chew the oversized bite.

"Walt!" Mom said. "Are you okay?"

His head tilted back with a single chuckle that, with nowhere else to go, released itself as a puff of air through his nose, and somehow, on the surface of bulging cheeks, a smile emerged, bringing forth his two dimples.

At home, Dad's lunches were simpler. A favorite of his was a cheesy sauce called Welsh rarebit. As bright orange as the Stouffer's box it came in, rarebit was something he could heat up himself and then pour over toast, just as he did with another standard issue, creamed chipped beef, also known as "shit on a shingle," he'd confide to me, the other "man" in the house. I'd laugh every time, tickled as much by our exclusive communion as I was by the naughty word.

Occasionally, Mom would overhear.

"What kind of talk is *that*?" she'd ask, feigning disapproval, or false naivete.

"That's what we called it in the Navy."

"Oh, that's man talk," she'd respond, passing through the room to her next task.

Dad would swear, but it was not crude, hostile, or obscene. Never F-bombs. Just his way of releasing big frustrations over life's little nuisances.

When I was in preschool and he was still able to go to work, I had just gotten myself dressed when I heard an outburst from the family room.

"Jee-sus Char-rist All-mighty!"

I dashed in to see Dad crouched over his cordovan wingtips with the snapped-off end of his waxed shoelace dangling from the butt of his fist. I laughed and couldn't stop. The scene replayed in my head throughout the day, making me giggle so much at school that my teachers and classmates must have wondered if I had some kind of behavioral problem. His comment wasn't the type of thing I could repeat or explain, so I just giggled, content to let them think what they wanted.

At that age, nothing was funnier than Dad saying a bad word. My favorite was "*buull*-shit," which seemed to come up a lot when he watched the news.

At the restaurant table, I'd finished all I was going to eat of my grilled cheese, leaving the crust on the plate like corner remnants of a split-rail fence. With his finger pointing upward, Dad raised his arm as far as he was able, halfway, to summon the server for the check.

As we left, Niki and Terry still talking, I shot ahead to escape being part of the scene that followed us in. Mom wheeled Dad down to the first floor and parked him against the outdoor wall of the store. Terry and I waited with him, while Niki and Mom went to retrieve the car.

Dad was draped in his gray herringbone cape—a hoodless wool poncho with a half-zip front—that Mom had designed and hired a tailor to make. Mom had given it to him for a not-too-long-ago special occasion, Father's Day or his birthday, in all likelihood. Coming up with gifts for him became a greater challenge as his disease progressed. Looking back, it's sad to review the "registry" of gifts we gave him over the years, each to mark his latest loss.

An electric razor so he wouldn't slice his face while shaving . . .

Loafers because he couldn't tie his shoes . . .

Pants with elastic waistbands . . .

Shirts without buttons . . .

A dictation machine because he could no longer hold a pencil or type . . .

A lilac bush planted outside his bedroom so he could enjoy his favorite smell in the spring . . .

A mirrored mobile over his bed to bring movement and light to his ceiling . . .

Bed sheets with bright patterns . . .

Cassette tapes Terry and I transferred from his old 78 rpm records . . .

A clock that projected the time onto the ceiling . . .

Bright wallpaper on the one wall he was able to see . . .

A brick doorstop wrapped in a needle point sleeve that Niki, the fine artist of the family, painstakingly crafted to keep his bedroom door open so he wouldn't feel shut off from the rest of the house . . .

Gifts. All thoughtful. All given with love.

All heartbreaking.

As Terry and I waited with Dad outside Lazarus, he sat with his most common demeanor, a look of resigned acceptance. My hands and feet were cold, and I couldn't understand why Dad never seemed to get chilled. Maybe because men, once fully grown, don't get cold. Or maybe it had something to do with him being from Buffalo. "People in Ohio don't know what cold *is*," he'd repeat throughout my childhood. "You get six inches of snow down here and the whole town shuts down. I used to walk to school in four feet of snow and thought nothing of it."

Yes, he'd really add the bit about walking to school in four feet of snow—the rare instance when he sounded like every other grownup.

As he sat, I watched the shoppers pass by with bags, walking with purpose, seemingly oblivious to the joy of the season, not even moved by the live carols coming from inside the store. Out of nowhere, a woman broke from the free-flow formation of the crowd. Middle-aged, long coat, expressionless, she walked up to Dad, reached across his lap and dropped something into his hand, then vanished as quickly as she had appeared. Moments later, Mom's car came up High Street and turned right onto Town, a slightly less-busy cross street, where she parked the car tight against the curb, just past the intersection. Spotting her arrival, Terry unlocked Dad's wheelchair and pushed him to the car. I followed, dreading the public drill about to occur.

Getting Dad in or out of the car always drew attention, putting us center stage in the most embarrassing scenes of my childhood. This one was compounded by the immense size of the audience on a downtown street, surrounded by the backdrop of holiday revelry to which we were providing the sobering contrast of a young family dealing with disability.

With the car still running, Mom emerged from the driver's side, stepped into the traffic she was holding up, swung around the back of our car, opened the front passenger door, and pulled out the transfer board, a smooth pine plank with tapered edges. The routine began and continued like a methodical engineering exercise. With grunts and groans, she positioned Dad's chair at an angle, removed his left armrest, lifted his left thigh, and wedged the board under his rear end. Sliding him across the board and into the car seat, she pulled the wheelchair and the board away from the car, lifted his knees one-by-one, placed his feet on the floor of the vehicle, reached across his body to fasten his seatbelt, and, making sure he was safe inside, shut the door.

"All these people here," Mom lamented, "and no one offering to help."

Niki and Terry took the wheelchair around to the back of the car and started folding it when Mom said, "Girls, let me do that. It's cold. You kids get in the car. And get in on this side," pointing to the sidewalk. "I don't want you getting hit by a car."

Like most mothers, Mom warned us of obvious dangers as though they were obscure safety tips privy only to parents, a habit she still practices, and one, predictably, I have "inherited" as a father. She also, at least while she was present in any given situation, insisted we not help. Many years later she explained she didn't want us to "resent" our father, a concern I never understood. Even as I dealt with my boyhood embarrassments, I never resented Dad. I wanted to hide from the public drama of disability—the canes, the crutches, the wheelchairs, the fatiguing father everyone seemed to feel sorry for, the ultra-conscientious mother whom everyone admired.

Just all the damned attention.

But I didn't resent him. If I resented anything, it was MS, which robbed Dad of his health and me of having the life afforded to other boys with able-bodied dads. They could do things together. Go places. Navigate the world as father and son. I had to learn on my own, the hard way, without a mentor, through mistakes and missteps. Rather than resenting Dad, I hurt for him. I wanted him to heal. He, such a kind, accepting, bright man, didn't deserve to be disabled.

I was mad at the world and ashamed of myself that I felt embarrassed.

As Mom folded the chair, then leveraged it onto the lip of the trunk to slide it in the rest of the way, I sank into the back seat hoping no one I knew had witnessed this entire spectacle.

Dad couldn't help it. Mom was just doing what she had to do, and my sisters weren't the least bit embarrassed.

But I was.

What a bad kid I must be to feel this way.

The ride home was sullen. At a stoplight, Dad's voice cracked when he said to Mom, "Mary, some lady gave this to me while I was waiting for you to get the car."

He opened his quivering hand and revealed a quarter.

Neither of them said anything.

"People," Mom would sigh years later when recalling the story, "they just don't think."

Relief Pitcher

MY first memory of the Flats along the Olentangy River comes from my Little League baseball tryout. Waiting for my turn on the field, I sat next to Reed Liming, who was singing to himself one of the big hits of the day, "What a Day for a Daydream," by the Lovin' Spoonful. *How cool is that*, I thought, as he had the courage to sing around a bunch of jocks. Even Reed's smooth voice couldn't take my mind off the wretched stench coming from a trash barrel behind home plate. More than a half-century later, even though the original metal can has long since been replaced by a polyethylene one in the exact same spot, I still brace myself for the odor every time I pass by.

The olfactory trauma was horrendous, but my tryout stunk up the place even worse.

As I run past that baseball diamond today, I see something unconventional. A boy, at least thirteen, is taking batting practice with a woman who looks to be his mother. Of course, you see this all the time with toddlers and their moms throwing Wiffle balls. But this is serious stuff. She's throwing overhanded, dipping into an industrial-sized bucketful of hardballs he's knocking into the outfield, and the boy doesn't seem the least bit self-conscious. I've got to hand it to him because, well, to be honest, I *have* seen this at least once before. Not from the point of view of an onlooking runner. I was the kid holding the bat.

It was the summer my family moved into our new house. With a baseball tryout having gone south, my season was going worse.

"If you just had someone to play pitch and catch with," Mom said after a game. "All you need's a little practice."

I was a scrub. A bench warmer. One of those kids they put in during the late innings just to make sure everyone gets a chance to play.

Truth is, I was afraid of the ball. Small and hard, it came at me too fast, and I just wanted to get out of the way. I was terrified a grounder would hop up and hit me in the face. I wouldn't put my glove all the way down, and my skinny legs, bent at the knees and spread apart, became a croquet wicket planted in a pair of Keds.

Consequently, I was put in the outfield. Shortfield, actually, a position they'd created for players like me. The shortfielder stood between second base and center field. He was the tenth man on a team of nine, the team tonsil, a superfluous node stationed as interference in case a ball got past the second baseman or shortstop.

Usually by the time the ball would dribble through the infield and into the tall grass before me, it had slowed to a near stop. I could handle picking it up, but then there was the throw to the infield. I had a cannon in my right arm, yet no control. The heave could end up in the third baseman's glove or, just as likely, under the other team's bench. Once, in throwing to the plate, I gunned the ball over the chain link backstop. Impressive show of force, but a dead ball nonetheless, which stopped play, moving all the runners up a base—giving the other team *two* runs, rather than one.

My little league coaches often commented on what a great arm I had. A few even said I'd make a great pitcher—if I could learn control. None of the coaches ever took the time to teach me, though. The unspoken rule was, "That's your father's job."

The last time I'd tossed a ball around with my dad was when I was three or four. His hands weren't able to grasp a baseball, so he'd sit on the front stoop of our old house and throw me the football. I loved to catch his throws, elude an imaginary "tackler" or two, then tumble to the ground.

"Don't fall down!" he'd yell every time I caught it. But he was missing the point. We were playing *football*. Since there was no one to tackle me,

I'd have to act it out myself, even risking injury—like the time I fell into a patch of clover and a bee stung my pinky.

When it came to baseball, however, I was left to learn the sport from other dads, whose priorities were coaching their own sons, showing little concern for me, or not being aware that my father was physically unable to teach me.

My baseball coach seemed to view me as a nuisance, a shy kid with undeveloped skills. He wasn't mean, just impatient, favoring the boys who were further along, especially his own son. The coach intimidated me, but so did all men. He seemed every bit masculine, with short salt-and-pepper hair. His son was our team's best pitcher, or at least the one most called upon for duty.

We were the boys of McCracken Plumbing, a horrible team. Even dressed like one. Our bright red caps clashed with our maroon T-shirts, which carried the name of our sponsor in mustard lettering. By midseason—and depending upon how our respective mothers did the wash—many of the shirts had faded to brown, purple, or rose.

It was a Tuesday evening, and we were playing on the diamond behind the former Linworth Elementary School. We were down 26–0 in the top of the final inning. No mercy rule in those days. We'd been in the field so long that my mouth was salty from chewing the cowhide knot on the thumb of my Rawlings glove "autographed" by Mickey Mantle, and chosen with my mother at Woolco, a local discount department store.

The good news for McCracken Plumbing and our fans: There were two outs.

The coach's son was on the mound. He was tall, lanky, and awkward. His windup was slower than a long pendulum, delivered with a motion as straight as six o'clock. His pitches, soft.

I stood in shortfield. He released his pitch. The batter swung and the ball lifted high into the air, right at me. Feeling like a soldier in a foxhole, I watched the grenade bear down. Terrified, I thrust my glove under the ball, waist high, Willie Mays-style. Like my teammates and spectators, I was afraid to watch, so I closed my eyes. The ball dropped right into my glove, just below the webbing, striking the underside of my knuckle at the base of my index finger. Because I was frozen with fear, my glove had no give and the ball bounced out like a bad hop.

Even the motorists out on Route 161 must've heard the groans. My coach dropped his shoulders, looked downward, and shook his head. My error failed to stop the bleeding, and they went on to tally another nineteen runs that inning.

Final score 45–0.

And this was baseball.

Before the last game of the season, the coach told us we could choose the position we'd like to play, depending upon the number we drew from a hat. By pure luck, I selected "one."

"I'd like to pitch."

A tremor went through the team.

"You want to *pitch?*" the coach asked.

I nodded my head.

As I walked to the mound, my team held its breath, and, feeling there were a thousand eyes on me, my confidence plummeted, and I exchanged my natural throwing motion in favor of one that imitated my coach's son. Exactly sixteen pitches later, after walking in a run on consecutive balls, I was relieved of my pitching duties and thrown back into shortfield.

It was my first lesson that the surest path to failure is abandoning your own methods in favor of someone else's.

* * *

If you just had someone to play pitch and catch with . . .

* * *

"Grab your bat and ball," Mom said from the kitchen on a Saturday afternoon. "I'm gonna throw you some pitches."

"You?" I asked, half-thrilled to get an invitation to play and half-terrified that one of the few older boys in our nascent neighborhood might see me playing with my mother.

"I'll show *you*," she dared. "Don't forget I had five brothers."

We went across the street to one of the many vacant lots in our new housing development. The clay soil was covered with Olentangy shale. Thistles and weeds pocked the dry ground. The lot, cresting on a modest hill, flattened out about thirty feet from the newly poured concrete curb that ran like bleached borders along our street. The fresh asphalt smelled like oil, glistened like coal. On the plateau of that lot, soon to be showcasing another prefabbed house, Mom and I stood about ten paces apart. She had the ball in her hand.

I addressed the plate, stretching my bat across it, then took a few practice cuts. Like the pros, I spaded the batter's box with my sneakers to secure my footing. Mom stood by in her knee-length denim shorts and sleeveless cotton blouse, a pastel floral print. On her feet were blue canvas tennis shoes with white laces and pointed toes. Instead of socks, she wore footies. Even so, any self-consciousness I had about being spotted with my mother was now being overruled by the excitement of having a bat in my hands. As it turned out, there was little chance of being seen anyway. On the first pitch, throwing underhanded, Mom served up a perfect—and fat—strike. The meat of my bat connected with the center of the ball, and I swatted a line shot that would have proved a thing or two to my coach, his son, and the rest of McCracken Plumbing. Unfortunately, less than a second later, the baseball smacked Mom squarely on the outside of her right calf. Her knee sprung up, her torso folded, and she grabbed the lower half of her leg with both hands, determined not to fall.

"Oh, oh, oh," she moaned, hobbling around in a tight circle, trying not to cry.

Me, too, as I saw she was also trying to be mother *and* father. This was her reward. A burst blood vessel three inches below the knee that made her limp for days. Some ninety-one years later, the bruise is still there.

Puffy. Darker.

And no smaller.

* * *

Not giving up on my baseball career, Mom later suggested I play that summer in the Junior Jets League—named after Columbus's Minor League baseball team of the day and sponsored by the City Recreation Department. They play three games a week, she explained, and the coaches are rec leaders, not dads, "so maybe you'll get some real instruction."

It took no salesmanship on her part. I signed up, and the extra practice paid off. By the time I was twelve, I made Worthington's traveling team, the premier youth squad in the area, and the only one that traveled in those days. Not only did we go to surrounding towns, but we sometimes even played under the lights at ballparks that had manicured grass infields. Just like on TV. Because we represented our city, we wore dapper durene uniforms like the big leaguers of the late sixties. White baseball pants and shirts, red and black piping, with black letters and numerals that had been stitched on. We had red elastic belts, and slipped our feet into black baseball socks with red and white horizontal stripes. We even got to wear rubber cleats. Sewn across our chests, in shiny black letters, was the name of our sponsor, Worthington Jaycees.

On my back, I proudly wore the number 4.

* * *

Although fielding was my weakness, I could hit. I batted 1.000 through the first nine games of the season. All singles, an occasional double. Only one homer in my "career," and that was because there was no fence. I smacked the ball right up the middle and it kept rolling and rolling and rolling. I kept running and running and running. I can still see the coaches' arms waving me around third, the team going crazy, never thinking they'd see Nez hit a homer. Not with these skinny arms. Still, our official statistician—the dad of one of my teammates—scored it only as a double. "If there'd been a fence," he said, "you would've been held up at second. So I thought a double was fair."

But there wasn't a fence!

Those damned numbers guys. Always stomping out the joy.

* * *

Dressed and ready to head to the ballpark early in the travel team season, I walked into the master bathroom to talk to Mom, who was at the sink getting ready to go to my game. I closed the hollow sliding door that led to the bedroom where Dad was stretched out. "Mom," I asked in a hushed tone, "are you bringing Dad?"

"Of course I am," she said in full voice, apparently not getting the signal that I wanted to keep this conversation between the two of us. "Why? Don't you want him to come?"

"No, Mom, it's not that, it's just that you pull up in the car and then get the wheelchair out and then everyone starts looking and it creates a whole big scene and—"

"But he's your *father*."

"I know, Mom, but . . ."

Just then Dad called to me through the closed door. Ashamed for how I felt about not wanting him to come to the game, I felt worse that he'd overheard me. I slid the door open and stepped into his room, my eyes not meeting his.

"Hey, about your game today," he said, "I'll stay home."

I thought I'd feel relieved, but I was surprised by the depth of my hurt for him.

Perhaps his love for me ran so deep that his concern for my feelings overruled his desire to watch me play ball. Or maybe *he* was relieved. MS is an exhausting disease. Leaving the house wore him out. Sitting in the sun incapacitated him. I'll never know for sure why he agreed to stay home. He wasn't one to talk about such things. Now looking back, I can't imagine how much it must have hurt him not only to overhear what I'd said, but also, through no fault of his own, to be deprived of the incomparable joy of watching his only son grow and participate in life, something I could fully appreciate only when I had children of my own.

Letter from Dad

"WHAT'S this?" Mom asked Dad as she came home from work and saw a small, gift-wrapped box lying on Dad's overbed.

Dad, trying to hide his excitement, said nothing.

"My God!" Mom said as she unwrapped a diamond ring. "What's *this* for?"

"Today we've been married for ten thousand days."

Mom was touched to tears.

Alone with his thoughts, day after day, having long since lost his ability to use a pencil or a calculator, with eyesight that could no longer read, and without the help of an internet still decades away, Dad, who could recall obscure chemistry and math equations from high school and college, had done all of the calculations in his head, complete with leap years.

Mom couldn't contain her surprise and joy.

At dinner afterward, we joked about how Dad had arranged the surprise through one of Mom's friends, who knew a jeweler. Dad had an uncanny way of getting owners of stores to bring their inventory to his bedside so he could pick out gifts for Mom.

"So . . ." Mom mused, ". . . ten thousand days, times three . . . that's thirty thousand meals I've cooked, and God knows how many dishes I've washed."

Dad broke into his movie-star grin and said, "Probably a quarter million dishes!"

They both laughed.

"Walt was a hopeless romantic," Mom said many times. "He had a marvelous smile, a wry sense of humor. His courting was dramatically embellished with French phrases of amour. The only love letter he ever wrote to me was written in French."

Mom and Dad met in August 1949. Unable to get a job in Columbus's saturated teachers' market, Mom, discouraged and desperate for money, went to work at Ohio State as an administrative secretary in the College of Business for Junior Dean Charles Reeder, who was also a professor of commerce. In her interview, Mom told him she didn't take shorthand.

"That's okay," he joked, "I'll talk slow."

Dr. Reeder's main role was as a student adviser. It wasn't long, however, until he saw how competent Mom was with her duties, and he delegated to her much of the routine course selection and scheduling for his advisees.

"Late one afternoon," she said, "I noticed a student who was waiting in line to get information. He was tall, had ash-blond curly hair, a lean, well-built physique, and was quite good-looking. He was wearing a khaki bomber-type jacket, which gave him a no-nonsense, masculine look. He definitely was not the preppy, letter-sweater and white-bucks type. He had been in line for quite some time."

When it was his turn, she finally motioned him to her desk. "As we talked," Mom continued, "I pulled his student file and saw that he was from Gowanda, New York, Cattaraugus County—wherever that was—and a transfer student from the College of Engineering." She also noted that he was a veteran who had served as a pharmacist's mate in the Navy during World War II, and his academic record was good.

"He was nearing completion of his requirements and came to discuss suggestions for electives. Because I was gung ho about the humanities and liberal arts, I encouraged him to try some of these courses."

He showed interest and enthusiasm for some of her suggestions, and before the meeting was over, he asked her if she would have a beer with him at Larry's Bar after work.

She wasn't much of a beer drinker, but said yes. "We had our beer. I couldn't finish mine so he finished it for me."

Dad later told her that he knew at that moment they were made for each other, because there would always be beer left over for him.

While Mom's explanation of their meeting was characteristically detailed, Dad's was succinct. "I went to the dean's office for some advice, and I've been getting it ever since!"

To go on their first official date, Dad borrowed a suit from his roommate, Stan Zalar. A fellow Slovenian and OSU student, Stan had been telling Dad for some time about this wonderful woman he'd taken on a date. Only later did they find out they had dated the same woman—my mother.

After meeting Dad, however, Mom told Stan that he was "just too calm, cool, and collected" for her. Stan never got over her but remained steadfast friends with Dad and Mom, visiting whenever he came through Columbus, always teasing Mom by repeating he was "just too calm, cool, and collected."

Dad was fond of telling us about the night he proposed to Mom. He had taken her to the Seneca Hotel in Columbus, where he had arranged with the orchestra leader to play "Body and Soul," while he'd present Mom with the engagement ring, a quarter-carat "perfect" diamond set in a platinum band. As he took the ring from his pocket, the orchestra instead played "The Tennessee Waltz." Dad was disappointed as hell at the mix-up, but took it in stride, and "The Tennessee Waltz" became their theme song, which we heard about every time it played on TV, typically *The Lawrence Welk Show*.

They got married in Columbus at St. John's Church, of course, where multiple statues of saints stood among the odors of burning incense and candles from the altar, spaghetti sauce from the priest's living quarters, garlic from the parishioners, and fresh bread from the neighboring Wonder Bakery. The ceremony was attended by only a few friends and family members. Their black and white wedding photos show Mom and Dad bubbling over with happiness, surrounded by their smiling parents and relatives.

As a child, having never seen Dad stand straight up without a cane, I was amazed at how tall he was in the photos, how healthy he looked, and how masculine and debonair he appeared. I felt pain that MS had taken subsequent healthy years from him. From our family. And from me. In one photo he's smiling with Mom at the top of the church's staircase. Who knew that just a few years later it would take several good men from St. John's to carry him up those twenty-some steps in his wheelchair so he could attend Mass with his family.

The wedding reception was at one of the city's finest Italian restaurants, Cenci's, where the photographer unknowingly captured a photo of a guest—the wife of an immigration attorney invited by Mom's father—sneaking out of the kitchen with some chicken she'd helped herself to as the reception was coming to a close.

In our family lore, she is known as "the woman who stole the chicken."

The wedding was on March 29, moved up from June after the Navy notified Dad that, now that World War II was over, he'd been recalled for service in Korea. Wanting to qualify for officer's training school, Dad had driven to the veterans' hospital in Cincinnati for a physical. On his wedding day, he received a letter from the Navy saying his service would no longer be needed. No explanation. In hindsight, my parents wondered if the Navy had spotted something about his health that was a concern. At the time, however, Mom and Dad just thought it was a strange response and went off to their honeymoon.

Their wedding was on a Thursday, leaving only a long weekend for a honeymoon because Mom had to work the following Monday, and Dad, still in college, had class. With a pittance to their name, they had little choice for a honeymoon except to go forty miles southeast to Lancaster, Ohio, where there was a hotel with a bridal suite. Because they didn't own a car, they were driven to the hotel by Mom's brother's best friend, a man who, strangely enough, had taken her on one or two dates, and who, according to his sister, still pined for her. After three nights of splurging on caviar, steak, smoked fish with scrambled eggs, and champagne cocktails, Mom and Dad took a Greyhound bus to Columbus, where they had planned to take a taxi home. It was there that Dad admitted to Mom, "I hate to tell you this, but we don't have enough money for a cab." They took the city bus to their new home, where they began their marriage in a ground-floor apartment on Ninth Avenue that had been converted from a garage into living quarters.

"He never fretted about money," Mom said. "He always said the money would come from somewhere, somehow. He lived in the moment and always tried to make things nice," whether it was champagne cocktails on their honeymoon, or the caviar hors d'oeuvres he ordered at Doersam's Restaurant when they dated.

"It was I who always worried about the money," she said, and repeatedly teased Dad about how they came back from their honeymoon broke.

Ten months later, Niki was born. At 5 pounds, 6 ounces, "her little feet seemed so tiny, no more than an inch and a half long," Mom said. "I had no idea what feelings giving birth to my firstborn would well up in me. I had never felt more joy."

My parents had some good times, particularly in the early days, yet life got hard for them fast.

When Dad told his parents that he was marrying a Sicilian, Pa was not happy. A native of Idrija, Slovenia, Pa was outraged at Italy for their oppression during World War II, and for the twelve Battles of the Isonzo during World War I, in which thousands of Slovenians ended up in Italian refugee camps and died of disease and malnutrition. Dad knew Pa was no fan of the Italians, but he was sure of his feelings for his future bride and wanted to make them clear to his parents.

After Grandma Nez died, my sisters and I were cleaning out her attic, and we found a letter Dad had written to her and Pa in 1951. It looked brittle but wasn't. It was smooth and heavy in my hands, as if it held the weight of Dad's heart. Having been folded for so many years, the seven-page letter resisted being opened. I tucked my thumbs into the crease and pushed on the underside with my middle fingers. The letter snapped open, creating a point in the center of the pages.

It smelled like old playing cards.

On the upper left side of the first page was the Ohio State crest, engraved in scarlet. Above that, a small translucent smudge from the oil of a thumb. Each successive page of the ivory stationery, its edges jaundiced by age, had a similar, yet fainter, smear.

This letter had been read a lot.

How strange it was to realize that I had never really seen Dad's handwriting. But how wonderful it was to be looking at it. In my early years, before MS had seized the use of his hands completely, he would try to sign his name to things like my school permission slips. It was always an ordeal. It would take him forever to pick up the pen. Because he could not bend his fingers enough to maintain his grasp, the pen would often fall to the table or the floor. At times he would resign himself to asking me to position the pen in his right hand. Quivering, his hand and forearm would pivot spastically across the page in broad, jagged strokes, like a worked-up polygraph needle.

The result was the shadow of a signature.

The penmanship in this letter showed no signs of disability. It flowed from a young man with dreams who had begun to assert himself.

His handwriting was straightforward, with a subtle flair. It suggested a man eager to communicate his feelings, yet somewhat impatient with the process. Most of his capital letters were not in script and remained independent from the rest of the word, which he wrote in cursive. His loops were sometimes slightly larger than necessary, although not at all extravagant, as if the freedom of the circular motions gave him temporary reprieve from the detailed demands of legible penmanship.

Each line of cursive was fairly straight on the page, although imperfect. He seemed to have given some extra care to achieve symmetry. There was an occasional heavily crossed out word, and his spelling was flawed in spots, which I found surprising but comforting.

He had used a fountain pen, presumably the one I had seen many times in the back of a drawer at home. Cordovan colored with a silver ring. The nib, stained with ink, had been dry for years. As I read, I realized that even though I had never seen his handwriting, it was quite familiar.

It looked like mine.

Many of the lines stand out in my memory.

Feb 12

Dear Ma & Pa,

    Thanks for the birthday presents. I almost forgot about my birthday—too many other things to think about . . .

    Mary and I had plans to get married in June after I graduated. I've known her for a year and a half and have been going with her for over a year. Plenty of times she made me feel happy when I got sad about school. In her, I found something to help me enjoy life. We go to church, talk, go to a few shows or else go to see friends of ours and just talk or play cards. I've always been happy with her. We argue a little bit now & then but we get over it in a few minutes. She's a good girl for a wife, that's why we're going to get married ...

I'm not a kid anymore & I can do a little thinking. Mary also isn't dumb. If it were something that we thought of overnight it would be different ...

I know that you don't like the idea but sooner or later every man, or almost every man, decides that he'd like to get married. I'm not doing this to make any of you mad. In fact I want your blessing. I know all of you have done a lot for me but so has Mary. She helped me in a lot of ways that none of you could. I appreciate all you've done for me. That's why I still want your love and understanding ...

She doesn't complain much but she never lets me get lazy either. I wish you had gotten to know her better—you'd find out that I made a good choice ...

I hope you're not mad because I'm not doing this to hurt you. You always wanted me to amount to something and with Mary I know I will.
Love
Wally

... for richer, for poorer, in sickness and in health ...
How little we know of marriage at twenty-four.
Or what life will ask of us.

Sage Advice

MOM and Dad never gave me the sage advice to marry someone I enjoy talking to, but they were a daily example of it. As Dad's health declined, their conversations revealed the core and the depth of their connection. They'd talk about everything, and Dad's intelligence and humor always delighted Mom, who was every bit as smart.

As for TV, they'd watch *Firing Line*, and although they disagreed with the conservative host, William F. Buckley, Jr., they loved his command of language and his repartee with the liberal John Kenneth Galbraith. They watched *Washington Week in Review*, but also *Columbo*. Dad got a kick out of comedians, whether they were on *The Tonight Show Starring Johnny Carson* or their own sitcoms. He often told me lines from comedians he'd watched the night before.

One of his favorite bits was the late David Brenner's now-classic line about the dumbest thing ever said to him. David was on a bus, sitting on a newspaper, when someone asked, "Are you reading that?"

David stood up, turned the paper over, sat down, and said, "Yes."

Dad also liked a sketch from *The Bob Newhart Show* where a man was showing off his ability to take anyone's name and say it backward.

"What's your name?" he asked Newhart.

"Bob," he replied.

Dad was the youngest child of his Slovenian-immigrant parents. An older brother, Justino, died of pneumonia at six months, and an older sister, Jennie, named after her mother, died in the 1918 Spanish Flu pandemic, along with two other relatives in the home within forty-eight hours. Born February 4, 1927, Dad turned out to be the only surviving son, with two older sisters, Sophie and Jessie.

"He got enthusiastic about learning new things," Aunt Jessie told me. "You know, he'd come home and be enthusiastic about something he'd learned. He was also very aesthetic. He cared about people and had a sense of humor."

"At twelve, he had a bicycle and a paper route," Jessie recalled with a chuckle. "On collection day, he'd collect his money and spend it all on pop and ice cream before he got home."

Dad's mother, Grandma Nez, sailed to America at age sixteen, "alone and scared to death," she recalled, rejoining her family in Gowanda, New York. She was kind and accepting, and called me "Ettik-ee," in her Slovenian accent, which, of course, my friends wouldn't let me forget. To go to a movie with her was embarrassing, for if a mildly sexy scene came on, she'd yell at the top of her register, "Oh, Mar-EE-ah!" Whenever she sent letters to the family, Dad would read them aloud in her accent, which was among the funniest things he'd ever do. She insisted that I was a "good boy," which I thought was grandparent embellishment, until one day, she cited evidence. I was walking home from school and moved a neighbor's empty trash can from the middle of the street to the curb. Little did I know she saw the whole thing from our front porch, and said, "Ettik-ee, you know that four kids walked by that can and you were the only one to pick it up. You're a good boy."

A low bar, but I was happy to accept it.

She died when I was twenty. The following week I had surgery. Alone and afraid in the middle of the night, I felt her presence come into my hospital room and lay her hand on the bandage covering my right ear. Once I was calm, she moved across the room to an empty chair, where she "sat," just as she did when I was a little boy.

"Grandma," I communicated to her through thought, "what can you tell me from the other side?"

"Just be good to people," she said and remained there until I fell asleep.

Just be good to people.

Words I'll never forget, words that guided her life. She operated her own unofficial Slovenian settlement agency. As she'd get word that Slovenians were arriving in Gowanda from the Old Country, she'd go to the train depot just down the street and take them into her home, helping them get on their feet and teaching them English. Serving others was a role she'd take on her entire life, the least of which was making fried chicken for special events at the Slovenian Club across the street, and always being at home to let the beer and liquor man into the club to restock their supply.

She never got paid for her duties.

Dad's father, Pa, or Jacob, had come to the United States on a passport he "borrowed" from a cousin. As a Slovenian, Pa had been drafted into the Austrian Army, but he anticipated the First World War and immigrated to America as a young man. He had a nice head of hair until he got the flu and double pneumonia, which cost him all but enough to comb over his vast bald spot. One day Dad came home from the barber with his plentiful hair buzzed into a stylish crew cut. Pa was almost in tears.

"All that beautiful hair going to waste," Pa lamented in broken English.

A few years after Dad left home, Pa was diagnosed with heart disease, and nobody from his family told Dad. Two-and-a half years before I was born, Pa had a stroke and fell down the basement steps. Dead at sixty-five, a month after retiring. His first Social Security check arrived in the mail the day he was buried.

Dad's voice would break when he'd speak of the cruel irony.

* * *

Gowanda is a village split between two counties, Cattaraugus and Erie, and is attached to the Cattaraugus Reservation. It takes its name from the Senecas, "a beautiful valley between the hills." The primary businesses were the Moench Tannery, which provided products to the Brown Shoe Company until it closed in the early 1990s, and the Peter Cooper Glue Factory, which took Moench's chrome-tanned hides and boiled them into more animal glue than all of their competitors combined. The

26-acre, $17-million-a-year business earned Gowanda the title in the 1930s, "America's Glue Capital."

As a child, I'd sit on Grandma Nez's porch and look beyond the catalpa tree in her front yard to see trains pulling into the factory with animal skins piled over the sides of the cars. The stench, with the air turning pink and clothes rusty, was unbearable, while the Cattaraugus Creek, running through the village, changed colors depending upon what waste the factory discharged on a given day.

Years after the glue factory closed, the Environmental Protection Agency named the former Cooper complex one of America's worst waste sites, finding that its "cookhouse sludge" contained chromium, arsenic, and zinc, and in 1998 placed it on their National Priorities List.

Pa worked there most of his adult life and hated every minute of it.

Dad considered taking a year after high school to work at the glue factory, but his football coach, Howard Hillis, a tall and broad-shouldered man, told him, "You'll start earning money and you'll never go to college." So, at sixteen, Dad went to college. He was accepted at Cornell University, where he couldn't afford the tuition, so he chose Ohio State over Michigan, which notified him a few days after Ohio State.

I've often wondered if Dad's illness was caused by growing up across the street from the glue factory. But there were other suspects, too, such as the scarlet fever that went into his kidney, bloated him, and nearly killed him as a young child. The harmful unknown chemicals he was exposed to in Okinawa when he was in the Navy. And there were some studies indicating that MS was more prevalent among people who grew up in cold climates.

As with many MS patients, the symptoms started showing up in his twenties. He worked at the GE plant in Cleveland, while he took a year off from college, and was never put on the assembly line because of his "lack of coordination," according to Aunt Jessie.

"Right after we got married," Mom said, "he started having trouble with his eyesight. We went to an ophthalmologist who gave him a prescription for eyeglasses but didn't mention any other diagnoses. Sometime later we were told that the eye doctor's notes indicated that he thought Walt might have MS." Then Dad began stumbling now and then and was slow on the brake when he drove, having a fender-bender the night I was born. Three days later, he was officially diagnosed with MS.

"I soaked you with my tears," Mom told me of my first few months in her arms. "Your father wanted a son so badly. You should have seen him the day you were born. He was so proud."

Soon thereafter, Dad's hopes and dreams of a bright future came to a crashing halt when he lost his job as a foreman at a construction firm because "we can't have a man who walks around looking like he's drunk," the company president said. Even though Dad had disability insurance through the company, the president disqualified him from receiving payments because he said his disease was a pre-existing condition. Mom went to the State of Ohio Department of Insurance to try to get the decision reversed, but got nowhere, as prior to the Americans with Disabilities Act, the disabled had no standing and were completely dismissed from society, viewed as an inconvenience to be hidden from the healthy to keep them from feeling uncomfortable.

Another slap in the face to Dad.

A few years later, when it became apparent Dad would never go back to work, he attempted a writing career, dictating his work, mostly plays, to my mother, or into a Wollensak reel-to-reel tape recorder. The fatigue of his disease became too much to overcome, and he stopped the pursuit, his literary appetite partially sated by listening to Talking Books from the Library of Congress. On a regular basis, stacks of LPs, packaged in square, hard-shelled black cases secured by green canvas straps and tarnished buckles, would arrive by mail. They looked like covert government documents, which I was happy to let my friends conclude they were. The discs were recorded for playback at ultra-slow speeds, and played on a government-granted turntable with a lift-top lid that housed a mono speaker.

Talking Books were what Dad depended upon to fill his days. Classic plays, topical nonfiction, newspapers, and magazines, read by a deep-voiced narrator whose government-issued inflection was flatter than the turntable the record was spinning on. Yet, Dad was genuinely grateful to have this service available, even if the "latest" periodicals and newspapers arrived on our doorstep a dozen weeks after original publication.

"How do you know so much about what's going on in the world?" a neighbor would ask. "Well," he'd respond, feigning the smugness of a self-satisfied pundit, "I just listened to *The Wall Street Journal* . . . from three months ago!"

Dad had always been a reader and respected great writing. My junior year in college, as he lay in a hospital bed, I told him of my aspiration to be a writer.

"That's what the truly intelligent people do," he replied.

Intelligent people also design homes, a dream my father had formed during his halted career in the building industry. Ironically enough, his MS diagnosis gave him the opportunity, as he designed our modest one-story home without steps, inside or out, and with extra-wide halls and doorways to accommodate a wheelchair. Because the ADA was still years away, patients from Ohio State's Dodd Rehabilitation Hospital would often come by our house to learn from Dad's design. Although our home looks typically suburban from the outside, a friend of mine paid my dad the ultimate compliment when he said the inside of our house reminded him of Frank Lloyd Wright's "Prairie Style" design, with its rows of windows and open flowing spaces.

Building the house was not without conflict, though, as Dad and Mom would fight like hell sometimes during the construction. After the house was completed, he had a wry reply for anyone who asked his advice about building a new home: "Get a divorce first!"

As his disease progressed, the wide hallways went quiet in the mornings, no longer ringing with the *ting-ting* of his wheelchair's unfastened arm lock hitting the aluminum frame as he made his way down to let me know it was time to get up. He became confined within the walls of his "mausoleum," as he comically-tragically called the quarters of his bedroom, where he held court, not nearly often enough, with friends and family.

As sardonic as Dad could be, he venerated the men who fought in World War II, especially those who stormed Normandy on D-Day. When the epic film about the invasion, *The Longest Day*, was released, he made it his personal mission to take me to the theater. It was the only time that just the two of us went to a movie and might have been the first movie I ever saw. Dad was still able to drive then, although it struck fear in the heart of my mother, since, as I later learned, he had stopped car-pooling me and a friend to school on his appointed days because he had trouble moving his leg from the accelerator to the brake. On this particular jaunt to the movies, however, Dad and I arrived safely, and as we sat in the darkness of the theater together, I felt imbued with masculine glory, for it was with me, exclusively, that Dad had chosen to share this great historical event.

The opening credits, merged with the soundtrack of male voices in song, seized me, filling me with an awareness of the power of music and film together.

Every now and then, Dad would lean over to tell me something.

"The guy who wrote the song is also in the movie," he tipped. "His name's Paul Anka."

Later in the film, when an errantly dropped paratrooper found himself hanging from the pinnacle of a cathedral tower and was left to watch the battle from far above the village street, Dad whispered with respect, "He hung there for over two hours, pretending to be dead."

How proud I was to be privy to all of his inside information.

Dad's voice would often crack with emotion when he talked about the war and said many times, "Each generation has to learn. The best way to honor the dead is to not get into another war."

Lying about his age to make himself eligible for the service, he enlisted in the U.S. Navy because he "looked better in Navy blue than in Army green," he joked, and would often make light about his job as a pharmacist's mate on Okinawa, where he primarily checked sailors for venereal disease. "I was serving my country!"

Throughout my childhood, Dad was a testimony to the benefits of humor, as he had depended upon it to get through his daily ordeals, not only the physical and emotional suffering brought on by MS but also the frustrations of being a person whose vision and insight went far beyond most others of this culture. As I grew, I learned that Dad's knowledge of history and current events exceeded that of nearly everyone he knew. His passion for politics, monitored by a skeptical eye, engaged his mind and kept him connected to the world outside.

"Turn on the news," he'd summon every night at six o'clock. "I want to know what I'm supposed to believe."

Humor was the way he got through his inevitable decline, the uncomfortable moments, his unbearable pain. For all of his suffering, being homebound gave him time to reflect and spared him the daily aggravation of face-to-face interactions with those who, although healthy and holding down prominent positions in life, were dull, dimwitted, dense, gullible, and greedy. I've wondered, had he been physically able, how he would have fared in an increasingly corporate-driven society, where image reigns over truth, and conformity is rewarded over creativity. Where a wise man thinking for himself is considered a threat.

Like a life without music, a humorless existence would be merely a soulless flesh-and-bones slog through time. A fish comes to mind. So does a worm. Or any number of dour desk jockeys who hide behind their titles and their company policies, motivated by ego or survival, biding their time until retirement, lacking imagination or the courage to dig into their deeper selves and find a passion that not only satisfies them but also serves others.

If Dad had participated in the world, how would he have endured the restless routine of being a cog in a conventional system? Would he have been booted out? Left on his own accord? I'm sure he wouldn't have merely "survived" by surrendering to a life of "quiet desperation," as Thoreau called it. My guess is he would have followed his dream of owning a company that built houses, viewing it as a service profession that also was financially rewarding.

I heard a 78-rpm recording of a speech Dad gave in college in the early fifties, about his support of the labor movement. Dad's baritone voice was thick with Western New York inflection and dialect, which waned over the years, except for a few words and phrases. "Californ-ee-ah." "Sore-ee" instead of "sorry." And "hamburg" for "hamburger."

I heard in his speech intelligence and conviction with an underlying confidence he may not have yet discovered. Saddest of all, as I look back, is to see the potential of such a brilliant man snuffed out. "He never had a chance," Mom has said repeatedly, always on the brink of tears.

My heart breaks for him.

I often wonder how Dad would feel about my various pursuits. Sadly, he died at about the time I was emerging into adulthood. I was twenty-three, just out of college, and had my first job. There wasn't much that I had accomplished. Just a few articles published in the local newspaper, which now I understand pleased him primarily because it was important to me. He was likely more concerned with how kind I was to others, especially my mother, and whether I would be a man of my word.

Would he like my songs? My speeches? Would he think I was funny? What would he think of my TV show? Would he enjoy it or just watch it because I created it? Would he fall asleep instead, as he often did during other TV programs?

While I'm not sure he'd like all of my material, I'm pretty sure he'd be damn proud of me for creating my own path and doing some things that life didn't give him the opportunity to explore.

When I was really young, he took a post-grad course in broadcasting, even buying a pale blue dress shirt, an oddity in the early sixties, to mute the glare of the TV lights. From what I remember, his final exam—a news broadcast he had to deliver—must not have gone well. I'm not sure what happened, but Mom had gone with him, and when they returned, he said both of them wanted to crawl into a hole.

I have felt similar pain and embarrassment more times than I can remember.

Dad used humor for self-protection, a way to conceal his piercing intellect and the depth of his feelings. No wonder he was so often misunderstood. Throughout my childhood I'd been a daily witness to humor neutralizing sadness and suffering. How ironic it was for Dad that even though his eyesight was diminishing, he saw so much in the world that others didn't.

H. G. Wells wrote of a sighted man who falls accidentally into a valley of blind people. Thinking that he'll be king, he instead finds himself an outcast. I'm not sure Dad ever read Wells's *The Country of the Blind*, but he certainly would have connected with the protagonist, for Dad was the original "seer." How alone he must have felt, even before his sickness, to be one of the few people who could see the world as others couldn't. And then, because of his disease, to be all but isolated from contact with the outside world, except for his family and a few friends.

When my niece, Yvonne, arrived in this world as his first grandchild, he joked with Mom that he was too young to be sleeping with a grandmother, so he declared to everyone that he was to be called "Uncle Walt."

And when I came home once to a raging argument between my sisters and Mom, I walked straight into his bedroom, at the other end of the house, and asked him what was going on.

"I have no idea," he said, "but whatever it is, I'm sure it's my fault."

I can't tell you the number of times a neighbor visited Dad with the intention of cheering him up. After thirty or so minutes, however, it would be the neighbor who left with spirits lifted, smiling from new insight into a current event or a quip that would turn into a running joke between them. One of his most ardent visitors was his close friend, Darrell Baker, Chris's husband, who sold Lifetime Cookware. Dad quickly dubbed him "a pot salesman," which raised a few eyebrows among neighbors in the late sixties. Our family doctor, Dr. Durant, would make house calls to tend to him, and his favorite barbers, Hank and Rick Nini, whom he'd met in college and took me to as a young boy, would come by to clip his hair.

As hard as life was for Dad, two forces sustained him. The love of his family, particularly Mom, and a sense of humor that gave him reprieve from the pain of his disease and from a world of people who couldn't see, didn't want to see, or most infuriating of all, who were able to see but chose not to because it would challenge their complacency.

Dad knew the risk in being funny. Many people didn't understand him. Some were put off. "Most people just don't have a sense of humor," I can still hear him say. "Don't waste your time with them. You're not going to change their minds and you'll just wear yourself out."

Losing Contact

IN August, the scent of the grass drifts from sweet to musty. The high school playing fields fill with teams and marching bands for summer drills. Coaches bark, whistles blow, and drumlines hammer out cadences, as if giving marching orders to get back in step for school. Even though it's been years since I've been part of this routine, I still get excited this time of year, I suppose, because I'm conditioned to it—the anticipation of meeting new friends, undertaking new projects, and returning to familiar tasks with a fresh outlook. As much as I mourn the loss of summer, the beginning of school feels like a second chance to make a New Year's resolution.

Summer heat beats down from the sky in June and July, but in August it rises from the ground. As I'm running, my body boils from the inside out, searing the last of any toxins, releasing them in a layer of heat that clings to my skin like a wetsuit.

I love it.

These workouts always take me back to the months before my freshman year in high school, my initiation into summer training, spent on my own, learning to endure the heat as well as discovering the joy of solitude and the private elation of transcending my own limits. I had turned to running when I realized that a coach's decisions couldn't be arbitrary in track. The fastest runners ran in the meets. Period.

I was also propelled by impending fear as I entered high school. Fear of upperclassmen. Of not reaching my goals. Of the varsity coach, who was a legend in Ohio, as much for his winning teams as for his unwillingness to bend with the times.

Once team workouts began, I met the legend himself, Coach Les Eisenhart. He carried his stopwatch in his jockstrap. "A man's natural pocket," he said. In his late fifties, he was tall and lean, his face worn with wrinkles. He had a broad smile and laughed easily, but only with other coaches, never with us. His graying hair was cropped on the sides with a tuft on top that looked like it was combed by a licked palm.

"You know what we say around here, fellas: 'Hair today, gone tomorrow.' All I ask is that you keep it above the ears and off the shirt collar."

Never mind that it was the seventies and we were competing against teams from Cleveland and Cincinnati who had ponytails halfway down their backs.

"If you don't have the money for a trim, I'll give you a coupon," Coach said.

Eisenhart stored coupons from the Ohio State Barber College in his desk drawer. "Two bucks," he said, stroking his coif in mock vanity. "They do just as good a job as those fancy places you go to, and they're right up north here."

No one I knew ever took him up on the coupons, but when one member of our team ignored Coach's overnight deadline to get a haircut, he found himself under Eisenhart's shears before he was allowed to practice.

He wasn't always so "lenient." When a teammate mooned an opposing team from our bus, Eisenhart found out and kicked him off the team. "We don't need some horse's ass who thinks it's funny to stick his bare ass in the air," he told us. "I told him to go down the road."

"Look, fellas, it's the same for everyone around here. You either abide by the rules, or you go down the road."

"Go down the road" meant to quit the team, and Eisenhart despised nothing more than a quitter.

When he addressed the team, he'd stand in the front room of the field house between the chalkboard and the shiny black metal door of the coaches' office. The room smelled like Cramer Atomic Balm and cat piss. I was sitting on the concrete floor with most of my teammates, while others sprawled on the spongy blue high jump and pole vault pits, which would be moved outside "once we get a break in the weather," as Eisenhart put it.

"Fellas, there's some new rules this year from the Ohio High School Athletic Association," Eisenhart read from his ever-present clipboard, occasionally glancing over his half-glasses to make eye contact with no one. "I'm telling you, fellas, my eyes aren't what they used to be. I used to be able to see a nit on a gnat's nut."

Those of us who were still listening laughed. Even though Eisenhart would say coarse things from time to time, he was not a crude man. Only unsophisticated and certainly not gifted in the language arts. Looking back, I almost feel sorry for him for his lack of oratorical skills, although it was a source of humor to all of us.

A shop teacher, he was organized, pragmatic, and unpretentious, his fashion sense dictated by comfort and economy. He wore soft-soled street shoes with "matching" double-knit slacks and a V-neck sweater, each its own shade of burgundy. When he dressed up, he wore a sport coat with a bolo tie for reasons I never understood, since he was not from the Southwest, but from Columbus North High School, less than ten miles from Worthington down High Street. Somewhere in my memory, though, I remember something about him and his wife traveling to Santa Fe in a mobile home. Presumably, that's where he picked up the bolo.

He had only one set of workout clothes. Faded gray cotton sweatpants, a pair of white Adidas flats with green stripes, and a navy windbreaker. In the rain he put on a poncho with a tan fishing cap, the bill sticking out as far as a canvas awning. The sight of him in that hat always broke us up.

As Eisenhart continued to address the team, Harrison elbowed me. "Look at Coach's jacket."

Eisenhart's windbreaker was snapped cockeyed. Neely saw it, too. So did Maynard. And Chadwell. Our shoulders shook.

Unaware of our reaction, or maybe ignoring it, Eisenhart kept reading.

"And so the relay runner with the baton must remain in the exzone change."

"*Exzone change?*" Harrison snickered. "Doesn't he mean *exchange zone?*"

Pockets of laughter were popping, concealed by coughs and throat clearing. To restrain myself, I dropped my head between my knees and dug my fingernails into my flesh. Blood pounded in my ears as I clenched my jaw, straining for dear life to hide my laugh from Eisenhart.

Thinking back, I miss the pre-practice meetings more than the workouts or the races. Enduring the monologues engendered empathy among us. Amusing, but usually painful in the same way it is to suffer through a bad speech. For more than two years, fear and my desire to please Eisenhart held my attention and kept me loyal to him.

I'd been proud to follow the outmoded rules that had driven so many other athletes to ditch track and instead play for coaches who didn't mind hair that hung below a lacrosse helmet or grew over the ears of a soccer player. Although I felt self-conscious in the hallways of long-haired upperclassmen, my quasi-military cut also announced that I was part of Something Special—the Worthington distance running tradition, led by Coach Les Eisenhart, an Ohio high school mile champion and one of the best collegiate runners of his day. Revered by his coaching colleagues, he was a member of the Ohio Track and Cross Country Coaches Hall of Fame. He'd been coaching at Worthington for twenty-six years, winning fourteen consecutive Central District titles and a state championship. No one could remember a year that our cross country team wasn't in the State Meet.

By my junior year, however, his mystique began to wear thin. I had grown tired of his rules, the physical grind, and his constant assault on my psyche. "I figure if I yell at you enough," he told us, "you'll want to prove your old coach wrong."

But that approach couldn't have been worse for me.

My onetime rival and now teammate, Ted Barnes, learned how to survive from his older brothers' experiences with Eisenhart: "I just don't listen to him."

I now realize Ted's approach was spot on. At fourteen, however, I didn't know how *not* to take Eisenhart's every word to heart. Nor did I know it would be okay to tune him out. More than okay, actually, and in fact the mentally healthy thing to do.

I had voluntarily and eagerly placed myself under Eisenhart's thumb since the day I walked into high school because I'd made the varsity cross country team as a freshman. Early that season at a meet in Lancaster, Eisenhart took my mother aside and said, "What I like most about your son is that he's a *competitor*." At that point in my running career, I was competitive. A friend told me I was so competitive he couldn't imagine me ever losing a race. Yet it would take years of effort to recover from the erosion of my confidence, which Eisenhart had a mighty hand in dismantling.

April of my freshman year, in the rain on a Friday at the Marion Night Relays, I'd run the race of my life, winning a varsity mile. I always ran well in the rain. At one with the dreariness, I felt that the adversity gave me an extra edge. My glasses would steam up, raindrops would further blur whatever clarity remained, welcoming me into a gray surrealist world where oxygen seems concentrated and in greater supply. Yes, I've since heard all the talk about rain and the positive effect of negative ions, but there was more to it than that for me. The greater the challenge, the harder I fought to overcome it.

After the race, Eisenhart dashed down from the stands in jubilation. "Looks like we've finally found our miler for the District," he said, "and he's a *freshman*. A tough, tough *freshman*." I was euphoric, as much from his approval as from my performance. My lungs burned raw from the cold air, and my teeth ached as if ice had been pumped into the pulp, the pains of victory I proudly accepted as the winner's laurel.

"Wasn't sure," I gasped, ". . . I could . . . hold off . . . that guy . . . at the finish . . ."

"Well, you did," Eisenhart interrupted, suddenly terse in response to my exhilaration. "Now go on, Eric, get your sweats on, start your warm down, and get out of this rain. We can't have you sick for the Districts." Then he cut off any further trackside celebration and headed back into the stands.

It was the only time when I was running for him that he'd ever called me "Eric." Usually, it was "Gnezda," and when he spelled my last name, he inverted the "z" and the "d."

"I'll spell it right when you're a star," he'd joke as his stock response.

I rode home from the race that night in the back seat of a sedan driven by a teammate's mother. Forty minutes through the darkness, illuminated only by the green lights on the dash. "A Horse with No Name" was pumping through the radio, and my victory ribbon was tucked inside my blue Adidas bag.

I felt like I'd just won the Olympics.

* * *

At Monday's practice, as I was warming up on the track, I happened to jog into Eisenhart's path. "Gnezda," he said, cocking his head to signal a summons into the infield. He spoke in a tone I'd never heard from him. His voice was quiet, confidential. "Listen, I did some checking. Do you know that's the fastest mile a freshman's ever run here?" He paused and locked his eyes on to mine. "I was pretty sure that would be the case," he said, then he continued to tell me it also was faster than a legendary American miler had run as a high school freshman.

To get Eisenhart's praise was unheard of, especially for a freshman, but to receive it privately, face-to-face, was beyond any encouragement I could have imagined. And then for him to have gone to the trouble to research the *freshman* times of one of my heroes, I felt anointed by Eisenhart, the man who, himself, might have been an Olympian had it not been for the Second World War. I was still a long way from the phenomenal high school feat Eisenhart was implying was possible, but I had four years left, and his face flared with possibility. "I think you can be one hell of a miler—*one hell of a miler*—if you want to be. *If you want to be.*"

When Eisenhart was at his most intense he would repeat himself, drop his clipboard to his left hip, raise his right forearm parallel to the ground, and rock his hand back and forth as if buffing the top of a shot put. It was an idiosyncrasy that became the way we, as teammates, would greet each other anywhere and everywhere. Partly out of mockery, partly out of respect, always as an affirmation of our bond. Even today when I see a former teammate, our hands start flapping before we speak.

"The mile's the toughest race there is," Eisenhart continued. "Not everyone's man enough to run it. Takes a rare combination of speed and endurance. *Speed and endurance.* You've got both. It's just going to come down to how much you want it. *How much you want it.*"

Sometimes the scene plays in my mind as an embarrassing cliché from a coming-of-age movie. Yet too much was at stake in those vulnerable years to dismiss all the emotion from it, even today.

I waited for Eisenhart to zoom further into my rapt eyes and fire the question point blank: *Eric . . . how much do you want it? How much do you want it?*

I longed to tell him that being a champion runner was more important to me than anything, that my life had prepared me for it. That as strong as he thought I was on the outside, I was even tougher inside. That I'd never quit anything. And never would. That a Gnezda knows how to persevere. That I would be The Guy. I just needed him to show me the way.

Instead, his eyes drifted into the distance.

"You know," he chuckled, "there was a guy here back in the sixties. I thought he was going to be a hell of a miler. *Hell of a miler.* Had it all. Speed, strength. He was tough all year long. Till the State Meet. Then he'd just shit down his leg. I mean, you could put a sign in front of him that said, 'State Anything,' and he wouldn't be worth a damn."

He tilted his head and shook it. "Never figured him out."

Silence.

"Coach?" I mumbled, trying to get the response I coveted. "I want it pretty bad."

His eyes returned to me briefly, only to disconnect. "Well, time will tell, Gnezda," he said. "You're young yet. You can't just wish it. You got to go out and do it. But we'll see what kind of man you are this Friday. I'm putting you in the Arlington Relays as our number one miler. I want to see if you can do it again. Now go run your warm-up and be ready for your workout."

He looked at his clipboard and walked away, over-striding as always did, leaning into each step, limping slightly from back and knee pain caused by running on cinder tracks in bad track shoes when he was at Ohio State.

My legs ached as I jogged around the track. The race I'd run less than three days before had taken my young body to a new level of exertion. Even though I'd run over the weekend to ease the effects of lactic acid, my calf muscles were stiffer than ever and my thighs were still sore. At school that day, my legs burned from the inside out every time I climbed the stairs. In class, slumping from boredom in my tablet-arm chair, I amused myself by watching my quads twitch involuntarily in my skin-tight bell-bottom jeans.

I didn't know it at the time, but what I needed more than anything else was rest. A few days of lighter workouts to give my young legs time to recover, not to mention a mental respite from incessant competition.

But that wasn't Eisenhart's way.

He ran us into the ground. Big meets on weekends, dual- and tri-meets with neighboring schools on Tuesdays, even followed once in a while by time trials to see who was going to run in the big meets on Saturdays. When we weren't racing, we were competing in lightning-fast workouts that would often leave us puking and doubled over with headaches from oxygen debt.

"Who wants it? *Who wants it?!*" he'd yell as we ran the backstretch. His raspy baritone voice snapped like a lash, cracking deep into our self-concepts. If we weren't running up to potential, there could be only one explanation as far as Eisenhart was concerned. We just didn't have guts. It never seemed to occur to him that our guts already had been spilled on the track earlier in the week during workouts.

I continued my warm-up, elated by what he had just told me in confidence. Well, at least by *part* of what he'd told me. Just the fact that he had taken me aside, something I'd never seen him do unless we were in trouble, was enough to put the wind at my back. Yet I also felt something I didn't have the words for—the dawn of disillusionment. For all his recognition of my potential, I was troubled by his apparent lack of faith in me. Perhaps over his years of coaching he had been let down by too many athletes who had proclaimed their willingness to pay the price to be champions, only to turn out to be "quitters." To cast doubt was his way of motivating. He didn't seem to trust that I'd turn out to be the runner he'd been watching for a year, even though I'd given him no reason to think otherwise. I knew better than anyone that I still had a lot to prove, yet in the aftermath of my greatest triumph, all he could come up with was "you're young yet" and a story about a guy who screwed up the State Meet every year.

Does he assume that's me?

Instead of "time will tell," I needed him to say, "I believe in you, and I'll help you get there."

But that wasn't Eisenhart's way either.

My legs hurt the rest of the week, the fast workouts not helping. Friday after school I rode to the meet with two teammates in the backseat of Coach's car. Upper Arlington, our archrival, is a richer suburb than Worthington. Black and gold, they are the Golden Bears, the high school alma mater of Jack Nicklaus, and the school our football team hadn't beaten in three decades. When it came to track and cross country, however, we were on equal ground.

Although clean, Coach's car, a pale-yellow Oldsmobile Cutlass, sagged in the rear from suspension problems. He dialed up the popular hits on AM radio. As we rolled up Zollinger Road alongside Upper Arlington's stadium, Neil Diamond sang his new release, "Song Sung Blue." It was the first time I'd heard it. Seeking refuge from my fear, I sank into the melody and let it lull me into the emotional terrain where I felt most at home—melancholy. Once there, I rolled uncontested into the cave of teenage self-pity.

No one came to watch me run... No one ever does... Mom's too busy... Dad can't... Everybody else's parents will be here... Or their girlfriends... I don't even have a girlfriend... I'm always alone...

I yawned from nerves as I got out of the car. The guys who had prelims—sprinters and those in the field events—already had set up our team camp in the visitor's stands. I stopped by long enough to drop my bag off and then walked languidly to the far corner of the infield, where I found a patch of grass to stretch out. The ground was cool, but the sun was still full enough this late in the day to give my face a welcome touch of warmth and reassurance.

I closed my eyes.

Just get whatever rest you can...

A small plane hacked away overhead, its motor grinding with the uneven chops of a lawnmower. My eyes popped open with a ludicrous thought. *Maybe it will crash right here in the stands. Then they'll cancel the meet and I won't have to run.*

Guilt now compounded my dread. I thought about soldiers at war and how terrifying an oncoming plane must be to them. *And I'm only running a race.*

Yet this race felt like a matter of survival.

I closed my eyes again. In time I lapsed into hypnagogia, the ethereal space between sleep and consciousness where awareness floats in fragments and noise travels underwater, rising to the surface now and then to startle us.

A starter's pistol echoes . . . A coach shouts . . . A hurdle is dragged from the track . . . A siren moans a few blocks away . . .

First call . . . Mile Run.

It came over the public address system like a doomsday announcement.

I sat up, lightheaded, my vision swirling from midnight blue to metallic green, then finally clearing.

C'mon, time to warm up, get it in gear.

Groggy, I jogged along the outside lane of the track, steering clear of any prelims. After my great race the previous week, Coach had made my varsity status official by giving me a pair of "swishies," a puffy nylon sweatsuit so named because whenever you moved it went "swish-swish." Hooded, it was royal blue with a round red patch on the chest embroidered in white lettering: "Worthington Track."

"When you step off the bus with those letters across your chest," we were told, "you strike fear into the hearts of your competition." Although we knew this was likely an overstatement, we were happy to buy into it because, well, actually, over the years a couple of guys from other schools *had* walked away from the starting line after spotting Worthington runners in the race.

My pride swelled as I ran past the stands. For years I'd been going to the high school meets, looking up to the guys in these trademark swishies, and now I was wearing them myself. My München 72s—Adidas's new training flats of blue suede uppers and three white stripes—were alternating in a poised rhythm on Upper Arlington's black rubberized asphalt track, which had lane lines alternating in white and gold. *Swish-swish, swish-swish, swish-swish* . . . I glanced at my feet, indulging in momentary adolescent self-admiration.

Maybe I'm feeling better than I thought.

The headwind on the backstretch had picked up. Ohio's spring winds are murder. The day can be bright and warm, but get on a southbound straightaway and a frigid gust will whack you backward.

"If you're waiting for the perfect day to run," Eisenhart told us many times with his hand flapping, "you'll never have it. You're never gonna have the perfect day to run a race."

It was, and still is, the primary Eisenhartism we love to repeat.

Second call . . . Mile Run.

Having jogged about four laps and broken into a good sweat, I did my stretches, then went into my strides—short bursts of speed, slightly faster than race pace.

The burning returned to my legs.

A few more accelerations to see if the ache might work itself out.

Still there.

Don't worry, you never know how you're going to feel until you're in the race.

Putting my spikes on was a ritual I preferred to do in private. Still in my swishies, I sat on the ground with my knees raised to my chest. Adrenaline-thick blood pushed into my stomach, shortening my breath, giving me momentary nausea. I got up on each knee to tie my laces, then stood up. My feet, sheathed in leather, undergirded with spikes like the tips of shark's teeth, felt weightless. I was ready to fly.

Final call . . . Mile Run.

The slow-motion trip to the starting line was always like a walk to the end of the high dive or what I imagined it would be like to be taking my final steps toward the executioner. Suffering was certain, and I wasn't sure what life would be like on the other end—if there *would* be life on the other end—so I moved in a trance of pensive inevitability.

Eisenhart was surely watching, although I couldn't tell from where. Except for his lone bit of advice before every race, "tie your laces in double knots," if he talked to us at all, it was to give us our lane assignments or to hand us the racing bibs we safety-pinned to our nylon singlets. He never talked strategy or gave us encouragement, except for once in a while with his patented phrase—"Gnezda [or whoever he was addressing], be the man today. *Be the man today.*" Usually, though, it seemed he was nowhere to be found until after a race.

I continued toward the starting line. I removed my swishies but had no idea who I'd handed them to. My spikes caught on the inside of my pants as I took them off, puncturing the cotton lining. I might have felt the cold air whisk my exposed legs and maybe a quick blow of the breeze caught the chest of my sweaty nylon singlet. But none of this registered. Like my competitors, I was absorbed in meaningless movements to calm the jitters—small hops, quick knee kicks, and short dashes from the starting line in anticipation of the gun that was less than a minute away.

The starter, his forearm in a puffy yellow sleeve, stepped in front of us and began his rote instructions. "Mile run . . . four laps . . . stay in your lanes until the break line."

I punctuated my pre-race ritual as I always did, by locking my knees, crossing my ankles, and bending down to press the ground with as much of my palm as I could.

"Runners, I'll give you two commands: set, and then the gun. Good luck."

This is really happening.

The starter raised his gun.

I stepped to the line, left foot in front, leaning slightly forward.

"Set . . ."

My weight shifted down and onto my back foot. Breathing stopped.

The gun cracked.

I sprung from the line, my fingers tingling.

The first part of any race is all adrenaline. You run on instinct and training, dashing to grab position on someone's outside shoulder so you won't get boxed in, and on a windy day, to shield yourself, or "draft." At the end of lap one, you start to feel the race. Adrenaline gives way to the first signs of exertion, and you settle into a pace within the pack and focus on staying relaxed yet alert.

Lap two is more of the same with the heat turned up.

Lap three is hell. Perhaps the longest interval in all of sports. You're far enough into the race to be writhing in pain but not far enough to see the end. The temptation to quit is immense. Adrenaline has vanished, agony sets in, and it's just a matter of hanging on while your heart, mind, body, and spirit battle it out. I've since learned that life has many "third laps." In relationships, projects, sicknesses, and, of course, creation. The price of perseverance always pays off in the end, but you've got to get through that arduous third lap to even be in the race.

My legs felt heavy. My knees were churning but there was no lift. No drive. No bounce. A distance runner's first commandment is *stay in contact with the leaders*. The idea is to remain with the pack so that in the final stage of the race you're in position to strike with your final kick, often in a split-second response to someone else making the same move first. If you've fallen back, though, even the strongest kick is worthless, especially in the mile, where runners have good sprint speed and can accelerate quickly.

Falling off pace rarely happens at once. A step. A few seconds later, another step. Then two. Your stride shortens. You might start telling yourself the biggest lie of all. *Just take it easy for a moment. You can catch up later.*

I was struggling to stay with the leaders. By the time I'd hit the backstretch of lap three, they were pulling away, and to make matters worse, there was no one to block the wind. With each attempt to accelerate, the pain in my legs pushed me back on my heels. To win a race, your body has to respond to what your mind tells it to do. Like an engine grinding without oil, my body only groaned in rebellion, so my mind eased off its commands.

What the hell, it's only one race. Eisenhart's not expecting me to run well today anyway.

The final lap was excruciating. With no prospect of reward, I let my form fall apart. My stride lost its cadence. My arms flailed. My head wobbled like a bobblehead doll. Had I not been in such pain, I could at least have kept up the appearance of being competitive. Perhaps Eisenhart, wherever he was, would get the message that I just had nothing left in the tank.

I crossed the finish line well out of contention, gasping for air.

As I walked back to get my sweat clothes, Eisenhart appeared beside me on the other side of the fence surrounding the track. He had a way of showing up out of thin air. "Gnezda!" His lips quivered, his eyes bored into me. "I can see running a second or two slower than last time, but not *that* much!"

"I know, Coach. Tired, I guess."

His eyes held mine a few moments longer, as if asking, *How could you do this to me?* Then he stormed away.

"Coach..."

"*What*, Gnezda?" he snapped, stopping and turning halfway around.

I dropped my eyes. I knew I didn't have anything to say. I was trying to ask for help, although I didn't have a clue what I needed or even how to begin to ask for it.

"Nothing, Coach."

He loped away in uneven strides. For the second time that day I had failed to get my point across to him. During the race I tried to show him, and afterward, tell him that I was being crushed by fatigue, inside and out, and whatever we were doing wasn't working for me. Strange thing, but even though I had run a bad race compared to the week before, my time was exactly what I'd run *two* weeks before when he shook my hand and congratulated me on "a good mile for a freshman."

His praise seemed like a lifetime ago, for now he was singing a different tune.

"Gnezda, you're up and down—always up and down."

One "bad" race provided hardly enough evidence to warrant a new refrain, but it didn't matter to Eisenhart. He was old-school. His only method of motivation was to tear you down.

The Quitter

EIGHTEEN months later, Coach Eisenhart's opinion of me hadn't changed. His car was filled with five of us heading up I-71 to the Ashland College Invitational cross country meet, a little more than an hour north. I sat behind him, my elbow against the door, my right knee knocking a teammate's left leg with each bump on the interstate. Coach's AM radio was again launching Top Forty hits into the unventilated air, with "Angie" making a direct hit in my brain and lodging itself as an earworm that kept burrowing deeper. From the first steps of my warm-up, through the parts of the race when my concentration lagged, until I fell asleep that night, my head would pulse with Mick Jagger's tormented "*Aiy-an-geh.*"

I'd ridden with Coach enough that just about every meet had a signature song.

Ontario Invitational: "City of New Orleans."
Newark Invitational: "The Night They Drove Ol' Dixie Down."
Lancaster Relays: "Taxi."

About halfway to Ashland, Eisenhart turned down the radio.

"Fellas, I don't know what got into me last night, but I had the strangest dream." He chuckled, lifting his wrist to check his speed. "I can't remember the last time I dreamed about a race. It was the damnedest thing. You were all there at the starting line . . . got off well . . . were running great... and then all of a sudden I couldn't find Gnezda. I looked and looked. And it turned out he'd taken off on a train somewhere."

He shook his head diagonally, seeming to be stumped as to the dream's meaning.

Truth was, even if he'd dreamed that I'd won the national championship, I still probably would've run a mediocre race that day. I was melancholy about life again and not at all enthusiastic about pushing my body when I was already hurting so much on the inside. By sharing his dream, however oblivious he may have been to its meaning or how it might affect me, Eisenhart further embedded the self-fulfilling prophecy, giving me permission to live up to it and surrender to the pain during the race.

Over the next few weeks, I ran well, finishing second in the league championship and fourth in the Central District, where Ted sprinted past me in the final stretch to beat me for the first time. "You came on like an ossifier!" Coach told Ted.

"An ossifier?" I asked. "What the hell is that?"

"I don't know," Ted laughed. "Maybe he said house of fire."

A few days later *The Columbus Citizen-Journal* wrote that Ted and I were Worthington's "two junior gems" who might just lead our team to a state championship.

For years, I had wanted nothing more. Now our chance stood right in front of me.

Our chief competitors were Upper Arlington, of course, and Cincinnati Elder, a large, all-boys Catholic school. Early in the season, Eisenhart had set up an after-school meet with Elder on our home course. "We'll find out where we stand today, fellas." Even our football team—rivals of another sort—rushed over from the practice field to cheer us on as we raced up the hill, their taped hands rattling the chain-link fence, their beefy voices bearing down through their steel face masks.

Despite their support, Elder nipped us.

By the end of the season, however, we were stronger, and in a large meet with many teams, we stood a great chance of winning.

The State Meet was always the first Saturday in November. I woke up that morning two hours before I'd wanted to. It was still dark. My muscles moaned for more sleep. With every failed attempt to relax, I grew more anxious.

The Quitter

I turned on the overhead light. On my nightstand was *Jonathan Livingston Seagull*, which Mom had given me months ago but I hadn't read. It was short and maybe the book would give me something more valuable than sleep. Inspiration. With my mind preoccupied and my heart already racing, I could no more absorb the story than I could comprehend a paragraph in the California Achievement Test. I finished the book unmoved, falling back to sleep just as Mom came in to wake me up.

Overnight, the Girls Track Club had put up red and blue signs in our front yards. Mine had a drawing of a skinny, dark-haired runner in mid-stride, wearing wire-rimmed glasses.

"GO ERIC! TAKE THE STATE!"

Mom had made special arrangements to have Dad looked after so she could come to the meet, which didn't start until late morning. Scott Harrison, our team captain, who lived one street over, picked me up in his dad's tan Buick, which had a horn that quacked like a muffled duck, thanks to Scott laying on it too long following a football game. This morning, we were quiet, though, as we drove to the field house, where the team piled into the coaches' cars for the fifteen-minute trip to the site of the meet, The Ohio State University Golf Club.

Back then, large cross country meets looked like small cross country meets. No one came but parents and perhaps a really devoted girlfriend. Our team jogged our warm-up in silence, drawing closer to each other than usual. Leaves crunched underneath, and the air smelled of autumn and analgesic.

It's said that track is an individual sport, cross country a team sport. In theory, you run as a pack for as long as you can, moving up in twos and threes to pick off your opponents.

"I don't care if you have to have a peter pull at the mile mark," Coach Smith, Eisenhart's assistant, said, "but stay together."

The starting line is a row of narrow boxes in which each team crams seven runners. Unlike track, where the lanes are staggered, the start of a cross country race is a stampede. Spiked herds dash toward a distant marker, where the course narrows, then often takes a sharp turn. You have to get out in front of the horde.

Which I did.

In doing so, though, I lost my teammates. Worse yet, I lost my head. While it's crucial to stay in contact with the leaders, you also have to stay within yourself. Run your own race. I'd been running with the lead pack all season. But this was the State Meet, for God's sake, and the frontrunners were really clipping along. Being a middle-distance runner, I had no business trying to hang with the elite distance runners. Once I reached that first flag, I should have done what I always did—what we were coached to do—ease off, settle into a reasonable rhythm, and keep an eye out for other Worthington jerseys to team up with.

I stayed with the lead pack, about four of us, all the way to the lip of the valley just shy of the halfway mark. Racing downhill takes more out of you than going uphill, I've always thought, because the legs do double duty, churning as fast as they can while holding back a body that's on the verge of lunging forward out of control. Your arms are under extra strain, too, as they work to maintain balance.

Recklessness requires denial, or at least a lapse in better judgment. I plunged down the hill with the pack, even surging forward to find myself shoulder-to-shoulder with the two leaders. We hit bottom at full speed. Momentum pulled me partway up the ensuing hill, but then my strength was robbed from me with the glib farewell of a con artist. I reached into my reserves, but nothing was there. Not even a whisper of adrenaline.

I'd been had.

I made it to the top of the legendary monster, gasping, my body bolting upright for air, pain flushing through my legs like fever. Only my arms could keep up a good front, swinging forward and backward faithfully, though feebly.

The leaders were long gone, along with any chance of recovery. Adrenaline, boosted by ego and emotion, had turned me into a fool. Waves of runners rose upon me from behind, dragging me into their undertow like flotsam.

"Aw, Gnezda!" Eisenhart yelled in disgust. "Don't quit!"

He was stationed in a grove just beyond the top of the hill.

Quitting wasn't what was going on. I'd run a stupid race. I'd known better. I'd run in the State Meet before, been in big meets. This time we had a real chance of winning, and I'd wanted the championship so badly I let ambition ride roughshod over reason, passion over patience. I'd tried to win it all in the first half of the race, but now the best I could hope for was that my teammates were running the race of their lives, and I'd somehow slip across the finish line unnoticed.

With spiritless strides, I came down the stretch with the also-rans, a position in which I was not used to finding myself. Crossing the finish line, I was herded into the chute, where an official handed me my place card. It was by far the worst race of my life.

I walked back to our camp. Everyone else was already there. I'd failed to score. I sat on the ground next to my sweats. A trail of thickened blood ran down the inside of my right calf like a strand of red shoestring licorice. The outside of my left shoe was sheared in two places below the ankle. Despite getting out ahead of the pack at the start, I'd still been spiked. I hadn't noticed it during the race, and I certainly wasn't feeling it now, doubled over from the one-two punch of disappointment and shame.

Incensed, Eisenhart charged into the circle. "Seven points!" he screamed. "Arlington beat us by seven points!"

We froze.

In an awkward reflex, Brad's father, Mr. Fallon, who was sending his second of six sons through Eisenhart's program, bellowed an oafish laugh. Eisenhart's glare cut him in two. The silence grew heavier.

We found out soon enough that we'd finished third. Elder had won the championship, but not by an insurmountable margin. I watched them celebrate in their purple and white, just as they'd done on our course two months earlier. Arlington would get the runner-up trophy. We'd leave with nothing.

I just wanted to get home.

Mom, who had arrived just before I took my place at the starting line, stood outside the perimeter, observing. The demands on her time prevented her from socializing, never mind coming to many meets, so she knew few of the other parents. The world of athletics was foreign to her. "Sports are fine," she said a million times, "as long as they're kept in proper perspective."

As a kid, I was so absorbed in sports that she fought me tooth and nail to come inside to read, do math, or fill in the blanks on a vocabulary worksheet. In fourth grade, my hands got so badly chapped from afternoons of playing basketball on the snow-covered driveway, I couldn't hold a pencil. Panicked I wouldn't hand in an assignment on time, Mom insisted I dictate my answers to her so she could write them on the back of the *Weekly Reader*. The next day, minutes after handing in the assignment, my teacher called me to her desk during reading time. "What's this?" she snapped, pointing to my mother's cursive. I showed her my fingertips, cracked open like fish mouths, yet she still didn't trust the work was mine and called home.

Mom's anxiety about my obsession with sports seemed somewhat quelled when she confided her concern to a father—a professor, no less—whose son had been on my Little League team. "Let him play all the sports he wants now," he said, "so that by the time he's an adult it'll be out of his system." She found his advice so reassuring that she found it necessary to share it with me, as if it would put my mind at ease, too. Yet my only focus in childhood was to pitch like Sandy Koufax, shoot baskets like Pistol Pete Maravich, or, in high school years, run the mile for the University of Oregon.

Having entered college at sixteen, Dad didn't have much opportunity for a high school athletic career, although he was a tackle on the football team that won a conference championship. "Do it as long as it's fun" was his mantra. Although I got the impression that he was proud of my achievements on the athletic field, Mom told me on one of our car rides to school that his greatest pride was my interest in politics. Furthermore, Dad's praise was always indirect, implied through his humor.

"Don't come home unless you finish at least second," he'd joke as I walked around the house in my varsity swishies, preparing to go to a meet.

"Second?" I said. "Last year it was third."

"You're a year older."

As Mom stood at the State Meet, out of her element and watching me slump in self-inflicted defeat, she must have been wondering what to say. How to approach me. What she could have done to protect me from the stings of failure.

Harrison called the team together to run our warm down, which we did in silence. The course, whose white line had glistened like fluorescent tape over the manicured grass only an hour ago, was now threadbare, pocked by thousands of spike marks, muddy on the turns. Stripped of its regal aura, the course looked beatable. But there'd be no more chances. Three of our top five were graduating. This had been our year to win the state title. Instead, we were jogging through the mud instead of stepping onto the winner's platform.

When we got back to the camp, our parents were still waiting. Mom said nothing. I told her I wanted to go home with her. On the way to the car, she pulled something from her coat. "I got this for you," she said. "I thought you should have one." She handed me a white T-shirt.

OHSAA State Cross Country Championships.

I thanked her, although I didn't feel I'd earned the right to wear it, and I certainly didn't want to be reminded of it.

The team met on Monday after school to hand in our uniforms and talk about the upcoming indoor season. "Gnezda," Eisenhart said as we broke, "I want to see you."

I stepped into his office. Eisenhart was surprisingly lax about letting us into his office whenever we wanted. He always kept the door open when we talked. Not this time, though. He closed the heavy, black metal door behind me.

"Gnezda," he sighed, "they're a lot of things I could get into about Saturday. A lot of things. But I'm not going to. I'm not going to get into all that—"

We stood next to his desk, our eyes meeting now and then. I waited for him to erupt, "to get into all that" anyway. How, if it weren't for me, we might be state champions.

He remained uncharacteristically calm.

"I'm more concerned about the kind of man you grow up to be," he said, his hand now in full flapping mode. "Running's one thing, Gnezda. But life's another. You're going to have people depending on you. You can't be a quitter."

I could see that he was trying to address the Big Picture. Using running as a metaphor for life, but all it accomplished was driving me deeper into self-doubt and inadequacy.

When I think about my childhood, the skies were always sunny. But now in my teenage years, everything had turned gray. I walked home alone, the sky over Evening Street an ashen scrim behind barren trees.

November and I understood each other.

* * *

Mom had always told me that one of my strongest traits was persistence. She even defined the word for me when I was too young to grasp the meaning. I had yet to set a goal I hadn't achieved. At three, I sent her heart into panic mode when I hopped on my sister's two-wheeler and, never having been on one before, rode it across the front yard. In middle school under Coach Smith, I'd reached all of my goals. Run best in the biggest meets. Set a school record. When he was packing up his classroom the day before summer break, he'd even introduced me to his visiting sister as "Worthington's next running phenom." I pretended I didn't know what *phenom* meant. "You'll see," he responded.

I had set my mind on making varsity as a freshman that summer. Day after day, in the hottest part of the day—rush hour—I ran six, seven, eight miles, learning that I could always do one more mile. Tasting the exhaust from idling cars at stoplights, smelling the mowed fields north of town. Stinging from sweat beads that rolled into my eyes. Acting like I didn't hear the catcalls from passing cars on High Street, didn't see the groups of older kids mocking my swinging arms as I churned by the Dairy Queen. "Mini-hoods," we called them. Long hair. Cigarettes. In groups, they'd jeer at you, but by themselves, they'd slink away. Still, I'd keep running. Alone. Almost always alone because with someone else, I could let down if they wanted to. But not by myself. I could never let myself down. In the fall, I reached my goals, becoming the first in my class to earn a varsity letter. Then I ran the fastest freshman mile Eisenhart had ever seen. Broke two minutes in the half mile as a sophomore.

Something along the way had gone terribly wrong, however. I'd been off to such a great start with Eisenhart. I thought again about what he'd told my mother: "What I like most about your son is that he's a *competitor*."

Now I'd become a "quitter."

I went deep down into my thoughts.

No one in my family's ever been a quitter. Mom and Dad stuck it out, even with his sickness. That's perseverance. His body may be crumbling, but his mind's sharp. He's more aware of what's going on in the world than anybody else's dad I know. And he still has his sense of humor.

What happened to me?

Maybe things have just been too easy. Mom's said over and over she doesn't want us kids to resent Dad for being sick, so she's tried to do what she can to make up for it. But maybe she's done too much for me.

And it turned me into a quitter.

At that age, you can't imagine that someone else has a problem. It's always yourself. Especially if that person is older and in a position of authority.

Like Coach Eisenhart.

* * *

When spring rolled around, Ted and I had the fastest indoor half-mile times in the state, according to our Bible for runners, *Ohio Track and Field*. As usual, however, Eisenhart tried to motivate us by pretending we weren't any good.

"Well," Eisenhart said out of the side of his mouth as he gave us the lineup for our first outdoor meet, "I guess in the half mile we'll have to go with Barnes and Gnezda. That's all we got," shrugging us off like fish too small to keep. While his approach did nothing for my confidence, Ted was downright pissed off but quickly let it go.

Then a couple of weeks later, our big dual meet came around—at Upper Arlington. Cold, damp, and windy. I hadn't been feeling well, but I ran anyway. Three quarters of the way through the race, Ted and I were leading. The rest of the field seemed to be way back. At payoff time, though, I reached for my kick and nothing was there. Bob Vance, an Upper Arlington senior who's since become a good friend, passed me coming down the stretch.

After the race, I started coughing. Violently. It wouldn't stop. I went over to the high jump pit and sat down. Put on my swishies. Slid my hands into a pair of tube socks to keep them warm and covered my mouth as I coughed. The coughs kept coming. I thought blood was going to come up. I was scared. Eisenhart came over and said nothing. Just looked at me as if I was faking it.

The following day, I didn't go to school. The coughing tapered off, but I had no energy. I stayed home for *three weeks*. No fever. No sore throat. Just tired as hell. Tests for mono were negative. Mom became so worried she even took me in to see if I had the beginning symptoms of MS.

In time, I realized I was just plain worn out. My exhaustion was beyond physical. I was beaten down emotionally. Tired of being the dedicated athlete with no reward. The well-behaved student. Of repressing who I was to conform to a role.

By the time I returned to school, the district meet was nearly upon us. Eisenhart told me he thought I should just forget about the rest of the season and put my efforts into recovering for cross country in the fall.

Sounded good to me.

In the meantime, as I sat at home all those days, I felt a pull to start playing music. Not just to play music, but write it, which was absolutely absurd, since I hadn't touched the piano since I was a kid. I'd been banging around on my drum set from time to time, but when it came to creating anything melodic, I was completely in the dark. Music became my release, offering me a way to explore my feelings, listen to my inner voice. If I could write songs, maybe I would feel heard.

I wasn't ready to quit running, but I needed someone to take my pain seriously. The psychic and physical pain Eisenhart had inflicted, the pain of my family life. A dear mother overstressed, a father deteriorating. The pain of being the only boy, alone with my dreams and ambitions without anyone to guide me.

I wanted to talk to Coach Smith about my depression. My conflicts. My discontent with Eisenhart. About what music was beginning to do for me. Yet the situation was awkward. He had begun dating Niki, and, therefore, was around the house often, but like everyone else, including me, he didn't understand what was happening.

"Are you down in the dumps again?" he'd asked me on more than one occasion through the years, usually after workouts. Depression would set in, and I couldn't bring myself to push myself. I guess that's why, in Eisenhart's words, I was "up and down, always up and down."

Finally, on a warm day at the bottom of my driveway, I told Coach Smith I was thinking about not coming out for the cross country team in the fall. What I was really saying was, *I don't want to quit running, but I need someone to listen to me. I'm hurting and need to know I still matter, that I can still believe in myself. I need to know that, despite what Eisenhart thinks, I'm not a quitter.*

The Quitter

For whatever reason, he got impatient and said, "Eric, I don't know what the hell to tell you. I mean, on one hand, you've been saying you're sick, but then I see you staying up all night playing the piano and talking to your friends."

I didn't feel understood, so I dropped the subject.

I didn't run all summer, and when August of my senior year came around, I didn't show up for the team meeting, leaving Coach Smith to break the news to Eisenhart that I wasn't coming out.

Eisenhart was incensed.

Without having to go to practice after school anymore, I grew my hair long and took my sweet time walking home, sometimes reading a book along the way, like some kind of intellectual. I'd stroll through our front door, say hi to Dad for a few minutes in his room, then head to the piano or downstairs to my drum set. I'd turn on a record and play along. Jim Croce. Janis Ian. Eagles. James Taylor. Carole King. Jackson Browne.

On a Friday night in the fall, I went to a football game. I stood alone outside the stadium fence on the north side, on that slope that leads down to the river—ironically, the hardest stretch of the cross country course. I noticed someone else standing several yards away in the shadow of the stadium lights. Turned out to be Cici, a classmate I hadn't seen in a couple years because she'd decided to go to the Linworth Alternative Program, a new experimental school in Worthington. Like everyone else, she was surprised I wasn't running anymore. She was a fabulous singer and guitar player and, before long, we were talking music. She had no idea I played drums or even liked music. Her country-rock band needed a drummer. Not long after, I auditioned and found myself in her band.

Playing early Bonnie Raitt songs beat the hell out of running quarter-mile intervals. Predictably enough, my choice made Eisenhart even madder. I was his second promising athlete to forsake running for music. A couple of years earlier, Ted's brother Gordon, another half-miler who'd broken two minutes as a sophomore, had gotten serious about his guitar playing and quit the team.

As a way to express my discontent or perhaps in a subconscious effort to retaliate, I wrote a song parody about Eisenhart to the tune of "Over the River and Through the Woods."

Over the river and through the woods to the barbershop we go . . .

I shared it with some guys on the team who thought it was hysterical. They put the lyrics up on the bulletin board in the locker room, where Eisenhart saw it and ripped it down.

Eisenhart told the team, "Don't even talk to Gnezda," his exact words, according to Ted, who, in typical fashion, ignored what Eisenhart said and became an even closer friend of mine, as he remains today.

I learned firsthand how serious Eisenhart was about ostracizing me when, during classes my senior year, I was walking down the empty hallway. Getting to the other end of the school was no short trip. Before the school was recently remodeled, our hallway was reputed to be the longest one in Ohio. Although it didn't quite measure the quarter mile that some claimed, the corridor was long enough that, on winter days, when ice made it unsafe to train outdoors, the track team would run indoors after school. Because the school was built on a gradual but substantial hill that ascended from the Olentangy River all the way to the center of town, the hallway sloped upward, from west to east.

As I walked down the staircase and rounded the corner from the east wing, I had a full view of the first half of the corridor. All clear.

Then a lone figure.

Is it the hall monitor? Shit, I don't have a pass.

No, it's not . . . Maybe it's a student . . . or a teacher . . .

Oh my God. It's Eisenhart!

Not even a stranger around to siphon attention. Just Eisenhart. Just me. Marching face to face in the longest hallway in the state of Ohio.

I moved away from the wall to make doubly sure I didn't give the impression that I was hugging it for security. But I sure as hell wanted to. His soft-soled shoes didn't make a sound, his unbalanced stride was as purposeful as ever.

What do I do? What's he going to do? Say hi? Stop me? Give me a dirty look? Do I say hi?

I watched for his cues.

He kept up his brisk pace. His arms remained at his sides, swinging in cadence. He held his head upright, his eyes locked forward. I did the same.

I stole a glance out of the corner of my eye.

Eisenhart's eyes didn't budge.

We passed with no words, no acknowledgment, leaving only the chilly after wind of a near miss on a two-lane highway.

I exhaled, and, having survived the encounter, my heartbeat jumped into my head, pounding louder, then slowly subsiding. Eisenhart had officially cut me out. Unexpectedly, I felt a sense of relief, as if that part of my life was over and I could look to the future. College, music—and long hair.

What I didn't realize, however, was how deeply his negative influence had rooted itself in my cells. "You're a quitter!" I'd hear those words for years every time I faced a risk. Consequently, I'd either run away from it or go into it not believing I'd succeed, fulfilling the self-expectation that I wasn't up to the challenge.

"Gnezda, you're always up and down, up and down," would echo in my mind when I embarked on a new endeavor. Since consistency wasn't in my nature, Eisenhart had made me believe that any triumph would be in my imagination or was destined to be short-lived. I've since come to understand that I'm not consistent in the way some people, including Eisenhart, define it. I'm persistent, but not a plodder. I live from the heart, so I have swings in emotion, mood, and energy, and therefore, my motivation levels rise and fall accordingly. I drive myself hard, meet goals, build to big challenges, sometimes exceeding my limits and the expectations of others, but the endeavor has to be worth the effort for me. If not, I simply can't gather the desire to rise to the occasion.

Not all of life's races are of equal importance. But they were to Eisenhart.

I needed a coach who understood and accepted this about me. One who, at the beginning of the season, would meet with me to pinpoint the meets that mattered, identifying the other ones as tune-ups, perhaps even looking at them as workouts. This way, I would have prepared myself, psychologically and physically, to peak at the right times.

A lot of champion runners take this approach. Yes, you have to maintain a high standard, but you can't ask your psyche and your body to push beyond their limits every single time out. It takes a lot of energy and recovery time to reach new plateaus. You build, plan, prepare for the opportunities that count the most.

Years ago, tennis legend Chris Evert was asked if she wakes up every day wanting to be a champion. Chris laughed. "Not first thing in the morning." Then she went on to explain that once she's forced herself onto the court, warmed up, and begun the workout, she feels the fire return. How many times have I heard other athletes and artists say the same thing? I, too, have felt a lack of enthusiasm sitting down at my piano to compose, packing up my gear for a gig, or tying my shoes (double knots, of course) for a run. But once I get started, the fire ignites within me.

That's not to say that championships and inspired art are unearned, random mistakes. The path for anyone is rarely a steady ascent that rises like stair steps, but is more commonly a series of uneven plateaus, punctuated by fallow spaces that, through effort and grace, transcend us into a few moments of glory and majesty.

If only I'd known it at the time.

If only I'd been able to explain it to Eisenhart.

If only Eisenhart had been capable of understanding.

* * *

My dream of being a champion runner wasn't the only thing torn apart. I spent my adulthood trying to prove Eisenhart was wrong about me, but I didn't realize it until well into middle age, and while these thoughts still haunt me, they now act more as an obstacle to overcome than one that continues to control me. As we mature, we learn who is safe to trust. As teenagers, however, we're at our most vulnerable, desperately seeking acceptance and approval. It was a mistake to give Eisenhart so much power, to take him so seriously, but he had been everything I dreamed of becoming: a state champion, a runner who held a district record that lasted for thirty-seven years, and a potential Olympian whose chance was swiped by a world war.

Above all, he was "tough."

I was raised to trust my teachers and coaches. Especially coaches, since Mom and Dad were not sports-oriented people. It would never occur to me to doubt a coach's advice. If there was a problem, it must be mine. If my legs hurt, it was my fault for being weak. If my mind wasn't ready for a race, it was because I was "soft." If my will to win faded, it wasn't because I was exhausted, but because I wasn't "man enough" to win. At least according to Eisenhart.

The Quitter

One of the most important skills we can learn in life is to advocate for ourselves. It takes courage to stand up to abuse, ask for help, express our needs, or assert ourselves so we're treated fairly. In relationships and in business. Sometimes it comes down to our approach—the old "it's not what you say, but how you say it." Not everybody has the courage, or the position, to confront someone else, and sometimes two people just can't work things out. Yet we owe each other an honest try.

It took years to see it, but the truth of the matter is Eisenhart quit on me. His one motivational tool was to beat his athletes down until they proved him wrong. When his only method pushed me away, he absolved himself by labeling me "a quitter."

It would take decades to get over the damage he did to my self-confidence. He influenced my mind and my body. Even his workouts stayed the same, failing to evolve with all of the new knowledge coming out at that time. For instance, the late Bill Bowerman, the famed coach at the University of Oregon, studied the success of New Zealand's Arthur Lydiard, who believed it was best to avoid hard workouts on successive days. "Train, don't strain," Lydiard said, maintaining that you want to finish a workout feeling good so that you're eager to run again the next day.

Eisenhart's teams would traditionally peak midway in the season, and by the time the State Meet came around, we were spent.

He was the wrong coach for the times and definitely for me. Coach Smith was the right one, although his authority was limited as the assistant coach. Years later, after he married my sister, I told him, "I wish you had been my coach in high school."

"Me too," he said sadly, then he added after a pause, "Do you know what you could have run as a senior?"

I shook my head.

"1:52," he whispered in the sad tone of what could have been.

Running was the only activity I committed to that I didn't take to its natural conclusion, leaving me with unresolved goals and lots of regrets. A few years later, Coach Smith asked me to coach with him, but I declined, still controlled by my anger at Eisenhart. How I regret that decision, although I did accept a coaching job at Worthington fifteen years later and loved it. I saw quickly that teenage athletes respond when you step into their hearts, listen to their dreams, and take them seriously. Many, many times I would have to hide my eyes as I teared up watching these distance runners put themselves on the line. I knew the risks they were taking and how they felt, win or lose.

The tears were also because I longed for another chance to do things right. To ignore Eisenhart. To not take him, or every race, so seriously. To not want to win too badly, to stay patient. To enjoy.

Just enjoy.

And to win a state championship, of course.

* * *

Shortly after Eisenhart retired, a race was named in his honor: The Les Eisenhart Cross Country Invitational. He had the honor of firing the starting pistol, and as the years wore on, he'd walk to his station with the aid of his folding stick chair that he'd use as a seat once he got into position to fire the starter's pistol. I went to the meet one year. After firing the gun, Eisenhart sat alone on the course. I watched him for a few seconds, then walked across the empty field to say hello.

I had no idea how he'd react.

He saw me and his face lit up. "Hey there, Eric!"

"Hi, Coach, I just wanted to say hi."

We hadn't spoken to each other in more than twenty years.

"You're quite the entertainer these days," he said. "I hear your songs on the radio."

"Thanks, Coach. I'm having fun."

He went on to tell me about some entertainer he and his wife enjoyed on a recent cruise, and I realized he was talking to me with the same levity in his voice I'd witnessed between him and other adults when I was younger. After all this time, it felt good to be talking man-to-man, as he would have called it.

"You know," he said, "I'm still competing at my age."

I don't remember the name of the sport, although I think he said horseshoes, and it became clear to me that competition was what he lived for, what brought him meaning. What got him out of bed in the morning.

I found myself feeling compassion for him. My need to compete had been supplanted by other things as I aged. Empathy. Service. I realized competition can be important at a certain stage in our lives, when we're out to discover our capabilities, but at some point, we need to rise above it and become focused on helping others. I'm sure that in his heart he wanted his runners to have the same feeling of success he had enjoyed, but he was hamstrung by having only that one motivational tool.

"I know we had our troubles, Eric, but I'm glad you stopped over. I really am. It's really good to see you."

I wished him well, we shook hands, and I left, seeing him through new eyes. He was just another guy out there trying to do his best despite his limitations.

Like the rest of us.

Sometimes, we just have to fight our way through life. We've got to outlast the forces hellbent on defeating us. Whether we're working to achieve a goal, pursue a dream, preserve a relationship, or, God forbid, battle an illness or injury in a hospital bed, it often comes down to a simple question:

"Who wants it? Who wants it?"

It's then that I'm grateful to Eisenhart.

Taking the Lead

EVERY now and then, I'll take the six-mile run through Colonial Hills. The course is hilly and I pass my old house, which is where I lived for the first seven years of my life. It always seems so small in contrast to my big memories. My dad sitting on the front stoop and throwing me the football. Watching the coverage of the JFK assassination, The Beatles on *The Ed Sullivan Show*. The Cuban Missile crisis. Puncturing my knee on a nail while our house was being remodeled and the fear of showing my mother the hole that went all the way through. Dumping hot tea on my bare leg. Sitting in the front yard and watching the Fourth of July fireworks from nearby Selby Park. Listening to the transistor radio I got for Christmas. Biking down the street with my sisters wearing our respective red, white, and blue windbreakers we were given for Easter.

Then there was the piano. An upright ebony instrument that dominated our family room. Mom, having heard through our music teacher at University School about a warehouse that sold used pianos, pooled our savings accounts to come up with thirty-five bucks, just enough to buy an aged behemoth with brittle tones, cracked keys, and a gummy, blistered dark finish. That was our piano until we moved into our new house.

Maybe nothing was more symbolic of our move than the piano. An "old" house into a new one, built in a neighborhood where no one lived yet. An "old" piano sold; a new one bought. A Wurlitzer studio model with a glossy American walnut finish. Mom and Dad must have reasoned that it would encourage us to learn how to play. Before I knew it, the new piano was nine years old and still filled our living room with the scent of fresh wood and felt. And sometimes music.

Once I entered high school, Terry had been urging me to try out for the musical. "It's such a good time," she'd say. Although I'd come to trust Terry on what constituted a "good time," I'd never been able to consider the musical because it conflicted with basketball. But a year earlier, being a smug sophomore, I began to view distance running as my ticket to immortality, so I'd been thinking about dropping hoops to train year-round in track. Between classes one day, the varsity basketball coach, standing outside his classroom, called me over.

"Coming out for 'ball this year?"

I was flattered, for I had no idea he'd been watching me on the court.

"Nah," I tested him, "I'm running winter track."

He lifted his chin, then nodded, dismissing me back into the stream of the hallway.

I had hoped he would see through my declaration and press the subject further, for at that age few things feel better than being pursued. But, without even a spoken reply, he'd taken me at my word, which put me in the position of having to as well. With that, my basketball career was done, opening up the possibility of trying out for the musical.

Had I only known that my decision would place me in the chorus of *Brigadoon*, wearing a kilt and ballet slippers.

Fortunately, all the other guys wore them, too, complete with sporrans, which we immediately took to calling our "hairy things" dangling from the front of our waists. Unlike me, however, most of the other boys didn't find themselves doing a sword dance during the wedding scene. Four of us had been chosen at random in early rehearsals with the understanding that all the guys in the chorus would be taught the dance and rotated through each performance. As opening night rushed upon us, however, Bronwynn Hopton, a choreographer who had the teaching talent to turn Eeyore into Fred Astaire, explained that she'd have to stick with the four who already knew the dance. And so there I was—downstage right—hopping over crossed swords, arms akimbo, with my hairy thing flapping with reckless abandon.

As it turned out, the dance, which I never forgot, thanks to Ms. Hopton, would come in handy decades later. Fueled with a rich blend of dark anxiety and caffeine-driven energy, I lost my senses in the kitchen one morning and, in my robe and slippers, launched into the dance. My daughters looked on with the astonished horror seen only in the eyes of pre-teens watching their dad make a fool of himself. But I had a ball, delighted as much by recalling the dance as by performing it, and, of course, getting under my daughters' skin. From that day on, as they navigated their ways through the overly self-conscious years of adolescence, it would take the mere threat of doing the *Brigadoon* sword dance in front of their friends to make them back down from whatever their misguided proposal might be.

Back when I was in high school, however, I was unaware of any benefit that being in the musical would have on my parenting, but my sister had been absolutely right. The musical had been a blast, and I discovered a whole genre of girls who had an eye for thespians in the same way that cheerleader types took a shine to basketball players, kilts and ballet slippers notwithstanding.

Now as a junior, I was hoping to get a speaking part. But first I had to get through the audition, which included singing a solo in front of teachers and, worse, my peers. "Edelweiss," one of only a few songs sung by a male in *The Sound of Music*, had just a single repeating verse and chorus, which would limit the risk of forgetting the words. It was a good choice for my upcoming public humiliation.

Helping me learn the song, Terry played the accompaniment on the piano. I peered over her shoulder, singing the first couple of lines.

"Make sure you enunciate," she directed. "And pro-*ject*!" She took her hands off the keys and pressed them to her lower stomach, in mock operatic fashion. "Breathe through your diaphragm so you're not so breathy. Joel's really big on that."

"Joel" was Mr. Haney, the choir director, a slender tenor who wore Haggar pants and Hush Puppies. Among ourselves, we called him by his first name. His comments could be as clipped as his short red hair, topped by a tussock that matched his goatee. Aggravation would trigger a tug on his hair. Anger, his beard. Rage seemed to simmer under his surface like tremors beneath a fault line, which, looking back, may have been one of the reasons I felt a kinship with him. Another was that he, too, was a sports fan. "For some reason," he told me a couple times, "people seem to think that if you're a musician you can't love sports."

Yet, as red as his face might get—igniting his hair in electric orange—his eruptions never fully developed, suppressed by abrupt sniffs and hair tugs that left us bracing ourselves for tantrums that never developed.

Once he got to know you, he was chummy, although at arm's length. "Well, good morning, Mr. Gnezda, how'd your track meet go this weekend?" He even smiled during a Christmas choir rehearsal when we replaced "No-el" with "Jo-el." But his good moods could never be counted upon, so we knew it was wise to be prepared both for his artistic temperament and with our assignments.

Putting her fingers back on the keys, Terry again waltzed into the song's introduction as we continued rehearsing in the living room. Taking her advice this time, I drew a deep breath into my diaphragm, stretching my belly as taut as a balloon inside a papier-mâché globe, and sang the opening lyrics. As my mouth closed around "greet," an unexpected pocket of air pushed up from my stomach. In reflex, I gasped, sending my tongue into rapid spasmodic slurps that sounded like a dog lapping up suds as they were sucked down a drain.

My knees buckled as I collapsed in a fit of laughter. Terry rolled off the piano bench. We crashed to the floor at the same time, wheezing in hysterics, sending a quake through the house.

"Oh my God!" Mom screamed, ripping through the louvered doors. "Who's hurt?"

Splayed, rolling, Terry and I couldn't speak.

It took Mom a few moments to figure out that we were laughing, not crying, then she exhaled, pressing her palm flat against her breastbone. "Thank God," she said, "I thought the bookcase had fallen on someone or you'd had a heart attack."

Once again, Mom could be counted on for overreacting. Which, of course, only made me and Terry laugh harder. To her credit, Mom eventually laughed, too, although more out of relief than amusement. Another example of how Mom, faced with life's greatest challenges, was as tough as they come, but a simple thud on the floor could make her come unglued.

Terry and I took a few more stabs at rehearsing, but we couldn't stop laughing, so we called it a day.

I was self-conscious about singing in front of anyone except Terry. From the time I was little, she and I would go into my bedroom, turn out the lights, point the gooseneck desk lamp at our faces, put on a record, and sing into hairbrushes.

"Ladies and gentlemen, Sonny and Cher!" I'd say to introduce our imitation of the pop music icons of the sixties to our imagined audience. In unison, we'd drop our "mics," bringing them back to our lips just in time to sing the next phrase in "I Got You, Babe."

With her long thin legs, and me a few inches shorter at the time, we had cast ourselves perfectly.

On our imaginary stage, I discovered a strange sense of security beneath the spotlight. The beam, shining directly in my eyes, turned the periphery black, providing the illusion of solitude. Meanwhile, being at the center of such concentrated light awoke the impulse to return my energy to the same stream that was focused on me. Absorbed in a connection that now transcended my immediate surroundings, I welcomed the eyes of an unseen audience, real or imaginary, that lived beyond reach in a sea of mysterious darkness.

In stark contrast, there was no such safety in the harsh fluorescence of the choir room, where the auditions were held. When my name was called, my heart jumped from my chest and into my shirt, as if pounding the word, "NERVOUS!" like a flashing marquee. The room couldn't have been more still as I walked across the linoleum tile floor, my nubuck Wallabees, gummy soles smoothed down from wear, not making a sound. I could see the faces of everyone, staggered in ascending rows, looking at me as I stood in the curve of the grand piano. Joel and his panel of judges sat with notepads in the middle of the top row, just beneath the windows. Classmates waiting their turns wore expressions of scrutiny and comparison. Their stares tightened the very stomach muscles I would need to "pro-*ject*!" and soaked the last drops of saliva from my mouth.

Harrison's mother had agreed to accompany me on the piano during my audition. She'd been a music major at Mount Union College and was the director of the bell choir at the Worthington Presbyterian Church. She was bubbly to begin with, but her enthusiasm overflowed because I had been able to accomplish something she hadn't—convincing her son to try out, too. I looked at her to signal I was ready, and she smiled back and played the introduction to "Edelweiss." When it came time to sing, my tongue was as stiff as burnt bacon, making every "d" a "th," and my clammy hands, gesturing with such ease in rehearsal, couldn't bring themselves to venture far from my sides. No matter how much I'd prepared, I was still caught off guard by how transparent I felt now that I could see my audience. Unlike running in a race, my nerves didn't calm once exertion began. The anxiety meter kept twitching away, spiking when I spotted indifference in the audience, dropping at the sight of receptivity. Eye contact, the importance of which I'd learned in speech class, was almost impossible to maintain while doing something so personal as singing. To merely glance at a face was to take a chance at rejection.

Up on the top row, the drama director, Miss Hottenroth, was smiling. Interminably buoyant, she had a voice prim enough to preside over a village garden club. But she was fiercely dedicated to her job and to us, having a gift for filling us with confidence and helping us transcend the teenage need for feigning indifference to appear cool.

Joel, sitting a couple seats over from her, seemed engaged in my audition. Or at least he wasn't gnawing on his lower lip, which he did when he was impatient or annoyed.

I finished the song to perfunctory applause and, without daring to look at anyone, returned to my seat, my hands still shaking. The sides of my face heated up and the damp spots on my shirt beneath the armpits turned cold, sending up the sour scent of sweat and vinegar.

I fashioned a pose of nonchalance, but inside I was desperate for reassurance. A comment, a tap on the shoulder, a wink. If I'd been running a race, I would've known how I'd done the instant I crossed the finish line, but in this world of auditions I had only limited experience with, I'd have to live through the anxiety of waiting for the directors to announce their decisions the next day.

With auditions completed for the afternoon, we chatted our way through the heavy, wooden double doors of the choir room and into the hallway, releasing our tensions with self-deprecation and overstated compliments to each other solely with the hopes of getting them returned.

I felt I'd done okay. But not great. Throughout the year, Joel had tapped other guys for solos in choir. I'd never been one of them. Nor had I been in any of the school plays. So, the next day, I was surprised to find my name on the callback list.

During this next round, about a dozen of us, mostly upperclassmen, read and sang from *The Sound of Music* in various combinations. After about an hour, the judges stood, their arms wrapped around their legal pads.

Miss Hottenroth took charge of the proceedings.

"Okay," she said, "Jeff, will you stand next to Cathy . . . Jim next to Sharon . . ." She dropped her eyes to her notepad and raised her pencil like a conductor's baton, punctuating each name with a tap in the air. ". . . then Eric next to Lisa . . . Dave to Diana . . . Scott . . ."

We stood still, they surveyed us, huddled up and re-emerged with gratified faces of consensus. They angled and twisted themselves like a team of sculptors surveying their work one last time before adding their signatures.

"Okay, thank you, everyone," Joel announced, and he told us the cast list would be up first thing Monday morning.

* * *

That Sunday night, I was surprised to get a call from Diana, a soprano classmate with sapphire eyes and long strawberry-blond hair whose voice would earn her admission into the Indiana University School of Music. We were just getting to know each other, brought together by being in choir and mixed ensemble.

"Hey, you want to go down to the school and see if the list is up?" she asked.

"Whadaya mean?" I asked. "Do you have a key or something?"

"No, but you know how Joel said it would be up first thing tomorrow? Maybe he already put it up and we can see it from outside."

"But it's dark, Di," I said.

"You got a flashlight?" she asked.

Her plan was ridiculous, but I signed on immediately. It got me out of the house. With a girl. And on some level, I must have felt reassured that she—even with so much talent—was more impatient than I about finding out the results of our auditions.

Di picked me up and we drove to the school. For me, this mission felt like I was on the cusp of juvenile delinquency. On school property. In the dark. About to peer through the window with a flashlight. We walked from the dark parking lot to the west wing, as they called it, where one set of double doors framed large windows of institutional glass. I cast a beam into the hallway.

"See anything?" Di asked, her nose against the glass, her hands cupped around her eyes. The pale-yellow circle of light climbed the wall, begging for the baleful soundtrack of a Hitchcock movie.

"Wait. Stop," Di said, grabbing my left arm. "That's it!"

She was right. There it was, the cast list, posted high on the wall just left of the choir room door, fifteen feet away, at an angle. Certainly not readable.

"What's it say?" she asked.

"I don't know," I said, suppressing my inclination to be sarcastic in order to keep her favor. "Can't read it. Can you?"

Even close up, Joel's handwriting took a sharp eye to decipher, so from a distance there was no chance. He wrote in scrawls of block letters that looked like chicken tracks, or rows of incomplete asterisks.

"Well, can you tell if any of the names are long or short?" Di asked.

"No, I really can't," I said, and we headed home.

By the time I arrived at school the next morning, a crowd had already formed in the hallway in front of the list. I jostled my way into the crowd and, with the one-eyed self-absorption of an adolescent, I looked for my name, starting at the middle of the page, working my way down.

Not there.

Daring myself to confirm my biggest fear that my name would not appear at all, I looked again, this time starting at the top.

And there I was—on the first line—my name right next to Captain von Trapp.

I'd gotten the male lead.

I was stunned.

It hadn't even occurred to me that the lead was possible. Being in the final lineup during callbacks led me to think I might get a speaking part, but there'd been no other hints along the way. Over the last few weeks, my peers had been throwing names around in speculation, and I was never even mentioned.

I read down the rest of the list, but in my excitement, I was unable to concentrate on who else got parts. My eyes kept snapping up to my own name just to make sure. Yep, there it was. Unmistakable. For all of the shortcomings in his penmanship, Joel, unlike Coach Eisenhart, knew how to spell my last name.

Classmates, depending upon what they'd just learned, peeled from the group with smiles or in silent disappointment. Some even in tears. I felt safe in the crowd, shielded from having to meet anyone eye to eye. But turning away from the list would be a different story, requiring social skills I hadn't yet cultivated. False modesty, after all, can be more annoying than conceit.

"Hey there, Captain," Connie teased, "are you still going to talk to us now that you're a star?"

Meanwhile, people I didn't even know were approaching me, and people I already knew were looking at me with brand new eyes.

The sudden, unexpected attention jolted me. I withdrew with ambivalence. I liked it, but it also left me feeling exposed and vulnerable. I continued working my way toward homeroom when Greg approached and stuck out his hand. "I just wanted to say congratulations," he said.

Greg, a handsome senior who had moved to our school at the beginning of the year, had a smooth tenor voice that had been earning him attention from the girls.

"Thanks," I said, returning his handshake. He seemed to be waiting for me to add something. "Well, hey," I covered in haste, "congratulations to you, too."

His face fell flat and I knew I'd said something wrong. But I had no idea how wrong until later in the day when I found out that, to everyone's astonishment, Greg hadn't gotten a part. Now I understood why he'd met my response with silence. Why his eyes had welled up and his handshake had wilted. Why he'd shrunk away when the next person came running up to me all excited. He'd been big enough to congratulate me, even though he was devastated, and my reply only rubbed salt in his wound.

I felt like a heel.

When I walked into choir that afternoon, Greg was sitting in the far end of the room. He was talking to a girl who looked to be consoling him. Behind me, familiar voices came bouncing through the doorway. I joined my fellow and newly named cast members in teasing each other about the roles we'd gotten. Girls joked about putting pillows under their habits to look pregnant. "Are nuns allowed to smoke? I'm going to."

Among the crowd was Di, who was cast as the Mother Abbess, a role that was spot on, as she would use her prodigious Hoosier-bound pipes to belt out "Climb Ev'ry Mountain."

"Here, here," I commanded Harrison, who had been cast as my butler. I could tell my teasing pissed him off, but he played along.

I could feel Greg looking on. Although for the moment I was wrapped in the robe of peer acceptance, I couldn't insulate myself from the rejection he must have been feeling. I wanted to tell him how sorry I was for what I'd said and how wrong I thought it was that he didn't get a part, but I didn't know where to start. *How* to start. I hadn't yet learned that injured feelings can sometimes be repaired by admitting your mistake at the first possible opportunity, offering a heartfelt apology, and, with genuine humility and remorse, asking for forgiveness. I was afraid that anything I'd say would only make the situation worse. Hurt him more. Make me a bigger jerk. I figured it was too late to do anything about it, so I just let the whole thing ride.

That day was the first time many of us had experienced our talents being assessed "in the marketplace." For some of us, it was glorious. For others, brutal. Now having spent my adult life as an artist, I know both sides. The elation of approval but also the sting of being passed over. The soft strokes of acceptance are affirming but ephemeral. The sharp stabs of rejection penetrate, linger, and, despite the mind knowing otherwise, always feel personal.

And, whether we admit it or not, they last forever.

* * *

The cast received our librettos as we left for Christmas break, and we were told to have our lines learned when we returned in January. Hard to imagine now, but in those days, you couldn't just run out and rent a video, surf the cable channels, or log into a streaming service to find your favorite movie, since none of those formats existed. If the film was long gone from the theater, as *The Sound of Music* was, your only hope of seeing it was if one of the TV networks broadcast it as *The Movie of the Week*. My only reference to Captain von Trapp was Christopher Plummer nearly a decade earlier, when Mom and Dad had taken us on another rare family outing to see a movie.

Unaware of the historical significance of the film, and not particularly engaged by Julie Andrews singing with a bunch of kids on a bed, I had dozed intermittently throughout.

All I had was the libretto, so, in learning the part, I approached my assignment by isolating my lines and merely memorizing them.

That's where the trouble began.

As an actor, you have to be aware of your character's motivation every moment of the scene. And, especially as the lead, you need to know the story and the characters inside out. But, being thrust into thespianism with little experience, I entered rehearsals delivering my lines simply by rote.

"I'm an Austrian!" I said to a Nazi, as if introducing myself to a group of campers with, "Hey, glad to meet you, I'm from Ohio!"

"Captain," Miss Hottenroth interceded, stiffening her chin to illustrate the appropriate tone, "let's show some defiance here. The Third Reich has invaded your country and is ordering you to report to their navy. You're letting them know in no uncertain terms that you don't consider yourself a German. And never will. You are an *Austrian*."

Once again, with feeling.

The Nazi repeated his cue.

"I. Am. An. *Austrian*," I replied.

Miss Hottenroth nodded with approval, followed by a reassuring grin that exuded her calm faith that, given time and proper direction, all her student actors would grow into their assigned roles.

"Keep in mind, Captain," she reminded me, "you don't like what's happening to your homeland."

That bit of direction woke me to the larger responsibility of acting and, when it came time to sing "Edelweiss" opening night, I dug deep into the captain's torment. "Well, you did it, Captain," Miss Hottenroth told me backstage after curtain. "There wasn't a dry eye in the house."

I'd always remembered my first laugh onstage, which came as a complete surprise. In third grade, I'd written a spoof of a detective series for the school talent show in which the villain would shoot his victims and make them fat. The script was mostly wordplay, which evidently appealed to the adults in the audience, for they went into convulsions at the first joke. Which, honestly, I didn't know was that funny. The room ignited, beaming an unknown light into my heart.

But to make an audience cry. That was new. And, like the third-grade laughter, their tears weren't something I'd consciously tried to evoke. I was just telling a story, this time through a song. The laughs had bathed me in approval. To learn that I'd made an audience cry, though, introduced me to an additional power afforded to a performer, although it left me feeling vulnerable, for I had unintentionally allowed strangers to peek inside and catch a glimpse of my personal sorrows I thought I'd managed to keep hidden.

I was discovering the level at which human beings universally connect, sharing common experiences and similar emotions. No way I would have been able to articulate it then, but now, having spent decades performing, I see that the depth and width of an audience's boundaries were being revealed to me. From laughter to tears. And everything in between.

Or as a minister once told me about a good sermon, which I've come to find also makes a satisfying show, "You've got to make them laugh, make them cry, and make them feel like they got some religion."

The Sound of Music provides all of these elements in abundance. Yet, the captain is not a character who is often thought of as providing comic relief.

Except when I played him. Opening night. By accident. Another moment that still makes me mumble to myself at 3 a.m.

I was nervous. Dry-mouthed nervous. It was Friday night, and after my track workout, with only about an hour before makeup call, the butterflies were making me nauseous.

"You've got to eat something," Mom said predictably. "Anything. You can't go onstage with an empty stomach. You'll faint."

Always saying whatever she could to inspire confidence.

"I'll scramble you some eggs."

"No thanks, Mom, I think I'll go to Burger King."

I wasn't exactly headed to Sardi's, but the two-mile drive down High Street to dine alone would fill my longing for self-reliance on this big night. And, much to my credit, I'd come a long way since the only-peanut-butter-and-chocolate-milk days, having grown into cheeseburgers sans lettuce and tomato—and pickles. A plain, flame-grilled cheeseburger, some fries, and a chocolate shake were the only things that sounded the least bit appetizing.

Until I sat down with my order.

I could eat nothing.

Even the chocolate shake fell upon my indifferent palate, my tongue taut against the roof of my mouth, collapsing the straw. I re-wrapped my uneaten meal, stashed it back in the bag, and slipped it through the swinging door of the trash bin.

I've since learned techniques for dealing with nervousness—breathing, meditation, visualization—but this clumsy attempt at self-care only drove me into deeper panic. By the time I made my entrance onto the stage, I may have been dressed the part of a revered captain, but beneath was an imposter.

Early on, a scene called for me to pick up a cup and saucer and walk across the stage. Casual. Calm. Debonair.

Except that my nervous hands were trembling so much that the cup rattled against the saucer like sixteenth notes on a closed hi-hat.

All the way from stage left to stage right.

A current of uneasy laughter pulsed through the audience.

Populated by parents, family, and friends, the audience at a high school production tends to be patient and forgiving, thank goodness, and when the captain entered again, they seemed to have excused, if not forgotten, the unscripted percussion solo. And to my surprise, the gaffe broke the ice for me, too. With my pretense punctured, I no longer felt the pressure to live up to perfection. I relaxed and began enjoying myself in the role of the captain. My defensiveness eased, making me less afraid of the audience, I began to build a connection with them, culminating with "Edelweiss."

It was the first of many lessons that showed me that while performers have to be supremely prepared and have talent, what wins the hearts of our audiences is the willingness to show our human imperfections and vulnerabilities. Plus, embarrassment never kills us and usually results in better stories afterward.

Taking the Lead

During the second night of *The Sound of Music*, in an attempt to silence any dish-rattling from a nervous captain, a crew member had taped the cup to the saucer. Unaware of this well-meaning gesture, I entered the stage calm and composed. I lifted the cup, and the saucer rose with it.

Prep Period

ONE of my high school teachers, Mrs. Saylor, lived less than a mile north of me. It's been years and years since she resided there, yet every time I run by her old home, my mind sees her son throwing hard pitches to his dad on the sidewalk in front of their house. I was a child then, a few years away from meeting Mrs. Saylor, who would turn out to be one of the most influential teachers in my teens.

In my senior year, I would cut Spanish class on a regular basis to visit Mrs. Saylor during her prep period. My Spanish teacher, Mr. Benalcázar, a wonderful man, never seemed to mind. A native of Ecuador, Mr. B had come to our school three years earlier to fill in for a Spanish teacher who had left midyear because she was pregnant. He smiled constantly, radiating his unabashed joy at being in America, where he had come to escape political threats from his homeland due to the work he and his wife had been doing for the poor in Ecuador.

Mr. B was possibly the shortest person in the school, and he spoke virtually no English, which only made him work harder to connect with us. And we loved him for it. We loved him even more for showing how much he wanted us to succeed. For instance, if you approached him during a test and said, "Mr. B, no comprendo," he'd respond by gleefully whispering the correct answer to you. So it was no surprise that, just about every day, I'd no sooner sit down in his class than I would rise to tell him that I had very important business with Mrs. Saylor.

"Es okay," he'd nod, smiling, of course, and I'd slip two doors down to a vacant classroom where Mrs. Saylor sat alone at a desk, engrossed in grading papers. My knock on the door was always welcomed with a warm smile and receptive eyes, overlooking the stacks of student essays and spiral notebooks beside her.

"Sit down," she'd say, asking me what I was up to on a given day.

She had been my English comp teacher, and we hit it off as the result of a persuasive speech I gave about Watergate. In putting the speech together, I'd learned the word "exonerated" and felt as if I'd found a silver bullet.

Who could ever lose an argument with "exonerated" in it?

"If President Nixon wants to be exonerated," I said to open my speech, adopting the tone of the attorney I imagined I'd be someday, "he should simply release the tapes. If he's got nothing to hide, then he's got nothing to fear."

My classmates sat with dead faces. Afterward, and to Mrs. Saylor's astonishment, she had to practically palpate them to induce only two responses.

"I'm sick of hearing about Watergate," said a redhead, thin and wan and sour.

"I'm sick of hearing about it, too," I said. "That's why Nixon should just tell us the truth."

"But he's our president!" another voice protested. It was the girl who'd later graduate as our valedictorian. "You can't criticize the president!"

I hurled myself against the back of my plastic chair. Mrs. Saylor, also clearly troubled by the class's apathy, tried to pursue the issue, but the bell rang, releasing my relieved classmates to sleepwalk into the hallway.

I stayed behind to talk to Mrs. Saylor.

"I'm with you," she said. "I just don't understand why people aren't up in arms over this."

I began staying after class more frequently. The next year, although she was no longer my English teacher, I continued my visits. One day I got up the courage to ask her to read a poem I'd written—a satire of Julie Nixon Eisenhower, who I'd seen deliver a Pollyanna defense of her father on the *Today* show.

I placed the poem on the desk in front of her. My heart pounded. She took forever to finish it. Said nothing.

My solar plexus tightened.

She looked up, nudged the page back toward me.

I knew I shouldn't have shown it to her.

"Is this your only copy?" she asked.

"Well, no. I can get another."

"Then will you sign this one for me?"

I stood looking at her blankly, my arms still folded in self-protection, having no idea what she was getting at.

"I'd like you to autograph this for me."

I smiled skeptically to let her know that I was onto her joke.

"No, really," she said, her face sincere, insistent. "I might be glad I have it someday."

Autograph? How do you sign an autograph?

Surely my ordinary signature wouldn't do. So, pinching the tip of the pen hard enough to strangle the ink right out of it, I improvised, creating an "E" so tall and thin that it looked anorexic. My "G" was a hasty sketch of a three-inch C-clamp. When I returned the signed poem, even her extreme politeness couldn't hide her what-the-hell-is-*that* look. Had it never occurred to me that she'd seen my "real" signature scores of times on the essays I'd handed her in class?

Temporary awkwardness overlooked, our talks continued. The topics grew beyond politics to books, movies, religion. She introduced me to the Bible as a literary work—the Psalms, the Song of Solomon, the Book of Job. And I'd bring in the lyrics of Jim Croce and Jackson Browne.

"Isn't this a cool title?" I asked, placing the lyrics to "My Opening Farewell" in front of her. I had typed the words out on the electric Smith-Corona that Mom was using to draft her PhD dissertation.

Mrs. Saylor took her time reading through each word of the song. "I like it," she said.

"Isn't it cool the way he puts that?" I said. "I mean, it's like when someone really means something to you, you don't just say goodbye and it's over. It can take a long time. Many farewells. It's like the first goodbye is just the opening farewell."

"I've never thought of it that way," she said, "but you know, you're right."

"And this line here," I continued, "look at it. Look how he lets you know what he's losing without saying, 'I've got a wife and kid.'"

"Yes," she said, "he creates a picture. Shows us, not tells us."

"Like a movie."

"Do you have any more of his lyrics?" she asked. "I'd like to see them."

Mrs. Saylor looked to be in her forties, and apparently her clothes closet was a hatchery for pantsuits. Her contact lenses made her blink like Lucille Ball slicing an onion.

"You know who one of my favorites is?" she asked.

"No," I said, flattered that a teacher would want to share her musical tastes with me.

"Elvis."

"Really?" I responded, repositioning myself in the chair to disguise my discomfort at the thought.

"Yeah, I know. My daughter says, 'Mom, how can you like *El*-vis?' But there's something about his voice that's just, well, there's almost a spiritual quality you notice when he sings gospel or those slow ballads of his."

"Guess I've never really listened to that stuff."

"I think you might like it, Eric. I'll tell you what. How 'bout if I bring in a couple of my favorite Elvis albums and you bring in your Jim Croces and Jackson Brownes? We'll trade them for a couple of days. I like to do that with people. It helps you appreciate new things."

I listened to Elvis behind the closed door of my room. All ballads. He did have a spiritual sound to his voice in a TV-evangelist sort of way. His vibrato was splashed on like Hai Karate aftershave, yet buried beneath his layers of sequins and celebrity I heard the remnants of vulnerability, the voice of a man still harboring the aches of a boy left alone, shy and feeling like a loser. He reached me for the first time.

The greater revelation, though, came from two of the songs he sang. "Help Me Make It Through the Night" and "For the Good Times," written by Kris Kristofferson. I'd heard them on the radio, but they didn't connect, having been sung by country singers who seemed twangy and outdated. Elvis brought them to me in a new way, and I began to wonder what made a song work for different singers. I started to look on records for the small print in the parentheses beneath the songs—the names of the songwriters.

Who are they? What's their background? How much training did they have?

Now that I wasn't running, music became my full-time passion. I felt an overwhelming, involuntary pull toward the piano, although I'd barely touched one since ending my short-lived lessons as a seven-year-old. Mrs. Peltason, an elderly German lady who spoke broken English, had gotten mad at me because I'd left a fingertip-sized smudge of peanut butter on the upper right corner of a page in my lesson book. *"Eez dot any vey to show respekt?"*

Her strictness drove me away, and I took up drums with a nice man who directed percussion for The Ohio State Marching Band, and now, for reasons I didn't understand, piano had reeled me in again. The lushness, the power, the tactile pleasures of hitting its keys. I asked Karen Nelson, the accompanist for our school choir, to show me a C-major and C-minor chord. From there I taught myself other chords and their inversions. I learned key signatures and started to understand basic progressions. When there was a song I wanted to learn, I'd figure out what I could by ear, picking out the bass line to guide me. And when that failed, I'd consult a songbook. As long as the guitar chords were written above the staff, I could accompany myself as I sang along.

I became a rhythm guitarist on the piano. I tried taking piano lessons three more times in my life—during my high school and college years, and in adulthood—but they were short-lived, as I could never get beyond the drudgery of doing those damned exercises and scales. My passion was really to write music, and as I learned the craft of songwriting, I taught myself to play piano.

"Mrs. Saylor," I told her one day in the empty hall just outside my Spanish classroom, "I know this sounds crazy, but I think I'm a songwriter."

Her blinking eyes brightened.

"I've been figuring stuff out on the piano and, well, I feel like my fingers belong there. Like I've found my instrument or something."

Her overloaded arms were clasped around a bundle of books and homework assignments. Still, she listened without moving.

"Yeah, it's like music includes everything I love to do. It's physical, like sports. But it's also emotional, and you have to use your brain, too. It encompasses everything. The heart, the mind, the body. And the spirit."

"It's wonderful to know that about yourself so early in life," she said. "I didn't find out I wanted to teach until much later."

"Really?" I said, not knowing how to follow up on adult disclosure. "I've always liked to write, you know," I continued, "and now with music, well, I don't want to sound stupid or anything, but I feel like I was meant to write songs. Even though I haven't written one yet."

"Well, when you do, I'd sure like to hear it."

I don't know if, in the years since, she's ever heard any of my music, for we lost touch. But what I do know is that I've gained an "adult understanding" of how extraordinary her commitment was. I certainly never thought about how much of her personal time, and therefore her family's, she gave up in order to spend her prep periods talking with me. Sure, I thanked her now and then, but not with the full measure of gratitude she deserved. I simply had no way of seeing the magnitude of what she was doing for me. The artist in me was awakening, and she was the first to listen with an earnest, enthusiastic ear. Free of fear. Of doubt, of judgment. She trusted my inner voice long before I would even know what that meant.

Quality Time

THE after-school sun was streaming through my bedroom window as I slipped *Late for the Sky* from its album cover. A puff of air popped me in the face, bringing with it the slightest scent of cardboard and glue, which always reminded me of the first album I ever owned, *Meet The Beatles!* I placed the Jackson Browne album on my turntable, triggered the arm, cranked the volume, and shut my door. Spinning at 33 rpm, *Late for the Sky* was blasting through my Magnavox speakers.

Alone, at last, in my own space, on my own time, I stretched out on my bed, my hands cupping the cotton comforter like seashells in cool sand. Eyes closed, but fully awake, I drifted. Jackson Browne hadn't been discovered by the masses yet, so I felt I still had him all to myself. His music was pure, his lyrics crisp, and his arrangements lean. His plaintive voice soothed me like a palliative drug slipped to me by a friend who understood my teenage pain because he'd lived through it himself.

Loneliness. Loss. That bottomless longing for love.

Deep into side one, David Lindley's slide guitar climbed to its final moan, releasing "Farther On" into the crackling grooves between songs. Savoring the after tones, I sank into the anticipation of the opening notes of "The Late Show," the song that spoke most deeply to my need for connection.

A scream raced through the hallway—raw, sustained—audible only now that the music had faded.

Dad! Oh my God, it's Dad!

I jumped from my bed and ran to his end of the house. This was not his usual call for help, but the wail of a man being tortured.

Arriving in his room, I saw that his wheelchair was gone from his bedside and his room was filling with steam. I ran around his bed and into his bathroom, where I found him on the floor of the shower, buckled under a torrent of scalding water.

"Dad!"

I slammed the faucet knob back into the wall.

"Dad! I'm sorry! I didn't hear—"

He heaved for air, his flogging mercifully over. He lay facing away from me in a semi-curl, his back red, his crooked legs twisted between the steel braces of the wooden shower bench, which he had designed himself in anticipation of the day he could no longer get around.

"I slipped off the bench," he said, "grabbed for something and hit the goddamned knob."

His shower stall was fitted with chrome grab bars, but over the past year his grip had weakened.

"Guess my arms are shot now, too," he said, stinging from the hot water and even more from the humiliation of his disease.

His skin looked too tender to rub with a towel, so I patted him down.

"Why didn't you tell me you wanted to take a shower?" I asked.

"I didn't want to bother you."

My heart sank that I hadn't at least checked on him before I sealed myself in my room.

Thank God I wasn't wearing headphones.

I stepped into the shower stall and slipped my arms under his shoulders from behind, locking my hands to my wrists over his chest. His skin was sticky and hot. My jeans and denim shirt would be rough against his back, but even so, I had to get him up. Spreading my feet as far as the stall would allow, I lifted from my legs, my grip tightening. He groaned. Halfway up I saw that his wheelchair was unlocked. If I didn't set him far enough in the seat, the chair could scoot out, dropping him to the tile on his tailbone. So, I lowered him back to the floor, propping his torso against my legs as I twisted myself to clamp the wheels. Again, I lifted him, this time chest-to-chest, a position that gave me more leverage.

He dropped safely into his locked chair.

We were both winded. He sat with his head slumped over his thumping chest. I stepped behind him to make sure he wouldn't see me arch my back to relieve the stiffness in my lower spine.

The steam had dissipated, but the air was still heavy with heat and moisture, his bathroom smelling as it always did—like sickness, a fusion of pharmaceuticals and body functions. I put my hands on the wheelchair grips, my knuckles pressing into the underside grooves of the molded plastic.

"Want back in the shower," I asked, "or back in bed?"

"I'd like to take a shower if I could. You know, it's nice to feel like a human being occasionally."

His caustic asides were growing more frequent as his ability to take care of himself diminished. He didn't seem to say them out of self-pity or bitterness, but because he felt betrayed. By MS. By his body. By life.

Nevertheless, his comments were daggers, confronting me with how much he was suffering and how powerless I was to do anything about it. Many years later I'd realize that his remarks had been invitations. He needed to talk. He needed to be told that he mattered. He needed to be reassured that his life counted for something. But as a teen, I wasn't attuned to such signals.

Unlocking his chair, I rolled him back into his shower and lifted him onto the lacquered bench, beaded with water.

"Say, before you go," he asked, "would you mind putting a little soap on this?" His hand, in a mild tremor, was trying to clasp a white washcloth, nearly worn through. Squirting a dab of his Phisohex into the center of the cloth, I dashed it under the warm water now streaming from the shower head and worked it into the closest thing to a lather I could produce from the antibacterial lotion.

"Would you have a minute to run it over my back?" he asked.

I took off my shirt, partially drew the curtain to keep the rest of me dry, then reached into the shower. Soaping most of him, including his underarms, I then moved to the final step of our protocol, arrived upon wordlessly the first time I helped him shower. I handed him the washcloth and he stuffed it between his legs.

Quality Time

While he sat on his bench to rinse, I pulled back his wheelchair and dried it off. Then him. After lifting him into his chair, I positioned his feet on the footrests and wheeled him to his bedside. Experience had taught me that, without clothes, his body wouldn't slide on the wood transfer board, so I grabbed him chest-to-chest again and sat him on the mattress. Clearly exhausted, he had a hard time remaining upright. Guiding his flaccid arms through his undershirt, I rolled him onto his side to slip on his boxers, pulling them under one hip, then over the other. I shifted him onto his back, wedging his pillow behind his head, and brought the sheet up over his waist.

Having parked his wheelchair against his bed, I rinsed out his plastic urinal and placed it in the center of the empty seat, well within his reach.

"Say, Eric," he sighed, his eyes on the ceiling, "thanks for giving me a hand."

"Sure." I shrugged.

He always acted like he was such an imposition. When I was little, he did feel like a nuisance sometimes. He'd call for help and I'd challenge myself to see how fast I could run into his room, lock the leg rests of his chair into place, lift his feet onto the metal plates, and fly back to the couch to watch whatever game I had on. Or when I pushed him in his wheelchair, I'd make a race of it, now and then catching his toes on the furniture. Even though I could tell I was irritating the hell out of him, the most he'd ever say was, "Careful!"

But it had been years since I had responded to him in that way. My impetuousness had matured into the realization that this is what we did together. This is how we bonded. Other guys and their dads went to ball games. They went fishing. Camping. Hunting. Golfing. But Dad and I just hung out. Calling from his bed, he'd ask me to do something—get him some Maalox, open a window, or empty his urinal, and then I might sit in his wheelchair and we'd talk. Politics. Sports. Old stories from his days growing up in Gowanda, which he'd told a thousand times but I never grew tired of hearing. Tales from "Bare-Ass Beach," where the boys would skinny dip while the girls would watch from a hidden view . . . The time he and his friends tipped over an outhouse, door down, unaware their neighbor was still in it . . . Or his job at Gowanda State Hospital, a psychiatric facility, where he told his friend to apply for a job and he did, only to later discover he'd mistakenly been hired by a patient posing as an administrator.

Even when we didn't talk, I was satisfied just to be in his company. His love was unspoken. Demonstrated through the quiet endurance of his suffering.

I placed my fingertips on his shoulder. His eyes were still fixed on the ceiling, his stomach rising and falling with each breath, the pulse in his neck still rapid. It reminded me of when I was a little boy and I'd put my head on his stomach and it would bounce with each breath, making me laugh and filling me with a feeling that I would one day recognize as love.

I wanted to tell him he was never any trouble, only that I hated what MS had done to him, but that he'd never once let me down. I wanted to tell him that nothing was more important at this moment than being with him. I wanted to lie down next to him, hug him hard and say, "Dad, I love you."

I inhaled to speak, but was unable to dislodge the words. He remained motionless, the signs of his exertion persisting, as if he, too, were trying to summon courage. Measuring my exhale to hide any hint of unease, I lifted my hand from his shoulder and reached into his nightstand.

I took out his comb and ran it through his thin, damp hair.

Resistance Running

No sign of anyone having been at the high school track all week. Not a footprint in the snow or even in the parking lot leading to the gates of the stadium. I step into the crown of the drift covering the curb, piled by the plows that had come earlier in the week, then jog down the hill to the track, the wind blowing through the nylon mesh of my running shoes. The running surface is ideal. Only nature could have created such perfection. About four inches of powder covering thin flakes of ice that collapse into a bed of snow at the base, providing traction and a cushion that would be the envy of any running shoe company.

How different things were back in my high school days. Far from keeping us away, six or seven inches of snow would have brought more of my teammates out, if only for the adventure. When Gary Smith was Eisenhart's assistant and was in charge of off-season workouts, he was forever creating ways to make them fun. He told us about how when he was a track athlete in Lakewood, Ohio, he'd run the Lake Erie beaches in the summer. "Resistance running," he called it. With no beaches here in Central Ohio, he got creative, as he always did, sending us off into fields of deep snow. Sometimes in boots. Yet after the workout, we'd still circle the track in a warm-down, crunching through the first couple of lanes, mashing the snow into narrow paths that would be the first to melt once the temperatures rose. We were a community. A culture. Damn near a cult.

We had a personal connection to that track.

I still do.

Over the years I've celebrated on this track in triumph, beginning with my sixth-grade victories. Left downcast after failure. Spilled my guts during workouts. Pulled out fragments of rubberized asphalt from my palms, forearms, and torso after diving for the tape and skidding across the surface. Mostly in these later years, however, I've spent mile after mile in reflection, working through pain, conflicts, decisions, and yes, even at this age, fantasizing about winning the Big Race, usually by hanging back on the shoulder of the imaginary fourth or fifth runner, then blowing everyone away as I come off the final turn into the home stretch.

I've cried on this track, too. It was early June 1998, and had been a long five months, beginning on—I'll never forget the date—January 13, a Tuesday. I was pulling into a gig when my sister, Niki, who'd been Gary's wife for twenty-two years by then, called in tears, incredulous.

"Gary has pancreatic cancer."

"*What?*"

"Yes, they didn't need to tell me. The doctor handed me a form to take to the lab that said, 'Ca-Pa,' and I knew."

My insides were sucked into a dark, bottomless hole.

"What am I going to do?" she asked, inconsolable.

Quaking in my own emptiness, I had no answer. All I could tell her is that she would not be alone. "I'll be there for you. *We'll* be there for you. You won't go through this by yourself."

After we hung up, I sat in my Ford Explorer for the longest time. Stunned. Remembering how, just two weeks earlier, on New Year's Eve, Vicki and I double-dated with Gary and Niki, went out to dinner, took in *Goodwill Hunting*, and then came back to their house and sat around the dining room table with their kids. Gary left to lie down on the sofa. The rest of us were having fun projecting into the next twenty years. Where would we be? What would we be doing? Gary suddenly roused himself, came in and said, "I know one thing. In twenty years, I'm not even going to be a-*round*."

Looking back, how eerie it was that the following week he wasn't feeling well enough to join us as we all went out to dinner to celebrate Niki's birthday.

As I sat there in the driver's seat after the call from Niki, my mind eventually snapped back into the present tense, and I wondered how I was going to get through my gig, face people, act like everything was okay, entertain them. I'd operated on autopilot before, but this challenge was on a whole new level. I'm not good at hiding my feelings, which is why I'm an inept liar, yet once I started the show, I suppressed what was going on inside of me long enough to make it through.

Then on January 30, a Friday night . . . another date chiseled into my brain . . . the Ohio Track and Cross Country Coaches Association inducted Gary into their hall of fame. As I told the audience that night, it was among my life's greatest honors to have been asked to introduce him for induction.

The hundreds in the room knew of his diagnosis, a death sentence hanging in the air that no one dared mention. He wasn't actually eligible for induction until the following year, but "due to extenuating circumstances," as they phrased it, an exception was made.

I had three days to prepare. I couldn't imagine how I was going to keep my composure and limit all I wanted to say to a few minutes. Had I been advising someone else, I would have said to gather the courage to bore down into the core of your sorrow. Feel the depths of your pain. Let your emotions ebb and flow until, with each wave, you wring out the tears like water from a saturated sponge. Once you're onstage, the residual dampness will still convey an appropriate level of authentic emotion, yet allow you to remain composed enough to lead the audience through their own grief. I would remind them that you can talk yourself blue in the face trying to *tell* your audience about someone, but the most efficient and effective way is to *show* who that person is through a story.

All well and good for someone else. My intense motivation to do my best for Gary, however, the man who'd been so much more than just a coach, was suddenly supplanted by the fear that I couldn't live up to the task. Such a situation so often feels like panic, but, in hindsight, reveals itself to be an intersection of two choices. Grow or fail.

I've taken both turns at that junction, only to find the regret that comes from shrinking in the face of a challenge is permanent and far more agonizing than the temporary discomfort of transcending our boundaries. I had no alternative but to commit myself to creating a tribute worthy of Gary. It was then that, without being conscious of it, I followed my own advice and returned to step one, getting to the depth of my feelings.

I paced my house, office to family room, living room to hallway, kitchen to dining room, back to the hallway, repeatedly, sifting through twenty-nine years of memories. In time, I remembered a spring afternoon in eighth grade. My gym class, all guys, dressed in our requisite whites. We were outside waiting for our teacher. Instead, here comes Gary with that distinct walk—his heels lifting in two motions from the balls of his feet—wearing loafers, in his stylish sport coat and wide, colorful tie. Smiling, as he so often did when he was doing what he loved most, working with kids.

"Mr. Balconi had to leave early," he said, "so I'm your gym teacher today." We almost applauded. We loved Mr. Balconi, but to have Gary—Mr. Smith, or Coach Smith to us—as our gym teacher was a special treat.

Of course, he had no lesson plan. He taught and coached on instinct and always seemed to produce magic.

"Let's do some calisthenics," he said, directing us into a circle, making it up as he went along.

Jumping jacks, sit-ups, leg lifts, and his favorite drill, hopping on one foot for an extended period.

We were about to get down on our hands and knees for push-ups when I heard him shout in his strapping yet affectionate tone, "Turner!"

Stephen Turner, not dressed for phys ed class, was standing alone several feet away, observing, wearing street shoes, his arm in a cast.

Turner's face lit up just to hear Mr. Smith call his name.

"You think you're going to get out of this just because you have a broken arm? Get over here!"

Turner, now beaming, joined the circle, a place where, socially, he'd never been.

"Steve, how 'bout a push-up?"

I thought Gary was nuts. Turner hadn't been on any athletic teams, and Gary was asking him to do a one-armed push-up. I was bracing for a humiliating disaster.

But Turner got down in the grass and, on one arm, did a push-up. Then another. A third.

"C'mon, Turner," Gary yelled, "you're Superman!"

Turner's pace quickened and we gathered around him, calling out the number of reps in unison. "Seven . . . Eight . . ." A kid who'd never been at the center of anything was now being cheered as the class hero by a circle of his peers.

I don't recall how many push-ups Turner did on one arm, but I wouldn't be surprised if it was more than the rest of us did on two. More importantly, I saw a life change that day. As Stephen Turner walked out of class, his chest was broader, and he stood straighter than when he walked in.

That's what made Gary so brilliant. He had a gift for getting us to reach down and do things we never thought possible. He motivated by building us up, making us *believe* we were capable of breaking our own barriers. Anyone who'd ever been his athlete, student, or one of the many coaches he'd mentored, knew exactly how Stephen Turner felt that day.

When I hit upon that memory of Gary, I'd drilled into the water main. Tears burst forth in a torrent, and that became the story I chose to tell about Gary for his induction into the hall of fame—after, of course, I'd spent two days telling and re-telling it to myself as I paced the floors of my house, refining and "wringing out the sponge" so that I could maintain my composure in front of the audience.

What remained a secret is that as I turned around and hugged him onstage after my introduction, I said, "I love you, Gary," to which he responded, "I know you do."

Always the lovable hard ass.

* * *

The next few months brought the inevitable ups and downs of a terminal diagnosis. The relief that chemo wasn't making him feel sicker . . . but the middle-of-the-night trips to the emergency room. The validation from hundreds of cards and front-page newspaper coverage . . . but his spontaneous outbursts of tears over nothing in particular. Encouraging test results . . . but concessions that the latest treatment fad, shark cartilage, wasn't curing anything. The night Niki and Gary celebrated Valentine's Day with a candlelight dinner of filet mignon and stuffed baked potatoes that Niki had cooked at home and taken to his hospital room . . . but the afternoon his kids and I had to steady him as he walked from the car to the bleachers of the regional track meet, where he was still coaching his runners. He coached into his final days, even from his hospice bed, where he discussed racing strategy on the phone with an athlete who was preparing to compete at the state meet.

Gary was born to coach. And to teach kids.

I'd known of Gary since the sixth grade, when Mom, working her way through grad school, supervised his student teachers from Ohio State. He was young then, twenty-four, in his second teaching job. She told me how he'd grown up without a father and that athletics were crucial in helping him navigate into adulthood. In addition to my mother's endorsement, all the older boys in my neighborhood were raving about the new teacher and coach, "Mr. Smith." How cool he was. How fun he was. And what a great coach.

I couldn't wait to get to middle school and meet him.

I finally did when he was my coach in seventh-grade basketball, and, as I recounted in my hall of fame introduction, "then he became my track coach, then my English teacher, then my cross country coach. Then he met my sister and became my brother-in-law . . . and moved two streets away . . . and the man I couldn't wait to meet turned into the guy I couldn't get away from."

All joking aside, though, I couldn't have been happier to have him living so close, and it was beyond anything I'd even dared imagine that he would one day be part of our family.

"Coach Smith," I still called him when he started dating Niki.

"Hey," he finally told me one evening, "Coach Smith is fine at school and on the track, but when I'm around here, how 'bout if you just call me Gary?"

Whoa. First-name basis. An anointing. A Key to the Kingdom of Cool.

On some occasions he literally did lend me the key to his new deep-green Pontiac Grand Prix with black bucket seats and a console shift. He let me take it on a date now and then. Or sometimes just to get a pizza. "I'll buy if you fly" was his chosen phrase, and he'd give me the keys and some cash. Free food and a flashy car. I cruised around town like a Division I recruit.

Resistance Running

How strange it is that no matter how close we are to someone, how well we know them, how much we love them, we don't seem to grasp their full essence until after they're gone. Free of physical form, they come to us unfiltered in spirit, more alive than in life. We are no longer influenced by their human idiosyncrasies, mannerisms, and (sometimes annoying) habits, so we let them in with our guard down, seeing their true nature for the first time.

As I ran on the track that day of mourning, the cascading memories made it impossible to maintain an even cadence, my stride varying with each flashback. With gratitude, I accelerated. With regret, I slowed, sometimes to a stop, bending over in tears. I'd made it down to the track, drawn more to trying to reconnect with the past than to run a workout. The gates, typically left open, were locked to the public, as the track was being prepped for resurfacing. Gary's friend Rich Seils, the athletic director, who had lost his wife to cancer and also stood by Gary through his illness, understood my request and lent me a key. The track's soft surface had been scraped away, exposing its rough, raw, unforgiving base, perfect for a personal excavation, with memories exhumed from beneath.

I thought about how on the first day of middle school track practice Coach Smith, knowing me only as a basketball player, assigned me to the group of quarter-milers. I left them and went to stand with the middle-distance runners. He came over and said, "Gnezda, you're no distance runner. Ain't you got no speed?"

"I *am* a distance runner," I said.

He smiled. "You run the quarter-mile and you'll eat 'em up."

The following fall, I played eighth-grade football. A wide receiver. At the end of the season, we were required to run a mile race at the Worthington Invitational, presumably as a recruiting tool for the high school cross country team. The race came down to me and Ted, and I edged him out again.

Gary was stunned.

"I told you I was a distance runner," I said in dry heaves.

"Well, you will be *this* year," he said.

In the spring, thanks to Gary's coaching, which included building plenty of healthy confidence in his athletes, I foolishly assumed I'd be hard to beat—until the first meet of the season, when I got wiped off the track by a middle school "kid" who had a hairy chest, a beard, and the beginning of a receding hairline.

"Sorry about your race," Gary consoled me on the bus ride home.

"Aw, yeah, what could I expect?" I replied. "He was a pube freak."

"A PUBE freak!" Gary laughed explosively. He'd never heard that term, and it turned into a lifetime joke between us.

The season concluded with the biggest race of the year, the Gahanna Invitational. The day before, Gary had sent me on an easy jog around the school grounds. When I returned, he asked how I felt.

"Nervous," I said.

He smiled. "You know," he said, perhaps attempting to lower the stakes, "it's always nice to win a trophy, but the real reward is all the things you learn on the way to getting the trophy."

I filed away his comment, knowing it was wise, but one I was too young to comprehend. It wasn't until my thirties that I finally understood Gary was the ultimate "process over results" person. It is the process that matters in life. My athletic awards are in dusty boxes in the basement, on infrequent display in my memory. The lessons I learned in pursuit of those awards, however, continue to guide me every day. Persistence. Patience. Tenacity. Teamwork. Faith. Discipline. Sacrifice.

The next day, as I stepped to the starting line of the Gahanna Invitational, Gary said, "No pube freaks in this race!" and I went on to win, with Gary sharing his typical broader perspective years later.

"You know what my favorite race of yours was?" he asked. "The Gahanna Invitational—because your dad was there to watch you win."

He was right, although it took me a while to understand that, too. That was the only race in my life that Dad was well enough to attend, and, for that reason it remains my favorite of all time.

* * *

The afternoon Gary went into hospice care, an erroneous special report surfaced in the news that comedian Bob Hope had died. Less than twenty minutes later, the story was recanted, but it had served its purpose of sending a chill through my bones. *Hope has died*, I thought as Niki called to tell me Gary's doctor had recommended he be sent to Kobacker House, the hospice inpatient unit. I tracked down Tony, their son, who was painting houses while on summer break from Grinnell College, and told him they were sending his dad to hospice.

Tony notified his foreman, left his ladder in place on the side of the house, and took off for his father's bedside, where he and his younger sister, Katharine, held Gary's hands through the week.

The last time I saw Gary smile was when Ted came to visit and said, "Gary, do you still want us to have a peter pull at the mile mark?"

With dusk descending the next night, Gary suddenly awoke and said to Vicki, who was eight months pregnant with our first child, Caroline, "When the baby gets here, tell her she was the beginning of the good times again." Then he slipped back into his cloudy, mysterious world.

Vicki chokes up every time she recounts that moment.

* * *

I woke up at home on June 10, wondering if it was to be Gary's last day, and I sat on the side of my bed with the morning light barely drifting through the window shades, dreading another "shift" on deathwatch.

How much more can he suffer?

How—why—does Gary deserve this?

An internal voice spoke to me: "These are the things that build your character."

Character? I scoffed. *Who cares about character? Nothing is worth this pain.*

I arrived at Kobacker House and, as the day wore on, I found myself bouncing between Gary's room and the hospice chapel, torn between staying with my family or going to a gig, ironically enough, at the annual cancer survivorship celebration at the Columbus Zoo Amphitheater. I'd written an anthem for the survivors, "Blossoms of Hope," and, as much as my family needed me, I also felt I owed it to the survivors to attend the event. I walked back into Gary's room, just missing his last breath.

"Goodbye, my son," his mother cried as she cradled his head.

The hospice nurse looked at her watch and dictated to her associate, "We'll call it 2:50 p.m."

Niki burst into tears. "That's the exact time the bell rings to let school out."

On the last day of school, no less.

Gary was fifty-three.

Within the hour, Niki encouraged me to go to the cancer survivor concert. As I stood onstage among the chorus of survivors I'd gathered to join me in singing "Blossoms of Hope," I looked out into the crowd and I was shocked to see, halfway back, my niece Katharine on a blanket. She had just finished her sophomore year of high school. She had just lost her dad. I couldn't imagine what she was thinking.

The next several weeks brought an overflow of condolences, highlighted by the entire chain-link fence in front of the high school track draped by a tenth of a mile of countless signs, bedsheets actually, spray-painted in honor of Gary.

If you have one good friend, you have more than your share. We were spoiled.

A Coach. A Teacher. A Father. A Husband. A Friend.

You meant so much to so many. We ♡ U <u>Always.</u>

You'll always live thru us.

* * *

Gary's public memorial service was packed. His family and friends spoke, I sang a couple of my songs, and more than 750 people—former athletes, students, colleagues—jammed into the high school auditorium on the summer solstice, twenty-one years to the day that my Grandma Nez had died.

I still smile when I think of his memorial service and the story Rich Seils told of the day he and Gary skipped a mandatory professional development day at school to play golf.

"Gary had an aversion to meetings," Rich said, "and decided to take advantage of that beautiful fall day. As fate would have it, after playing golf for forty years, Gary makes a hole in one and can't tell anybody about it."

The audience laughed.

Three years earlier, Gary and his coaching staff had gathered after a track meet at The Ground Round, a local hamburger joint. Beer started flowing, their voices got louder. The following Monday, Rich called Gary, telling him a woman had phoned him in the athletic office to complain about the amount of swearing she heard coming from the table of Worthington coaches. So the night of Gary's fiftieth birthday party, his assistant coaches surprised him with a sweatshirt and cap that sported the name of a competing school.

"These are for you to wear the next time we go to The Ground Round," they teased.

Immediately following his death, the school superintendent was approached about creating The Gary Smith Compassionate Teaching Award. He agreed, and every year the award honors teachers who go beyond their normal duties to make a difference in a student's life. In addition, former athletes and their parents established the annual Gary Smith Worthington Classic, a race including the route he had set up years ago as a coach. The race's motto comes from what Gary told his runners. "Run as hard as you can, then let your heart take you the rest of the way."

I'm sure Gary would be embarrassed by all the posthumous acclaim. The race, the shirts, the signs, the closed streets. The coffee mugs with his face on them. Yet he was almost universally loved by our community, and nearly everyone felt a need to express their reverence for him, from students and athletes to school bus drivers to the woman at the gas station who sold him his cigarettes every morning before school.

While Gary's teams won state championships, he was equally devoted to the athletes who had the least amount of talent. Whether an athlete was gifted or not, he treated them equally and misled no one.

A father of twin girls walked into his office as Gary and his assistant, John Bader, sat smoking cigars.

"My family's moving to this part of the state, and I want my girls to have the finest coaching available," the father said. He further explained that his twins were talented runners and he was interviewing coaches from different school districts to find the perfect fit.

"What can you do for my daughters?" he asked.

Gary took a puff, then laughed as he exhaled. "Not a damn thing," he replied.

The father was caught off guard by Gary's freehanded honesty.

"They've got to want to do it themselves," Gary said.

The girls enrolled in Worthington and they both became state champions.

Gary had little patience for rules—and especially egos—if they got in the way of doing what was best for a kid. What he hated most was a cheat. Gary was fair. As real a man as I've ever known. He was full of contradictions. A track coach who smoked, yet he had heart. He took his work seriously, but not himself.

"I had a professor who told me, 'Remember to never violate Rule Number One,'" he was fond of saying. "Never take yourself too seriously."

When Gary and Niki were starting their family, I visited them on Christmas Eve, arriving at their house with a bottle of 90-proof Finlandia. Over the course of the evening Gary downed a shot or two. I had half the bottle. Around midnight I staggered to the couch.

"What the hell are you doing?" he asked.

"Just going to crash here for a while."

"Like hell you are," he said, laughing and scolding simultaneously.

"Whaddaya mean? I'll drive home in a couple hours."

"I don't want my kids to wake up on Christmas morning and find their drunk-ass uncle passed out on the couch."

I'd learned to tell when he was kidding and when he was serious. This time he meant it, so this "drunk-ass uncle" rallied himself to the door.

"I'll pick up my car in the morning," I said.

"No, you won't," he said, "I'll drive you home now," apparently wanting to conceal any evidence of me whatsoever on Christmas morning. He headed to my car. I chose to walk, needing some fresh air, or, more truthfully, afraid that even a short car ride would make me puke.

Just for the sake of a little good-natured sadism between brothers-in-law, I didn't bother telling him that my ailing car, a brown Nissan Stanza with a standard transmission, wouldn't engage beyond second gear. As he drove through the snow-covered streets, the car bucked with his every attempt to jam it into third gear, which, I'm still only slightly ashamed to say, amused the hell out of me, for I could only imagine the names Gary was calling me as he crawled along.

Meanwhile, I hoofed through the elements for two blocks, more like Pooh chasing a heffalump than Dr. Zhivago in ardent pursuit of Lara, discovering the next morning a path of footprints that corkscrewed from sidewalk to neighbors' yards, to street, to sidewalk, back to the yards, and finally, home.

How could I have known then that there would only be a finite number of Christmases with him? New Year's Eves? Just plain fun times? Before I knew it, the years would pass and I'd be introducing him into the hall of fame, knowing that he would not live long afterward.

When I look back on Gary, as I do in some form every day, I imagine him bouncing down the front steps on the last day of school. The bell tolls, he smiles, and signs off with a wave, "Adios, motherfuckers!"

Olympic Dreams

RUNNERS from Uganda, Kenya, and Spain gallop by me like steeds passing Rocinante. While they're running a relaxed workout, I'm trudging along Pre's Trail in Eugene, Oregon, where I'm attending the World Track and Field Championships with my daughter Meredith, Vicki, and Ted, who's now living in Seattle and has come down to join us.

Pre's Trail is a four-mile path, named in honor of American distance running legend, Steve Prefontaine, who was killed in a single-car auto accident in 1975, just before his anticipated return to the Olympics a year later. A University of Oregon runner, Pre was who we all wanted to be back in my day. I learned the word "prodigy" when I read it on the cover of *Sports Illustrated*, which ran a story about him in June 1970. A year and a half later, as a freshman runner for Worthington, I traveled to Knoxville, Tennessee, with my teammates to watch Pre run in the NCAA Cross Country Championships. I'm not one to collect autographs, but I treasure Pre's. He signed it for me shortly after winning the race. Still with labored breathing, and in his warm-down with a half-dozen competitors he'd just defeated, he signed my program, and said, "Hey, don't you want theirs, too? We're all All-Americans!" Testimony to the "fraternity" of distance runners, and a fine example of how to respect competitors.

After his death, his words and signature became priceless.

The summer following that race, having become an ardent fan of the Olympic Games, I watched the trials in Eugene on TV. In addition to Pre, I became aware of another runner, Dave Wottle, who was from Canton, Ohio. Just a handful of years older than I. He'd run in the same high school meets I was running in and went to college at Bowling Green State University, less than two hours north, where so many of my schoolmates would go.

Having become famous in the trials for his powerful finishing kick, Dave was also known for his slight eccentricity: he wore a golf cap. After watching him make the Olympic team in the 1,500 meters and 800 meters, in which he tied a world record, my teammates and I had to have a hat like his. We ran into a paint store and they gave us painter's caps. Close enough for us. We trained in them all summer as we ran through town.

Once the Olympics finally arrived, I was glued to my TV.

"Stand by for the kick of Dave Wottle. If he's got it, he could make it!" said ABC sportscaster Jim McKay, who was caught up in the excitement. Dave was coming from far behind in the final turn of the 800 meters.

"And here he comes," McKay continued. "This is the bid for a gold medal of Dave Wottle. He's got one Kenyan! Can he make it? I think he did it! Dave Wottle won the gold medal!"

"He did it!" I screamed. "He did it!"

"The man who came out of nowhere in the U.S. Olympic Trials!" said McKay, his voice still peaking with emotion. "The first tremendously exciting moment in track for the United States in these Olympic Games!"

It sure was for me.

Three days later, on September 5, the first day of school, I arrived at cross country practice. Coach Smith was sitting on the brick retaining wall in front of the field house talking to a few guys who'd gathered around.

As I approached, I detected his serious tone, picking up a word here and there. ". . . terrorists broke into the Israeli compound . . . the Olympics have been suspended . . ."

What? What's happening?

The word "terrorist" was new.

After the workout, I raced home and turned on the TV.

Jim McKay was giving an update.

"The Olympics of Serenity have become the one thing Germans didn't want them to be: the Olympics of Terror. At this moment, eight or nine terrified living human beings are being held prisoner."

McKay reviewed the sad ironies of the day. Many of the athletes were weightlifters, yet had no control over the terrorists, and this was happening, of all places, in Germany, which kept security lax to show the world it was a changed country after the Holocaust.

As events wore on, the video, now iconic, told us pieces of the story, leaving more questions than answers. The hooded terrorist on the porch... the German woman dressed in a light blue suit negotiating with the terrorists... the law enforcement officers climbing the building in helmets and sweat clothes and carrying guns.

McKay guided us as the story inched along into the darkness. The hostages were taken from a bus to a helicopter, then flown to Fürstenfeldbruck Air Base, where the Germans had planned a rescue attempt.

"The latest word we get from the airport is that, quote, 'All hell has broken loose out there.' That there's still shooting going on, that there's a report of a burning helicopter," McKay said. "But all seems to be confusion, nothing is nailed down, that we have no idea what's happened to the hostages."

Then, late into the night, McKay, flanked by ABC correspondents Peter Jennings, Chris Schenkel, and Lou Cioffi, broke the news:

"We've just gotten the final word. When I was a kid, my father used to say, 'Our greatest hopes and our worst fears are seldom realized.' Our worst fears have been realized tonight."

And then he looked straight into the camera.

"They have now said that there were eleven hostages. Two were killed in their rooms this morn—*yesterday* morning. Nine were killed at the airport tonight."

"They're all gone."

I sat motionless. For I don't know how long. Nothing like this had ever happened. *At the Olympics*, for God's sake. In front of the whole world.

I couldn't believe it.

What were other people feeling?

How would our world change?

These questions, and many others, tossed in my head all night. I left for school the next morning, sure that it would be all we'd talk about. In the hallways, at lunch, in class.

But as the day wore on, not one mention from anyone.

That day, I realized that if I were looking for my education to reconcile relevance with the world, I would have to put the pieces together myself.

* * *

Nearly four years later, after my first year of college, when I'd long since given up running competitively but still enjoyed watching world-class races, Ted and I were driving on Route 23 when he asked, "Eric, you wanna go to the Olympics with me?"

"You serious?" I said. The 1976 Games were going to be in Montreal. I'd heard he'd gotten some tickets but figured he'd already invited someone. "Well, hell, yes!"

Our plan was to stay in a youth hostel.

"A youth hostel?" Mom asked. "Are they safe?"

My mother, who could track down Italian "family" in The Stone Desert, got on the phone. Before I knew it, she'd located "relatives" to stay with for one night in Mississauga, Ontario, on our way up, and other ones who were willing to be our hosts for two weeks in Montreal. Their names were Fred and Juliette. Fred was Ukrainian, and Juliette Italian. They were retired. He spoke broken English and was a cheerful man, forever in his lounge chair in front of the television. Ted called him "The Mad Russian."

"Hey," The Mad Russian told us in his well-approximated English, "there's a TV show you might like tonight." At midnight, The Mad Russian and Juliette joined me and Ted to watch *Tele-sex*, a half-hour show on regular TV in which a man, then a woman, stripped to music in their own fifteen-minute segments.

Feeling confident that the French were more relaxed about porn, Ted and I went to an "art" theater in the French section of town. When we tried to buy tickets, the owner spoke to us in French. We told him we didn't understand. Then in English he said, "Why do you want to see the film? You don't speak French!"

"We're not here for the dialogue," I said.

He didn't laugh, then shooed us off.

So much for French open-mindedness.

At the games, we watched the former Bruce Jenner earn his gold medal in the decathlon, and Finland's Lasse Viren win the 10,000 and 5,000 meters, as he did in Munich. We mourned that the late Steve Prefontaine did not get a chance to re-challenge him.

* * *

Eleven years later, in 1987, I was working as a freelance producer and on-air talent for a syndicated TV program titled *PM Magazine*. I had been hired to write and star in music videos of some of my funny songs. But when the executive producer changed, so did my role.

"I love to hear you read," the new producer interrupted me from behind her desk as I recited a script I'd written. "I want to expose the world to the serious side of Eric Gnezda." Shortly thereafter, she asked me to go with the *PM Magazine* crew to Germany. "How would you like to do a fifteen-year retrospective on the Munich Massacre?" she asked.

She had no way of knowing my interest in the subject, but I couldn't wait. I'd never done anything close to producing a TV story, but I accepted her offer immediately. In the weeks prior to the trip, I read everything I could get my hands on about the tragedy, talked to people who'd studied the event, and got a layout of the Olympic Village so I would know my way around.

I was ready to go.

But not so fast.

Our contact from the Munich Tourist Office tried to discourage us from doing the Olympic story, asking us if we wouldn't rather profile Hitler's private bunker. They'd give us full access. Strange offer, I thought, but it foreshadowed a prevalent German attitude. They were more comfortable revisiting their Nazi history than what had happened in Munich. The Olympics, Germany's long-awaited chance to show the world that it was free from the ghosts of its Nazi past, ultimately set the stage for disaster, and they wanted no reminders of it.

We stood our ground, and I was off to Munich to do the story. When I arrived at Olympic Village, I was surprised to find it was being used for student housing at the local university, with the former Israeli quarters, 31 Connollystrasse, a guest house for visitors, leaving me to wonder who would feel comfortable staying there. Outside the complex was a bronze plaque that names the eleven Israelis and reads, "Honor their memory."

Not far away was Olympic Park, where Munich's highest hill, Olympiaberg, a *Trümmerberg*, or mountain of debris from the war, rises 164 feet over the grounds. Halfway up the hill, we were high enough to get a glimpse of the Olympic sports compound, including the beautiful pond and the iconic membrane roofs over the venues.

"This is good here," my photographer said as he moved to set up his gear.

Carrying the camera equipment is not easy for any photographer, but something inside told me to keep going, so as much as I hated to tell him, I insisted we continue to the top. It was a long path. When we got to the peak, we found a large cross. The photog set up his camera, and, as if choreographed, a dove perched itself on the horizontal bar, then flew toward the stadium.

He got the shot.

The extra steps up the path seemed to have been worth it, and my story felt like it was shaping up into something special. Until we met with a gentleman from German TV, who told me he had some footage we could use.

"I remember it like it was yesterday," he said, his glance reflecting off into the distance.

He showed me some archived TV shots and told me to let him know which ones I wanted. I chose about a dozen, excited to have them as the basis for my story. He then informed me that each one would cost about $1,000 per minute. I wasn't expecting that. There was no way we could afford any of the archives. And so, what started off as a promising story was turning out to be nothing more than a few seconds of a dove flying from a cross on a pile of rubble.

I was beside myself. My first story. A trip to Germany. And a failed mission.

What am I going to do?

I came home to my long-unkempt home office. As I was sorting through my own pile of debris, I came across an article from *USA Today*. The headline read: "The day sports changed forever; Mourning moments at Munich." In the article, dated September 4, 1987, Dr. Benjamin Berger, the father of one of the Munich hostages, David Berger, was interviewed. He still lived in Shaker Heights, Ohio, just two hours from me, and seemed willing to talk to the press, at least to *USA Today*.

Would he talk to me? Would I have the courage to call him? How do you ask a father who lost a child to relive the events surrounding his death?

I'd never done anything like this.

"Should I call him?" I asked Mike Harden, my late colleague at *The Columbus Dispatch*.

"You've got to," he insisted. "I promise you he'll talk to you. He'll *want* to talk to you. He doesn't want the world to forget."

Mike was a master columnist and a Vietnam veteran who often wrote about things he didn't want anyone to forget. I trusted him. I pulled together my courage and made the call. Dr. Berger could not have been more receptive. We scheduled the interview at his home on a Sunday before the holidays.

When the photog and I arrived, I took a deep breath and knocked on the door. Dr. Berger and his wife answered. They were smiling. But as I stepped into the house, I could feel a sea of sorrow. They invited us to join them at their table for lunch, then took us to David's room upstairs, which still showcased the laurels of a high school scholar-athlete.

"My agreement with my son," Dr. Berger said, "was that if he finished law school, he could seek dual citizenship in Israel." David, who won the NCAA weightlifting title in the 148-pound class, finished his MBA-law degree from Columbia University in 1969, and shortly thereafter, made Israel his home, where he was among the first to teach sports to the disabled.

Dr. Berger then invited us to go with him to see the David Berger National Memorial, which, at that time, was at the Mayfield Jewish

Community Center. A steel structure, the memorial consists of the five Olympic rings broken in half, resting on a base of eleven segments, symbolizing the athletes who died. But the broken rings also reach forward and upward, representing hope and optimism.

On the drive back from the memorial, Dr. Berger talked about the day after the attack. He told the media he wished for no reprisals, and he received a call from President Nixon.

"He was very nice and asked if there was anything he could do. I told him that I'd like my son to be buried here, and so he said he'd make sure the body was returned home."

David's body arrived on a U.S. Air Force jet.

We returned to Dr. Berger's house for the interview. I asked Mrs. Berger if she'd like to speak, too, and she declined. Her husband said that it helped him to talk about David, but that she preferred to stay silent.

Dr. Berger was patient and kind. Years of sadness seemed to have made him deliberate with his thoughts.

He talked about how he had learned of the attack.

"I was getting ready to go to work that morning when somebody called me up and asked if I was watching the morning news.

"From there, each passing moment was an eternity. The short-term relief when Reuters News Agency falsely announced that the hostages had been freed, followed by the unconscionable despair when he heard the words from Jim McKay: 'They're all gone.'

"I think if you lose a child, it is a loss that is never replaced by anything else," he said. "In any tragedy I think that we have to look for some positive thing to come out of it."

The story concluded with a shot of Dr. Berger walking around his son's memorial, with his voiceover saying, "The forces of good always have to be there to fight the forces of evil. And that's what life's all about."

Mike Harden had been right. Dr. Berger did want to talk about the tragedy. He wanted the world to remember. And I learned that even as a journalist, I could help a hurting soul.

A few months later, another surprise emerged. The story, which early on seemed bound to fail, earned an Emmy nomination. Although I was pleased with the acclaim from my peers, I was sad it came at the expense of someone else's suffering.

* * *

Over the years, I've remained a fan of the Olympics, even as they've become more tainted by politics, greed, and hype. I've kept in touch with where my running heroes are today through web searches and social media. Dave Wottle is a retired admissions officer at Rhodes College in Memphis.

In 2014, when I was an adjunct speech professor at Ohio Wesleyan University, I was gathering my teaching materials from my lunch table in the faculty dining hall, and I felt someone enter the room behind me.

"Hi," a voice said to what I sensed was a small gathering of people, "I'm Dave Wottle."

Something in my subconscious connected Dave Wottle and higher education, so I bolted around and there he was, the Olympic champion, standing in a suit, still thin. In an instant, I turned into the fawning fan everyone hates. I went straight for him, blowing right past the university president, who was introducing him to other administrators—the VPs, the deans, the provost.

"Mr. Wottle," I said, catching him off guard, "I can't tell you what an honor it is to meet you. When I was in high school, you were the guy we all looked up to . . . we wore the hats . . ."

The university crowd stepped back with a blend of surprise and curiosity, for they knew nothing of his history.

"I just watched your race the other day on YouTube."

"Did I win?" he asked, smiling.

"Just barely."

His sense of humor made him feel real.

I figured he was a guest of the university and would only be around for a day or two.

"I know your time is precious, but is there any way we could get together and have lunch or something while you're still here?"

"Well, sure," he said. And he wrote his secretary's name on the back of his business card—an *Ohio Wesleyan* card. "Give her a call. I'm here during the week."

And then, while shaking his hand in thanks, my parting words cemented my place in the Doofus Hall of Fame. "I thought you were taller."

After class, I called a former student of mine who was working in admissions at OWU. "So why didn't I know Dave Wottle was working here?"

"He's been here since January."

"Don't you know who he is?"

"Yes, he's a rock star in admissions. I didn't know about the Olympics until someone brought it up about three weeks after he started."

Apparently, the president of OWU had worked with Dave in an earlier job and hired him for a semester to help with admissions. He also apparently announced Dave's appointment in an email weeks earlier, which, of course, I didn't bother to read.

Dave and I met for lunch and he ordered a salad, so I tempered my regular eating habits and just had a sandwich. I was pleased at how down-to-earth he was. We sat like two guys with running stories to tell. Except I didn't tell any. I just listened. His history was filled with competing against world-class runners, while my memories were merely about great high school runners.

Dave had roomed with Pre in Europe.

"What was he like?"

"WILD! I mean WILD!" he said, without offering any examples, and I didn't press him.

I asked him about tying the world record at the Olympic trials, his tendonitis, and getting married the summer of the games, a move that didn't resonate well with the Olympic coach, Bill Bowerman.

As great as his 800 meters victory was, he said he was disappointed that he didn't make the final in the 1500, which he considered his best event. "I got cocky," he said, and "a guy from Denmark did to me what I did in the 800 to everyone else."

"What was it like to be an Olympic champion and then go back to college?"

"I was student-teaching at the time," he responded. "My supervising teacher didn't care about a gold medal. I had to have my lesson plans in or that was it."

We both had to get back to work. He thanked me for giving him a chance to reminisce, and I let him know what an honor it was that he'd spend his lunchtime with me. As we left, I asked him if he still runs.

"Not much. I play some basketball though. But running? You get sick of it, you know? My knees hurt and I don't want to be one of those old guys out there."

We both laughed.

Yeah, I've seen many of those old guys, dressed in outmoded running gear, plodding along in the outside lanes to stay out of the way, squinting to look at their watches.

I'm one of them.

Climbing the Ladder

IN the spring of 2001, Vicki quit her corporate job to stay home with our two girls and run my company, which included booking my speaking gigs. For six months, our business boomed. Until September 11, when the world changed. Facing an unsure economy, companies quit hiring public speakers who lacked "content," making things rough on a songwriter and storyteller who inspired and entertained but didn't unfurl a five-point plan guaranteed to bring success, money, or fame.

Once again, I felt like a refugee forced to change course while always on the move. "The road is at an end, but the journey isn't through," as I'd later write in my song "The Voice of Faith." But at forty-four, being a father and husband, I didn't have the luxury to wait until my inner voice spoke to me. I inventoried my interests, talents, and passions. Eventually, I heard my alma mater, Ohio Wesleyan University, was looking for an adjunct instructor in public speaking. Being foreign to the world of academics, I had nothing close to their requested "curriculum vitae." Worse yet, the person to contact was the provost, who was a professor when I was a student, leaving me to think, *this could be good . . . or this could be bad.* Nevertheless, I sent in my application, sans curriculum vitae, with a list of my hundreds of speaking clients, and hoped for the best.

I got an interview and was hired on a Friday. They needed a syllabus on Monday morning.

I called my art-teaching sister in a panic. "Niki, how do I write a syllabus?"

"Just write down everything you know, then organize it."

Everything I know? Do I know anything?

Over a sleepless weekend, I jotted down every last detail of what I had learned over twenty years in the speaking industry. My sister's advice was perfect, and by Monday morning I submitted a syllabus.

I hadn't been in a classroom for twenty-six years, knowing this time I would be on the other side of the seats, facing dozens of eyes daring me to teach them something. Not unlike my comedy club experiences, where the audience sits before you in cynical anticipation, as if to say, "Okay, make me laugh," which is good training for any communicator, because, whether you do well or poorly, once you've survived that, you will forever remember the concept of "audience."

Teaching, however, would be a different challenge. As I thought about how to prepare for my classes, I went through the usual "I hope they like me" thoughts before I dug down into the same essential questions I'd learned to ask before a speech or performance.

Who is my audience?
What do they have in common?
What do they need?
How can I make a difference to them?

I wanted to give more to my students than had been given to me, and get them thinking beyond themselves. I thought about my college years and what experiences stayed with me. So much of what I had learned seemed irrelevant. Cramming for tests was useless, of course, for as soon as the exam was over, I forgot nearly everything. One of the reasons I liked my journalism classes was that I couldn't prepare for tests by doing "a lot of book-beating," as my professor, Verne Edwards, called it. His tests were an opportunity to display the skills and knowledge I had acquired over the term. And I have to say it felt pretty good when a summa cum laude classmate expressed her frustration when I repeatedly outscored her on these particular exams.

"How do you do so well on Verne's tests?" she had asked me. "You can't study for them!"

I shrugged and kept my smugness to myself.

Journalism and speech are skills you can only learn by doing. So I decided to give my students every opportunity to "do."

Meanwhile, I had to get through the first day.

I arrived thirty minutes early. As the students rolled in, I sat in the front, saying nothing. Never good at small talk, I choose awkwardness over chatter. My heart pounded.

My God, these are just kids! When did I get so old? How do I reach them?

I welcomed them and told a story:

A FEW YEARS AGO, I made friends with a guy named John Bokros, a battalion chief in a local fire service, who invited me to participate in his Citizens Fire Academy.

"What kind of things do you do in it?" I asked.

"Oh, a variety of things," he answered, "like CPR, vehicle extrication, fire safety. You'll get to dress in our turnout gear . . ."

"Sounds pretty cool," I said.

". . . and you'll get to climb the ladder."

"The *ladder*?"

"Yeah, on the back of a truck. Ladder 111. We call it a straight stick."

"And how high is that?"

"A hundred-five feet."

I'd heard enough. There was no way I was going to climb any ladder. I've had a lifelong fear of heights. For as long as I can remember, I've had recurring dreams in which I was falling from a tall building, and right before I hit the ground, I'd wake up. But with dismissive curiosity I asked John, "How high is 105 feet anyway?"

"About ten stories."

"Definitely not for me," I said. All I could think of was when I took a tour of Ohio Stadium with my daughters, and I stood in the lobby of the premium corporate boxes in the Huntington Club, afraid to even look out the window at the parking lot. That was only six stories.

"Well, you can pass on that session if you want," John said. "It's the sixth week, so just stay home for that one."

"Okay, it's a deal." Except I showed up for the third week, and there, extending high above the fire station, was the ladder.

"Hey, what's with the ladder?" I asked John.

"Oh, we had to move Ladder Day up a few weeks."

"I see," I said, not hiding my sense of unease.

"Look, you can watch . . . or just climb thirty feet."

I looked up the ladder and couldn't even see the top. I chose to watch. But as classmate after classmate climbed and returned alive, my curiosity grew. I knew myself too well. If I didn't at least try, I would never forgive myself. My face must have been transparent, for John came by and said, "Well?"

Dusk was falling and the moon was approaching three-quarters. Streetlights were beginning to peek through the twilight. If I was going to climb, I'd have to do it now because it was not like I could change my mind overnight and walk into the fire station and say, "Hey, I'd like to climb your ladder today!"

People have been committed for far less.

"Okay," I said to John, "I'll go thirty feet."

"Good. You'll know thirty feet because it's the end of the first extension. You'll see a reflector on the side of the ladder."

Everyone was done, so they gathered around me, all aware of my fear. I climbed up on the deck of the truck, which was scary enough, and a firefighter named Brian gave me gloves and, with a double-pronged buckle, belted me to a blue rope that was tethered to the hands of another firefighter holding it beneath the ladder.

"Now, as you climb," Brian advised, "lift your right arm with your right leg. You always want two points of contact on the ladder. Just focus your attention on the rungs. Don't ever look down."

I began the climb, my feet stepping on the black, pleated grips of each rung. Brian was following behind me. Soon I saw the reflectors in my peripheral vision, signaling thirty feet.

I knew if I stopped, I wouldn't continue. I kept on, looking forward, moving my arms and legs in unison. About halfway into the second extension, I saw the roof of the fire station in the foreground. Brian picked up on the fact that I was getting scared.

"Hey, Eric, do you have any hobbies?"

"Yeah, napping. I love to nap."

Brian laughed. "This wouldn't be a good time to nap," he said. "You're doing great. Keep going."

As we reached the third extension, I noticed a few geese flying below in the distance, and a strange awareness hit me. *If I fall now, I'm dead . . .* which was actually a liberating thought. I had to put my faith in the ladder. I was trusting my life to it. The steps beneath my feet felt secure, my legs sturdy, thanks to my running, even as they quivered from nerves and the ladder swayed ever so slightly in the breeze. It was like I was watching a horror movie, divorced from reality. Although I was far beyond my comfort zone, as I came upon the fourth and final extension, the ladder narrowed again, giving me the illusion of sealing me safely in a tight cocoon.

"You're almost there," Brian said.

"About ten more steps?"

"More like fifteen," he said, which I knew meant twenty.

Brian's real talent was keeping me calm.

"Did you have any training in climbing?" I asked.

"No."

"You ever get scared?"

"I'm not going to lie to you . . ."

"Don't imagine you talk much about your fears," I added.

"No, no. But you know something, we always operate as a company. When we get a call, we never ask what race, what religion, who they voted for in the last election. We just know they need help."

Through the upper level of my peripheral vision, I saw the orange glow of the top rung. A few more steps and I reached it, pulling my chin just above my clenched hands.

"Wanna look around?" Brian said.

Without turning my head, my eyes darted back and forth. There was Otterbein Tower . . . St. Ann's Hospital . . . Route 270 . . . as if I were looking down on a LEGO village.

"Hey, look at Worthington," Brian said, referring to my hometown a few miles to the southwest. "Wanna wave at Worthington?"

"I'll wave to my kids." Then, without looking directly down, I also waved to my classmates below.

Although trembling, I felt triumphant. I wanted to savor every moment I was at the top because I had no plans to do this again anytime soon. I imagined what it must feel like to be rescued from danger, surrendering to someone like Brian, who knows what he's doing. I thought of John, who'd saved a coed from a burning dorm room, and now I had some idea how she felt.

What an exhilarating feeling it must be to risk your life to save another.

Then, out of nowhere, my mind went to the strangest place, and I blurted out, "You know what an American's greatest fear is?"

"No," Brian said.

"Public speaking," I answered. "And the second one?"

"No," he responded.

"Death. So, as Jerry Seinfeld pointed out, most people at a funeral would rather be in the casket than giving the eulogy."

He laughed, and with my eyes forward, not looking at the rung but at the setting sun, I began my descent.

Wow, I thought, *lots of people are afraid of speaking, but I've always been afraid of heights. Now I understand how they must feel getting in front of an audience.*

My downward steps continued one by one. And soon I heard some of the sweetest words ever: "Four, three, two . . . you're home."

I exhaled. Brian hugged me, John gave me a high five, and my classmates cheered. The firefighter who'd been holding the rope said, "Hey, funnyman, I wish someone would've had a camera on your face from down here. You were intense." Even the fire chief got in the act, saying, "I think I'll sign you up," to which I responded, "I'd love it, just as long as I get a desk job like you!"

A few years have passed since I climbed that ladder and faced my lifelong fear. And you know what? I have yet to have another dream of falling. But what I want to get across to you today is that to overcome my irrational fears, it took a team. A community. A family of people who cared. I didn't do it myself. A group of people were with me every step of the way.

And that's what this class is about. We're going to be here for each other every step of the way. ✦

The room was motionless. A student in the front row looked up at me spellbound and said, "That's a helluva story!"

A nice touch of validation, but now the real journey was to begin. I was done with being able to hide that I had no idea what I was doing in a classroom. I went through the syllabus, attendance, and other housekeeping matters. "As far as grades," I said, "if it were up to me, I'd go around the room right now and ask each of you what grade you wanted and give it to you. Then, with that out of the way, we could get down to learning. But for those of you who care about such things, let me say, focus on connecting with your audience and the grades will take care of themselves."

What I didn't tell them was that it took me a decade to learn to rise above myself and care more about what my audience was getting from me than what I got from them. And my students had only a semester.

I tried my best to provide an example through the "I've Been to the Mountaintop" speech by Dr. Martin Luther King, Jr. "MLK, of course, is also known for having a dream," I said. "But what did he mean by that? A dream can be anything. We might dream of having our own business, practicing medicine, being independent, being rich, becoming a professional athlete. What was different about MLK's dream?"

Usually, my students got the "right" answer in short order: Martin Luther King's dream wasn't just for himself, but for everyone.

"Yes," I responded, "he put others' needs above his own. That's service. That's leadership. The first step to leadership is putting some*one* or some *idea* before ourselves for the good of others. And, as speakers, that's what we're asked to do. To be leaders. To serve our audience. The greater need must come before our own."

We discussed the value of public speaking in the workforce. "If you can write and speak, you'll be sought out for leadership positions because you can express yourself and explain concepts and convince others," I said.

The theme of my course was "Connection, not perfection."

"Our goal is not to be perfect, but to be authentic," I said. "Everything we do communicates. From the moment we walk into a room, we're communicating. Before we even open our mouths, we're communicating. That's why it's important to be comfortable with ourselves, to not feel like we have to fill every second with words. When we're on a long car ride with a good friend, we don't have to talk all the time. We can sit together in stillness and silence and enjoy the ride. That's what we want to build with our audience. To have moments of stillness and silence in our speeches. Not only to let our words sink in, but to give us a chance to listen to our audience, to catch their cues, to respond to them with our eyes, our expressions, and our body language. Stillness speaks of security. Silence is power. When we combine those with authenticity, we build trust."

I'd tell them the story of how David Letterman said he learned to do comedy in his early years by watching Jay Leno at The Comedy Store. "It was just Jay talking to his cool friends."

"That's where we want to be as speakers," I said, modifying David's comment, "just talking with our intelligent friends."

"Speak . . . slowly . . ." I advised. "If that's the only thing you learn this term, it will have been well worth your time."

"What makes a good topic?" my students asked me continually.

"What consumes so much of your passion," I'd respond, "that midnight rolls around before you realize you've forgotten to eat dinner?"

I also added a segment on listening, the single most important skill a speaker can have, to which a student summed up my months of preparation in one sentence: "Listening is selfless."

I had a sudden appreciation for how Kurt Vonnegut must have felt. In the prologue to *Jailbird*, he wrote that a high school student sent him a letter saying all his works could be summarized in a single sentence. Vonnegut agreed and lamented that after all of his effort writing novels, a simple telegram was all he needed.

I had much to learn from my students. My default response to an ambivalent or indifferent audience had always been defensiveness, which I knew would be the worst possible reaction to a group of young people who were feeling insecure themselves while trying to figure out who I was. A couple of times early on, I gave in to it, but once I followed my advice and got out of my own way, the students and I got in sync and the classes hummed along.

For twelve years, I became a privileged witness to students discovering themselves. Developing talents they never knew they had. Cheering each other on. Taking enormous emotional risks. Failing, only to come back with their next speech and succeed because they grew from what went wrong the last time. I was reminded daily of what I learned when I was coaching distance running: When we take a young person's dreams seriously, they will constantly amaze us with their commitment, discipline, and achievements.

I also was surprised over the years by how many international students signed up for my class their first semester. Students from Pakistan, China, Japan, Ghana, Jamaica, Trinidad and Tobago, Mexico, Bhutan, and elsewhere. All spoke English as their second language.

"Let me ask our students from the U.S. a question," I said. "How many of us would volunteer to go to China, or Pakistan, or Ghana and take a public speaking course the moment we walked on campus?"

Of course there were no replies. My message was unspoken but clear. We need to honor the courage of our international students, we are lucky to have them with us, and we can learn a lot from them.

We had a few students from Vietnam. During a speech by An, a student from Hanoi, my mind went back to my childhood, seeing nightly carnage from the war on television. Yet this young man's speech revealed a gentle soul, a person I cherished and wanted to know better. I told my students about my thoughts and said, "You know, history's a strange thing. If this were forty years ago, An and I might be on opposite ends of a gun, and we'd never see the beauty that lies beneath."

Another night, I walked beneath the acorn street lamps illuminating the campus with a Jamaican student, Lathania. Contemplative and wise beyond her years, she stopped, scanned the nighttime sky, and, like all gifted orators, painted a picture in words that said it all.

"You know, the way I look at it is that back home there are places where people are very poor and crime is bad, so it can feel very dark. At the same time, there's so much beauty in the faith and community of the people. It's like the sky. When it's dark, you can see the natural, enduring light clearly. Here in America, people have so many things, but it can feel so empty. There's so much man-made light that you can hardly see the stars."

A freshman from China walked onstage during her persuasive speech, looked at the clock on the wall, and paused. Then she looked us straight in the eye and said in broken English, "In Beijing, it's 5:30 a.m.—and my mother is starting chemotherapy."

With one sentence, she brought us all into her life, made us walk in her shoes, and challenged us to imagine being half a world away when our mother is beginning cancer treatment.

A male student opened his speech with: "I've heard my dad say before, 'The hardest things a person can say to another person are I'm sorry, I love you, and help me.'"

He then told of a boy being home from college for Thanksgiving his freshman year and driving in a car with his best friend of five years. The friend leans over and says, "So who's this girl you've been crushing on? I've never seen you act like this before."

The boy responds that he'd rather wait until they're on their hike to talk about it. Once they're on the trail, "the boy plops himself down on a rock, stares at the patches of mold, the leaves on the ground, and his mud-caked boots, and eventually mutters, 'I guess we should get to the meat of the conversation, shouldn't we?'"

The friend leans against a tree, listening, "and the boy sits in silence, choked by internal conflict. Going through his head are questions of *Can I even say this? Will she be okay with it if I say it? And what will it do to our friendship?*"

"He takes a moment, in silence, looks up, and like the body expels vomit to get rid of the bad feelings inside, one phrase bursts from his lips: 'I'm gay.'"

He pauses and he returns to center stage.

"So how does this story end?" he asks.

The student continues that the girl is still his best friend, "and that boy I was three years ago, sitting on a rock, unsure about if he could even say two simple words, I don't even know him anymore. That one phrase, it's still one of the hardest things I've ever brought myself to say.

"And so I'd like to add one more to my dad's list: The hardest things I can think of to say are. 'I love you, help me, I'm sorry . . . and I'm gay.'"

Coming out is a lot easier these days, if, in fact, anyone truly cares anymore, but at that time it was courageous for him to come forward, especially in public.

Many students spoke about emotional issues, but I made it clear that, while class would be a safe place to reveal personal struggles, students by no means had to if they preferred to talk on other topics. One of the most passionate, and therefore most effective, speeches came from a finance major who showed us how a student who invested the cost of a pizza into the right funds weekly would be well on their way to being a millionaire in their thirties. Another student showed us how to set a table for a formal event, and the placekicker for the university's football team demonstrated how to kick a field goal.

Great speeches, with little emotional risk.

Yet, other students seemed to need to talk about their personal lives. A senior spoke about his friend who was in a wheelchair due to a drunk driving accident. Afterward, he felt it had lacked the necessary emotion, so he followed up the next week with a speech about why he had failed and what he had learned.

"What I know now is that my speech lacked emotion. I tried to hide my insecurities so that others would not judge me. After having time to reflect, I realized that hiding my emotions was not helping anybody. Pulling back emotions is like holding back potential and opportunity to connect with your audience. The key to these emotions, and giving an emotional speech, is to wring out your emotions. Wring them out through practice and preparation so that these emotions can develop into constructive thoughts, so that you can talk passionately about this situation that has happened to you. And I believe that is truly the challenge of public speaking. Talking passionately without getting overly emotional about a subject you truly care about. That's hard."

What bigger compliment can an instructor receive than to watch a student embrace what he's learned, make it his own, and then explain it to his peers in his own words?

At the end of the first year, the provost called me into his office and said that so many students wanted to take my class that they needed to add another section and create an upper-level course.

"Upper level?" I asked. "What do you want me to teach?"

"You're the speaker," he replied. "Whatever you want."

I decided to model the course after the writing workshops I had in graduate school. All of my students had the basic speaking skills down, so they would decide on the speeches they wanted to give, even the length, as long as they kept the audience engaged. I'd give one lecture at the beginning of the semester, then turn the class over to them. They'd speak, lead critiques, and structure the course however they wanted. It would truly be their course.

"The biggest challenge you'll have," I explained to students, "is how to deal with your freedom."

The first day of my upper-level class, I started with a PowerPoint presentation. Toward the end of the slideshow, a blank screen appeared.

"What's this?" I asked, giving my students a chance to answer. "A blank page," I continued. "Scary, isn't it? We've heard authors, composers, and speakers talk about the fear of facing the blank page. There are many blank pages in life. In fact, life itself is a blank page. So how do we fill it?

"One choice," I said, "is this way," and a canvas with borders and numbers appeared on the screen. "We can approach our lives like a paint-by-number project. We paint in the reds where we're told to paint in the reds. The greens where it says green. Blues in the blues. In life it's the same process. We reach our twenties, we get a job. We follow directions, we're offered a promotion. Time to get married. Have kids. And before we know it . . ."

Next slide: a completed paint-by-number on canvas.

"... we've painted our lives. There's nothing *wrong* with this picture. In fact, some of us may have one in our homes, or seen them in our grandparents' homes. Many people need this structure—in art and in life. The only problem is that some people strive for more. They want to create ..."

Slide switches to a Van Gogh painting.

"... a masterpiece. So that's our challenge. You've been given a blank canvas. How are you going to fill it?"

One student responded with a speech about his trip to Greece, where he'd studied abroad for a semester and had returned with some newfound meaning.

"I found the answer to life on my way to the restroom in Greece," he began. "I stopped to talk to the owner of the taverna where I was eating, and he mentioned he'd never left the island we were on."

"Never?"

My student asked him why.

"Because everything I love, and all that matters to me, is right here. My family, my friends, my business. I don't need anything more."

As simple and direct as the taverna owner's comments were, they made an immense impact on my student, who I observed had found an inner peace, a serenity that was not there a year before.

The class absorbed his speech. For me, it awakened the same questions that the Greek taverna owner raised in him. I reflected on my decision to stay in Worthington, the commitment to my family, and the advantages of maintaining lifelong friends. My thoughts drifted over to Grandma Nez's brother, Great Uncle Joe, who came to Gowanda from Slovenia at age three and barely ever left town. He'd traveled to Buffalo occasionally, had gone to Cleveland once, missed seeing the Statue of Liberty when he landed at Ellis Island because it was dark, but he never felt the need to return to New York City. He spent his life in Gowanda, where he owned a grocery store attached to his house. He rarely collected credit that was owed. He made Trick or Treat a legendary event each year, and the neighborhood kids loved him so much they planned a tribute to him in a nearby park after he died. He was jovial and even taught Vicki to polka the night she met him. He was happy with what he had, where he was, and who he was with. He needed nothing more.

"He's a man who's found what people call peace," said my Uncle George.

Good for him, but had I found peace? It was a fundamental question my student had brought from one end of the world to the other. All from a trip to the restroom.

A great speech can raise the damnedest questions.

Another student told us a story from her childhood, which brought anything but peace.

"At eleven years old, a man crept into my room, and he took something from me that I will never get back. After that night, a pattern emerged and proceeded for three years. To this day, I am haunted by the sound of a pickup truck pulling away late at night. When I close my eyes, I'm twelve years old again, bleeding in a bathtub, wondering if I'll ever feel clean again. I know it's hard to imagine, but I'm one of the lucky ones."

At fourteen, she was welcomed into "the arms, into the lives, into the home" of a foster family, and "able to experience the process of healing."

She asked us to imagine four students disappearing from the walkways of our campus every day. She spoke slowly, pausing to add emphasis to her words. "At the conclusion of the year, 1,600 lives would have been taken, leaving only 200 students on the campus. This is the reality for the 1,600 children every year who die as a result of abuse and neglect. Four children . . . every day, every year . . . die as a result of being abused or neglected."

Seventy-five percent of these children, she explained, die before the age of four. "This means that these children will never experience sleepovers, they'll never agonize over puberty or spelling bees. They'll never attend high school proms. They'll never experience the euphoria of first love. They'll never have the opportunity to have the college experience we are all sharing.

"As the years pass," she continued, "we are going to be facing some hard decisions. We will all leave this campus and we'll have to decide what career path we will go into, whether or not we will follow our dreams, or if we will reach for stability. Someday we may find love, and we will face the decision of whether or not we will start a family.

"Maybe we should ask ourselves if we have the capability to foster or adopt *one* child, to save *one* child, to give *one* child love, support, a fighting chance to make a positive difference in the world. I hope that when that time comes, when we ask ourselves that question, that the answer might be yes."

She concluded with Rumi's "The Way Things Should," then, after a brief pause, walked off the stage. Five seconds of silent eternity passed before her classmates erupted in applause. A ten-minute speech, no notes, except for the poem at the end. I was further astonished when she told me afterward that she had made the decision to give the speech that afternoon. "I felt like it was the right time to talk about it, and I always go with my gut," she said.

The speech no doubt had been boiling inside of her for years, and, as bad as her story made me feel for her, I was glad our class was the beneficiary of her courage.

In another speech, a student mentioned that he wanted to become a priest. Being a lapsed Catholic, I was curious about his motivations, so I asked him to have lunch.

"Why do you want to become a priest?" I asked.

"It's the only profession I know of where I can wake up in the morning and ask God what He wants me to do today."

"Hmm," I responded, "imagine what the world would be like if everyone on Wall Street or Hollywood or Washington would wake up with that question."

I'm not sure if my comment registered with him, but it did with me, and I try my best to keep it in mind every morning.

My concern about whether I was making a difference in the lives of my students was addressed through an email I received from a student four years after he had graduated. His father, a celebrated fire chief, had recently contracted a neurological disorder originally mistaken for Parkinson's disease, but which turned out to be multiple system atrophy. He died at fifty-nine.

> My father went downhill very quickly and he went very fast. The outpouring of love from friends, family, and the community as a whole was absolutely amazing.
>
> His funeral was difficult. I had known going into it that he wanted me to speak and say something on behalf of the family. Me

being his namesake, I took this as my duty. What I didn't realize was the four hundred-plus people in the church and the four hundred-plus outside listening or that I was the only one that was speaking and the eulogy rested on my shoulders. For all the big-deal politicians, firefighters, cops that loved my father, they all choked up and had a difficult time talking about him. All the people my mother asked couldn't handle the responsibility of speaking about this great man's life. At no point did I feel nervous or even upset. I went through the steps I learned from you and was brimming with confidence from "go."

I cannot thank you enough because without you and your class I would never have been able to do this, and giving that eulogy has been the single most important thing I've done in my life. I can feel it. I'm so proud that I could speak on behalf of my father. I know the message got through because for weeks after that I received emails, phone calls from people wanting to share my words with others. Thank you.

The ABC News affiliate covered the funeral, including my student's full eulogy. I was so proud of him, knowing that, through his work in my speech classes, he was able to pay tribute to his father, whom his family, friends, and colleagues called Superman.

Damn those neurological diseases that take a man down in his fifties. But did I ever understand how his eulogy was "the single most important thing" he'd done in his life. He will remember it forever, and I will always be grateful that he considered my class an important contribution to that lifetime memory.

Over my twelve years of teaching, I received many emails from parents, one from a mother, who copied the university president, thanking me for the "help and guidance" I'd given her son. He had a genetic brain abnormality that caused learning disabilities and trouble in social situations. "You have single-handedly had the biggest influence on helping him improve a skill he will use for the rest of his life."

Big words from a mother. How do you respond to them? I thanked her, of course, but to tell the truth, I felt that any words from me would be inadequate. I wasn't aware of his diagnosis, and I don't think I did anything other than treat him like everybody else. To be told I "single-handedly had the biggest influence" on him is more than my heart could hold. But I am grateful, grateful, grateful. Both for the opportunity to have such an influence on him, and to her for taking the time to let me know.

The summer after I quit teaching, a student wrote to me. "Currently, I am a police officer with the Las Vegas Metropolitan Police Department, and being able to talk to people has kept me alive. I have seen some hairy situations, and the gift of gab that I learned in your class has de-escalated situations."

From providing skills that a student with a learning disability will use the rest of his life, to being credited with keeping another one alive are compliments no teacher would ever dare imagine. The opportunity to teach, a career I'd turned to out of necessity, became one of life's greatest gifts to me. And perhaps with a few exceptions, it went well for everyone involved. So why did I stop?

It was time.

I could no longer be all the way there for my students. During my teaching years, I got my graduate degree, ran my business, wrote songs, began this book, and took care of my family. And thought about an idea for a TV series consuming so much of my passion that midnight would roll around before I realized I'd forgotten to eat dinner.

Tony

I LOVED watching my nephew Tony grow up and being part of his life. Giving him sports stuff. A Cleveland Browns jersey. My old baseball card collection. Signed memorabilia. Playing kickball in his backyard. Cookouts. Making him the star of one of my music videos for TV. Lifting him from the swimming pool when he was about three and in pursuit of his turtle ranking. Taking him to Cleveland to watch Nolan Ryan pitch in his retirement year.

A visceral connection.

A fusion of bloodlines.

One advantage of working for myself was that I could keep my own schedule. As an eight- or nine-year-old, Tony would come by in the middle of the day during the summer. No matter what I was doing—or whoever I was talking to—I'd drop everything because *Tony was at the door*! He'd usually show up with his bat and glove. I recall the time we went down the street to Worthingway Middle School.

He stood with his back a few feet from the tennis court fence, and I was about twenty feet away with the ball.

"Now remember, Tony, you don't want to kill the ball 'cause when you try to kill it, that's when you hit grounders, or foul tips, or you strike out. Just make contact."

Tony listened.

Tony

"Keep your hands together and your back elbow up. Step forward as you swing."

"Elbow up!" I yelled as I released the ball, underhanded.

He was fouling off, missing the ball, and hitting grounders. It didn't help that most of my pitches weren't any good. I switched to throwing overhand, inching toward him. He started connecting, so I threw each pitch harder.

"Now, Tony, what you want to do is smack the ball right over my right ear because in your league, that will be a base hit right up the middle."

Three pitches later. *Whack!*

My hat went flying, my glasses followed. My glove sailed and I was flat on my back, the ball just missing my head. When I got up, Tony was laughing so hard he couldn't even stand. Every time he tried to hold the bat again, he'd laugh and drop it to the ground.

He couldn't stop.

So much for practice that day.

* * *

As he grew, we shared other interests. I was never more honored to be his uncle than when he, in elementary school, invited me to be his guest at Special Friends Day. Then, in high school, he had to put together an oral report on some historical event that, to me, seemed to have happened just a day ago. We climbed into my crawl space and sifted through the stacks of magazines and newspapers I'd kept. The moon landing. The Reagan shooting. The *Challenger* disaster. His teacher was in awe that he'd come up with all those clippings, all available to him because I was a pack rat.

Tony loved to blaze a trail, forever forging his own way, from the time he was a kid into his teenage years when he sat down to figure out which lawn-mowing pattern would save the most time. I can't say the rows ended up looking even—definitely not classically suburban—but to Tony, that didn't matter. Even cutting the lawn was a creative endeavor.

Tony and I ran on the track together a few times when he started high school and was still trying to find his sport. I pleaded with him to go easy, "this is no race," but he kept pushing the pace, sapping my breath, making it impossible for us to talk. But that's all I wanted to do. More than anything. Just talk while we jogged. I wanted to get to know this boy who was too rapidly growing into a young man. But I also understood he felt he had to prove himself. As if he ever needed to. As if I'd love him more just because he could kick my aging ass on the track.

Tony tossed pitches to me, too, in the form of questions about life, school, women, and, when his newfound passion took hold, songwriting.

Like me, he taught himself to play the piano. I found joy in giving him my spare recording and sound gear, but nothing meant more to me than the day I gave him my car. The red Integra. With an aftermarket body kit and alloy rims, the car did have its appeal and a special place in my heart.

I can still see Tony and me standing in my driveway on the summer day he came to pick it up. He was sixteen and needed a car to get back and forth from his job making wood-fired pizzas. He'd walked the two blocks from his house to mine. We stood by the driver's door.

"Well, take good care of it," I said, "and be safe."

He promised he would.

I handed him the keys. "I love you, Tony."

Suspended silence.

"I love you, too," he said behind a laugh.

* * *

When I looked at him, I thought I was staring into the mirror long ago, right down to his curly dark hair, glasses, square jawline, and hazel eyes that threaten anyone with something to hide. Hell, he even wore a ten-and-a-half boot. In his twenties, he was so much like me when I was that age. Artistic, idealistic, and naive. I told him I thought he was allowing himself to be too vulnerable. Even now, *especially* now, my feelings sway between anger and tenderness. Anger at how he put too much trust in the world. Tenderness for his vulnerability.

And how much more vulnerable could he have been than on his motorcycle, in the path of a barely functional driver who failed to yield on a left turn.

Tony

I was working in my office when Vicki called.

"Tony was killed in a motorcycle accident."

Words that plunged into my soul.

Words that echo to this day, in slow motion, syllable-by-syllable, always with the same force as the moment I heard them.

Tony was killed in a motorcycle accident.

He was on his way to a wedding on Cape Cod, riding his motorcycle from his home in Baltimore to Vermont to pick up his sister Katharine, when, just outside of Highland, New York, he was T-boned by a Hyundai Santa Fe.

Taken away in an instant. At twenty-nine.

* * *

The night before Tony's funeral, we all got together in the bar at the Holiday Inn, where his friends who had driven out from Baltimore were staying. I was able to talk to two of his girlfriends, Hillary and Emily. I asked them the same question. "Did Tony know how much I loved him?"

"Oh, yeah," Hillary nodded, as if she were surprised I even needed to ask. Later, Emily had the same response, her brown eyes not leaving mine. She even told me Tony kept a picture on his nightstand of me with my two girls, all mugging for the camera.

And then she added something else. "Tony talked about you all the time."

"He did?"

"You'd be surprised how much your name came up."

"You're kidding."

"Tony was mysterious," she continued. "He didn't open up easily. But he told me early in our relationship that he would look for your approval as if it were his father's. You always seemed to be his hardest critic, but his stubborn attitude made it almost impossible for him to show gratitude for your concerns. I'm just speculating, but maybe he thought you could see too much."

"He thought *that*?"

Her sad smile confirmed it, submerging me into even deeper reflection.

"I had no idea."

"Yeah, he looked up to you. The only negative thing he ever really said was he looked up to you, but he was determined not to live the safe life you did."

"The *safe* life? What did he mean by that?"

"I'm not sure."

I continue to wonder about what Tony meant by "the safe life." That I'm still living in my childhood home? That I don't, as he did, sleep on the porches of strangers? Or sneak into Cuba? Or hop trains? Or ride motorcycles?

I told Emily about the last time I saw him, and how I tried not to say too much about his choice to ride a motorcycle.

"I just hope you're taking a safety class," I said.

"You have to in the State of Maryland to get a license," he replied with his dismissive smile that always made me defensive.

Tony and I were standing at the door of my mother's house on Christmas night. I, heading for home three blocks away. Tony, on his way back to Baltimore the next morning.

"Look, Tony, I'm not trying to tell you what to do. I just want you sticking around."

"I'm sticking around. I'm sticking around."

I didn't want to overstep my bounds, so I didn't say anything more.

"I wish you had," Emily told me, closing her eyes.

I wish I had, too.

Like words from a father to his only son.

* * *

The morning of Tony's funeral service, I woke at 5:30, still not sure what I was going to say during the eulogy. I knew I'd open by reading Charles Bukowski's "Roll the Dice" because it was an appropriate poem for him by one of his favorite writers. Niki, having lost her son a decade after her husband died, chose to close his service with the Tom Waits song he had shared with her the last time the two of them were together, "Jayne's Blue Wish," the lyrics she put on his memorial card.

Once everyone was seated, I remained in a cove behind the parlor, which was packed with mourners as motionless as the photos of Tony bordering the room. Of all the photos, the most heartbreaking to me was the one of him at about three, asleep in a tie and blazer on Christmas night, my gift to him tucked between his head and shoulder.

A football.

His favorite music drifted from the funeral home's ceiling, lingering like fog over our grief. All week the thought had tormented me and now it was really bearing down.

Damn it, Tony, you were supposed to be doing this for me thirty years from now.

I'd given eulogies before. Spoken and sung at more funerals than I can remember. But I knew this time I'd have to count on something larger than myself to take over.

I asked God for help.

I told the story of Tony knocking me down in batting practice and how his middle school band director, Jim Dowdy, had emailed me right after his accident with a memory that "flashed" through his mind. He told me how Tony had saved the day at a contest of the Ohio Music Educators Association. Apparently, a seventh-grade trio was short a member and Tony, "a popular eighth-grader," was willing to step up to learn the parts on the spot and sat in with them on trumpet, making a trio. "He literally put those two on his back and said, 'Let's go.'"

"He was about servanthood and relationships," Jim continued, "and in this case he used making music to be Johnny Appleseed, spreading his love wherever he went."

What a fitting epitaph for Tony. The older I get, I realize there can be no greater definition of a successful life for anyone than *spreading his love wherever he went.*

Following Tony's 11 a.m. funeral service, we went to the burial. It was beastly hot, the sun toasting me in my dark blue suit like an ant under a magnifying glass. The cemetery ground was rock hard and dry. I was a pallbearer, and as we rolled him from the rear of the hearse toward his grave, I made sure to be at the front of the group, flanking his left side, grabbing the swing handle with my left hand, my weakest. I needed to feel I was facing grief head-on. Even more, I'd needed to be the first to arrive with him at the last place any of us wanted him to be.

A few months later, Tony's grave marker arrived, and I would see what a wonderful job Niki did designing it, continuing the theme she,

Tony, and her daughters created for Gary. The strand of ivy engraved in Gary's marker swings over to Tony's in an imaginary reach across the patch of grass between the two of them, side by side. Tony at Gary's right side, just where he was ten Junes before, rubbing Gary's forearm for days on end when Gary was dying. Holding his hand. Tony's eyes in reverent observation, soft with compassion, his silence making his devotion all the more pronounced, displaying what D.H. Lawrence called "the courage of your own tenderness."

In the winter after Tony's death, I visited his grave regularly. Right after his grave marker was installed, his resting place covered in a veil of snow. I stood behind it, my breath visible, the traffic audible far away on Route 23. I paused, as if waiting for just the right moment to lift a shroud from a sacred tablet. I squatted and, with my right hand, swiped the snow from the brown granite.

Gary Anthony Smith
November 22, 1978 – June 17, 2008
"Tony"

I stepped back, stood at his right shoulder.

"Tony. Tony. Tony," I uttered. Just as I'd said during his service. Just as I still catch myself muttering to him in disbelief, in tenderness, even years later, when my grief seeps in and catches me by surprise.

I walked down the line of what has turned out to be our row of family plots. Tony never meant to be part of this symmetry. Tony wanted nothing to do with Worthington and its middle-class values or lifestyle.

Now he is here for good.

As I walked from his grave that winter day, my feet pressed the snow as if they, too, were in deep contemplation. I was wearing black, bicycle-toe dress shoes, not at all Tony's style. He was so proud of the boots he'd bought from the thrift store. "They were worn by a guy in prison!" he boasted.

The situation felt so unreal it played out as a movie scene. It was hardly the first time. Immediately after his service, his body having just been loaded into the hearse, I stood next to the Rutherford-Corbin limo waiting for everyone to get in. I watched a stream of mourners file through the double doors of the funeral home and into their cars tagged with purple flags. Relatives I'd not seen in years. People I'd never met. All silent. All stunned. I was wearing shades, but this time, unlike at my Grandma Nez's funeral, I wasn't trying to conceal my tears. Someone put his hand on my shoulder, asked me how I was holding up.

"I feel like I'm watching a movie," I said. "A really sad movie, so sad it almost feels real."

Tony's death was real, of course, so I suppose seeing bits and pieces of those days as movie scenes put a safe distance between me and the pain. Gave me enough space to be able to handle the unthinkable. Then again, maybe the "movie scenes" were about something else. I still feel the full force of Tony's loss, a loss so immense I feel it deserves the attention of the entire world.

* * *

All of these memories were front and center for me when I returned to Baltimore on business, years later. It was November, and with Tony on my mind, of course I went to Camden Yards. I recognized Baltimore had been the ideal place for him to begin his adult life. The city is a blend of history and contemporary restoration. The birthplace of Babe Ruth. The streets where Edgar Allan Poe spent his last night. The town where H. L. Mencken unleashed his satire.

A ballplayer. A poet. An iconoclast.

Perfect for Tony. From an early age, Baltimore seemed to hold an allure for him.

I remember the Christmas when Mom got him a baseball cap. He was eleven and had given her specific instructions about which one he wanted and how to order it.

"I got Tony the baseball hat he asked for," Mom told me, quite proud of herself that, under Tony's direction, she was able to navigate her way through a world completely foreign to her: licensed sports apparel.

"Which team?" I asked.

"Oh, I don't know," she said, "but it's the hat he wanted."

Turned out it was an Orioles cap, all black, a "throwback" with an orange bird embroidered on the front.

"Why the Orioles?" I asked him. I was privately pleased because I always carried a soft spot in my heart for them, too. Mostly because the '66 World Series was the first one I watched with Dad. The games were still played in the afternoons in those days, and I happened to be home sick that week, so I joined him next to the TV. Maybe it was some subconscious thing on my part, but there were a few subsequent years when I "got sick" during the World Series, giving me and Dad a baseball experience far exceeding box seats in the stadium.

"I guess I've always liked the Orioles for some reason," Tony told me. And he went on to explain how their "new" logo was an updated version of the team's original design from the 1950s. The previous year they'd lost their first twenty-one games, leading them to a miserable season, so for the upcoming year they decided to ditch their "cartoon bird" and go retro with what they called "The Ornithologically Correct Bird."

I loved how Tony's curiosity propelled him to dig into things and discover something new, an interesting fact, or a different point of view.

I love even more the photo I have of him wearing the cap that Christmas morning. Tony, Gary, and I are sitting on the sofa in my living room. All smiles. All so proud to be with each other, a small, exclusive club of the family's only men.

Now only I remain.

* * *

Camden Yards in November. The contrast is profound. In the summer, a crowded center of energy, anticipation, and release. The gray and cold of late fall make the grounds feel desolate.

An appropriate day to be thinking of Tony. His memory brings warmth. His absence, a chill. As I jog, I wonder about the small things, like where he'd park when he came to a game, who his favorite vendor was, where he'd sit, and if he'd come with friends or alone. I was almost sure he'd spent a lot of time, at least once, giving a careful reading to the Orioles Hall of Fame wall.

I went into the team store, hoping somehow, someway, they'd still be selling the cap my mother bought Tony years ago. They had everything but. The cartoon bird. The script "O." The camo cap. The Cooperstown. The pillbox. The bird swinging a bat. The green St. Patty's Day cap, and the red, white, and blue "Stars & Stripes" model the team wears on the Fourth of July.

But no "Ornithologically Correct Bird."

I left without a purchase, which is rare for me at a sports apparel store.

If only they'd had the cap, I think as I begin running again. To wear one would have put me in physical contact with Tony and opened up the possibility of someone asking *me*, "Why the Orioles?" Then I could tell them Tony's story. Our story. Which, after all, is what grieving people want the most—to talk about the loved ones they lost. Who they were. What they meant. How they slipped, or were ripped, from their lives. Talking about the loss is a salve providing temporary relief from the permanent pain that remains forever fresh beneath the surface of the hardened tissue.

Being in Baltimore both soothes and aggravates the wound. Even though it's been years now, the trip to clean out Tony's apartment seems like yesterday. Niki and I had been there for less than thirty-six hours, but it was one of those weekend trips that felt like a month. Packed with emotion. Activity. Loss. And love.

Jemicy School, where Tony taught, was still holding events to honor him. To celebrate him. They just couldn't seem to let him go.

I understood how they felt. And still do.

They dedicated a reading room in his name. *The Tony Smith Reading Room*. His students read original works, all written for him, the English teacher they adored.

His student Mackenzie said her favorite memory was the time she walked into class wearing shades and Tony asked if he could put them on. He kicked his feet up on his desk, put his arms behind his head, and told them they could earn some free time by sharing stories of things they'd done with duct tape. Challenging his students to think outside the box. I've seen the image before. His dad, when I had him for English in the eighth grade.

After the dedication of the Tony Smith Reading Room, the school had lunch for everyone.

"Not a day goes by when someone doesn't bring up something about Tony," Ben, the then-head of school, told me, putting his full plate next to mine and sitting down. "The impact he had—still has—on this school is unforgettable."

Pauline was sitting across from Ben. I could tell in an instant she was an art teacher. They looked at each other in agreement. "I can honestly say I don't remember anyone ever saying anything bad about Tony," she said.

Ben showed me Tony's classroom. When I stepped inside, I was surprised to see only about six chairs. But I guess that makes sense at a private school for kids with language-based difficulties. Or as Ben, dyslexic himself, likes to say, "kids who learn differently."

"When I'd walk by here," Ben said, his open hand extending into the room, "I'd never know what I was going to see. Tony on the floor with a group of kids around him, or dressed up in some costume. Whatever it took to get them to learn."

Ben smiled in reflection and told me one of his favorite stories.

"I'll never forget when Tony came in for his interview. How sweaty his palms were when he shook my hand. He was so nervous. But I knew within five minutes I was going to hire him. Just the way he talked about kids and learning and teaching. He was perfect for this program. On his application he wrote about how he wanted to be as good a teacher as his dad had been. And he certainly accomplished that in a very short time. He's what we want all our teachers to be.

"Tony didn't teach by teaching, he taught by modeling. The traits of a true educator."

Jemicy even renamed their annual arts festival after Tony.

At the first celebration Jemicy held for him the summer after the accident, Ben said, "Some people live very long lives and never make much of a difference. Tony Smith lived only twenty-nine years but made a huge difference."

Tony taught at Jemicy for two years. *Two years*. But he made such an impact they not only named their reading room after him, but also their arts festival. And, as I learned in yet *another* celebration of his life, the school's athletic conference named their sportsmanship award in Tony's honor.

Both celebrations were heartfelt. The first one featured a soccer game. A cross country race. A slideshow of his life looping the entire time, growing in radiance as darkness set in. Two guys in Tony's band played his songs by the bonfire for nearly two hours. "Tony was such a prolific songwriter," one member said before starting a song.

Tony

I ran in the race in Tony's honor, a loop starting and finishing at the life-sized metal moose sculpture in front of the school. A sign saying "Tony Smith Race" was fastened to the tip of its nose by—what else—duct tape. While I raced, I imagined what it must have been like to have had Tony as a coach after school each day. Standing by the road, on the side of a hill, holding his stopwatch, calling out encouragement to his runners, those kids who weren't used to having someone on their side, let alone cheering for them.

"I have a request," Tony told Ben shortly after he arrived at Jemicy to teach. "Give me your most difficult students."

* * *

Niki cried again when our plane left the runway. She was looking out the window while we gathered speed. She seemed fine until the wheels left the ground, the jolt of takeoff triggering something in her. Her head fell against the back of the seat, her chest gave way, her shoulders quivered. Her eyelids squeezed shut, trying to pump tears from an empty well.

The dry burst subsided as fast as it had come.

She was in the middle seat. I was next to her on the aisle. She didn't know I was watching. I wondered if leaving Baltimore made her feel she was losing her son all over again.

Baltimore is a town no one in our family had given much thought to until Tony moved there. The summer after the accident was the first time I opened Tony's front door, knowing he had walked those hardwood floors, climbed those stairs, cooked on that stove, and left clean utensils on the counter.

A memory stick jutted from the front of his desktop computer.

A bar of soap in his shower dish.

Towels and washcloths left hanging.

He was going away for a week, certain to return. In fact, he had planned to visit Ohio the week after the wedding. I couldn't wait to see him. I imagined us sitting in my basement or at the bar at the Old Bag of Nails, both of us now adults. I was going to ask him about his songwriting, his teaching, and his performing.

But, oh my God, how expectations change. After the accident, his friends came by his row house to clean out his refrigerator. Turn off his utilities. And back up the song files on his computer in case someone broke into his now uninhabited house, which seemed entirely possible, the way it was tucked into the end of the alley behind a vacant lot off South Broadway.

Niki sat among the boxes he had stored beneath his bed loft. She couldn't believe he'd held onto all those letters she'd sent him over the years. "I didn't even know he had read them," she said. "I'd send him things and then we'd talk over the phone and he'd never mention a word. But he saved *everything*."

Somewhere on his desk, among a jar of coins and all those nooks where he stashed things, I found my dad's dog tag from the Navy. I'd forgotten all about it. I didn't think I'd seen it since I was a kid. I was curious how Tony ended up with it. I showed it to Niki and asked if I could keep it. She didn't think his sisters would mind, so I slipped it onto the key chain I was wearing on my belt loop, a green carabiner my daughter Meredith got for me on the way back from a spring break trip to Tampa with Vicki when she was still in preschool. I didn't keep keys on it, just the rubber Florida "license plate" that said, "I ♥ You."

The inside of Tony's row house reminded me of the apartment I lived in after I graduated from college. No furniture. Next to no adornment. Only a workspace, really. Just books and the other necessities for living— a bathroom, a bedroom, a refrigerator, and music gear. I was surprised by how much stuff he had in that small place of his. A digital recorder and a studio mic left upright in its spider mount, as if he'd stepped into the other room for a sip of water between vocal takes. He still had the mixing board I'd given him.

Tony's Steinway upright piano was one of his many contradictions. How he railed against affluence, protesting it by wearing working-class clothing, choosing to live in a blighted neighborhood, and being adamant about not eating at a fine-dining restaurant. But when it came to his instruments and music equipment, he insisted on having the top of the line.

Packed in a road case against his staircase was his Fender Rhodes, as if it were ready to be loaded for his next gig. Niki said he'd just bought it. I always loved the sound of those keyboards, which they've never quite been able to recreate digitally. Leave it to Tony to have the real thing.

When I put my hand on the road case, I felt like I was about to open my past. I used to do gigs with a Rhodes back in the day. I enjoyed playing them, but they weighed a freaking ton. I remember thinking I hoped Tony's bandmates helped him carry it to gigs.

He'd always talked about making instruments, but I didn't know just how many he had created until I stood beneath the ones he'd hung across the length of his downstairs brick wall—until I saw more of them at Jemicy, where they're now part of the reading room named after Tony. Until I held the ones his friends brought out for his funeral to place on his casket and then took to Niki's with great care. Until I looked through the open boxes of instrument parts scattered around his house—bridges, strings, piano keys, hammers, pivots, and levers.

Tony taught a class on instrument making at Jemicy, and Niki had gone to Baltimore for a gallery opening where they were exhibited. No wonder they were considered works of art. Banjos and other stringed instruments using nearly anything imaginable for a resonance box. Turtle shells, enamelware pots and pans, an antique cheese box. Tony even turned a washtub into a standup bass. Not that anyone came even remotely close to fighting over his things after his accident, but it was amusing to hear how many inquiries we got about that bass.

As little girls, Meredith and Caroline were so taken by his instruments they requested I ask Niki if they could have one. For years now, two of them have been on display in my den, hanging above me as I work. The week of his funeral, Meredith made one of her own and gave it to Niki. Elastic hair bands running down the "neck" of a one-egg poaching pan.

The thing even twangs.

* * *

Seeing how central music was to his life was satisfying because it forged an even deeper connection between us. Out of love and concern, I told him, "If you're going to write about being a vagabond, be *today's* vagabond. Aspire to be Tony Smith, not Woody Guthrie. Write about your own experiences, your own relationships, your own environment, your own times.

"Your truth will be your listener's truth."

I regret being so direct with him.

The first time I saw him perform his own material was in a roadhouse in Marysville, Ohio. Under the name of Tony "Truck" Smith, a persona I hadn't known he'd created until we were driving to the gig together and I caught a glimpse of a stack of posters he'd printed up. A black-and-white photo of him in a trucker's cap, on an 8½ x 11-inch sheet of paper, lunar blue.

"Truck?" I asked.

A muted, self-conscious chuckle in response. "Yeah," he said, resigned to his anticipated fear of having to respond to a follow-up question, "it goes back to playing coffee houses in college. The guys started calling me Truck."

I nodded, leaving out the "hmm," knowing any utterance could be interpreted as judgment. I found out at his funeral that some of his friends even called him Truck. I thought it was cool. I wish I'd known. It would have been a fun addition to my nickname for him: Bones.

"Bones," he snickered when he saw it on my phone. But I could tell he was touched. Although not particularly original, it was my nickname for him. Many Tonys out there, but to me, he was always "Bones."

Truck could have been his artistic, coming-into-adulthood nickname. Or like the third, or alternate jersey of a sports team, reserved for special games.

As much as I know about him, there's so much I don't. So much mystery. As there always had been with him.

I wish we could sit in each other's space. This time I would just listen. Absorb. Enjoy. Without comment. Without judgment. Without giving advice. How much we miss when we're not truly present, when we're intent upon responding instead of just taking it all in.

Now I have no choice. Tony's not here.

All I can do is listen.

* * *

Grief is protean. It changes shape, comes at us from unexpected angles, collars us in new forms. As C.S. Lewis points out in *A Grief Observed*, grief also can feel like being concussed.

How strange.

But that explains my state some six months after Tony's accident, when I momentarily lost my mind at a traffic light and began a left turn into a line of schoolchildren crossing the street. Thank God the crossing guard jumped in front of them and blew her whistle at me before I put anyone in real danger.

I was horrified at what I had done. I felt the same astonishment at myself that exuded from the crossing guard's face.

How could you do this? You must be crazy!

The only explanation I have is grief. My mind was concussed.

In ensuing months, gutted by grief, as I struggled to find meaning in Tony's death, simply as a means to get beyond the sorrow, I wrote pages and pages of letters to him. A way to keep my connection with him alive.

A year passed until I had the heart to delete him from my phone directory.

I'm not forgetting you, Tony, I told him from within. *Not wiping you out of my memory, but it's time to get used to not having you around.*

Then my mind replays:

"*I just want you sticking around.*"

"*I'm sticking around. I'm sticking around.*"

I couldn't think of anything else to say to him. I just wanted him to be there. Wanted to be in his presence. Thought about how that's the essence of love.

Being there.

* * *

Tony was born the day before Thanksgiving. When I arrived at University Hospital to visit him and Niki in the wee hours, I was drunk, flaunting the odor of alcohol like a fool wearing cheap cologne. A senior in college, I was interning at Channel 10 and had caught the TV bug. I also had an emerging case of media hubris, to which early twenty-somethings are particularly susceptible. I strutted up to the maternity floor, only to be stopped by a couple of thirty-somethings in pastel nursing smocks who told me that visiting hours were long over.

"Look," I announced, "I've got a show to produce in LA tomorrow and I'm going to see my sister and her new baby."

Dumbfounded, they paused, and I blew by them.

No one followed.

Those poor nurses should have summoned security and had me strapped to a gurney until I sobered up, if not grew up. But they didn't even call to me.

My declaration had been a raw bluff, but I'd succeeded in selling them the role of who I wanted them to think I was, or who I thought I needed to be at that stage of my life to stake my place among adults. The cocky creative type, like the brash men at the ad agency where I'd worked over the summers. The self-satisfied reporters and anchors I'd been observing at the TV station. The urbane men I'd seen in the movies, or the behind-the-scenes showbiz pricks I'd read about in interviews. I was putting flyover country on notice that I was a man with a purpose, not long for the slow pace of these soft-in-the-middle Midwesterners.

Niki gasped with surprise when I shot through the door, cracked halfway, as hospital doors always seem to be. She looked exhausted but serene. The C-section had taken a lot out of her. She sat up in the pallid light, smiling, a plastic ID band around her petite wrist.

"How'd you get up here?"

I told her my story.

"You didn't really say that to them."

"Sure did."

She forced a laugh, too polite to roll her eyes.

I walked over to Tony, asleep in his Plexiglas bassinet.

"Hi, Tony," I whispered.

"Gary Anthony Smith," she said. "Gary and I wanted him to have Gary's name, but not be a junior. So we gave him Anthony as a middle name rather than Alan, and we're going to call him Tony."

"Makes sense."

"Of course, he'll still have Gary's initials—G-A-S," she chuckled. "Don't you think he looks like Dad?"

"Yeah, I guess he does," I said, figuring a mother is most attuned to that kind of thing.

"But I see some of Gary's family in him, too," she added.

"Definitely got Gary's hair," I said, touching Tony's bald head, not yet having the humility to be careful of what I make fun of for it's destined to come back around.

Gary wasn't at the hospital that night. He was home with their daughter Yvonne, but I would've liked to have seen him. When Niki was pregnant with Yvonne, Gary and I sat at Franco's Pizza and he told me over pizza and beer what a miracle it was that he was going to be a father. During his previous marriage, doctors had told him he couldn't have kids. The doctor had shown him his sperm cells under a microscope.

"Those damned things won't swim!" he paraphrased the doctor.

But now here was Tony, Gary's second child. A boy, no less. Coach Smith had a son. And I had a nephew! All my life I'd longed for a brother. Mom told me that she and Dad had been planning to have a fourth kid. But when he was diagnosed with MS, they stopped at me. No guarantee, of course, that the next kid would have been male, but at least there would have been half a chance of a little brother. And I wouldn't have been "the baby," the only boy, with a sick dad in a family of girls.

Tony was what I'd been hoping for all my life. A dream come true.

* * *

Since his death, I have become even more aware of who Tony was, what I can learn from him, and how much I admired him. He was intent upon drilling into falsehood and stripping away pretense in all areas of life. He was born an advocate for justice. When he was a little boy, he drew a portrait of his family. Everyone—Tony, Katharine, Yvonne, and his mom and dad—was drawn to proportion. Except instead of standing, each of them was suspended in midair, their heads at the same level, their feet dangling at the appropriate distances from the ground.

"All these years," Niki said, "I'd look at that drawing and think, 'that was Tony just being Tony,' looking at things differently." But now she sees the drawing truly represents his view of the world, "Everyone *is* equal. Literally."

Tony's death shook my foundation. In time, I realized that the night he was born, despite my self-absorbed canard about being an LA TV producer, my heart would always be most devoted to my family and those I love. It turned out I was never willing to sacrifice any of those things for an ounce of worldly success.

Am I living the "safe life?"

There's nothing safe about loving someone. Anyone. You're bound to get your heart broken.

Flippo

I'D drive thirty-five minutes to visit my friend Bob, who, after a stroke, had been checked into a state-of-the-art Jewish hospice all the way over on the east side of Columbus. When I entered his room on the first day, he'd been dozing. The nurse told me he hadn't eaten anything solid—just orange juice through a straw. But I saw an empty carton of Wendy's chili and an open wrapper of pastrami, half devoured, on his overbed.

That was a good sign.

His hair has been washed and, not having been trimmed in a while, his curls had been brushed back from his receding hairline into a silver wave, giving him the amusing but inapt air of a scholar.

He grumbled something unintelligible. In response, I placed my fingertips on the back of his shoulder. "Bob," I whispered. "Need something?"

"Go away!" he snapped, his eyes staying closed.

After twenty-one years of friendship, I knew not to take it personally. Instead, I withdrew to the sofa at the foot of his bed and reminisced to myself about the first time I stepped onto the porch of his home. His "welcome" mat greeted me with those very same words: *Go Away*. I rang his doorbell, chuckled to myself, and, in time, learned that he didn't always mean it. At least not for me.

I dissolved back into the immediate moment and saw that his hospital gown, turquoise with a faint pattern, hung far below his neck, his flat chest appearing sunken in contrast to his enormous belly. His legs, which had been failing him for a few months now, were stiff and bent beneath the white sheets.

He's seventy-nine, I remind myself. And I am suddenly amazed that over all these years it never occurred to me that he and my father were born less than a month apart. Bob got to grow old. Dad did not, and over twenty-three-plus years of fighting MS, Dad wore more than his share of hospital gowns, his legs, too, stiff, bent, and useless.

The two never met, but, like everyone else in Columbus, Dad knew Bob as "Flippo, the King of the Clowns," one of the many local TV clowns across America from the 1950s through the early '70s. Other cities had Bozo, Clarabelle, J. P. Patches, Blinky, Whizzo, Bungles, Corny, and Zeebo. But our clown was Flippo, and he was the most popular local TV personality Columbus had ever known.

Dad and Bob were both funny men, although their senses of humor were vastly different. Dad's was sagacious, Bob's was physical, with a vaudeville flair. They both had street smarts. Dad through intuition, Bob through experience.

As Flippo, Bob was costumed in a blue clown suit peppered with white pom-poms, a matching hat, an immense red collar, and white face paint with a red nose and lips. Keeping his daily Flippo gig for twenty-seven years, Bob delighted his after-school viewers with pranks, poking fun at the movies he introduced, and making personal appearances in the dozen or more counties the station served. His humor was beloved by both adults and children. There's no way to overstate his popularity. Flippo's *The Early Show* was *the* program Central Ohio watched daily, and "Flippo at the Fair," which ran live from the Ohio State Fair every summer, drew thousands of live audience members, plus even more who were glued to their sets at home. In addition to his comedy schtick, Flippo welcomed the biggest stars of the day to his show, from broadcast journalist Diane Sawyer, to actor Don Ameche, to comedian Red Skelton. He was a guest on Captain Kangaroo, and later on *The Tomorrow Show* with Tom Snyder. With a Q Score in the upper nineties, Flippo was gold in the ratings, delivering a huge audience to his station's biggest moneymaker, their local newscast, which followed his show.

All this, and the station never paid him more than $35,000 a year, he told me.

I met Bob years later, when his television days were behind him. By then I was a media personality myself and was asked to be in a downtown parade with him. Because he had been out of the public eye for about ten years, his appearance would be a surprise to the thousands of people lining the streets.

I was instructed to meet him in the basement of a downtown flower shop, where we were to be picked up secretly and taken to the parade site. I had been given specific directions to this makeshift greenroom, tucked into an alley. Nervous, I approached the door and knocked.

No response.

I knocked again.

Nothing.

Thinking I might be in the wrong place, I gave it one last knock, this time with my fist.

The door swung open. No one was there.

Afraid to enter this underground "cave," which grew more mysterious each moment, I remained outside.

"Come in!" I heard a bold, raspy voice say.

I poked my head inside and saw no one. "Hell-Oh?" I called.

A face popped out from behind the open door, wearing his famous white greasepaint and a red nose. No hat. When I entered, I understood why he was standing behind the door. He had nothing on but a sleeveless undershirt, his briefs, socks, and his big, blue clown shoes.

My introduction to the local icon.

About an hour later, I was on a float with Flippo, now in his clown suit. As we came around the corner onto High Street, the crowd went wild. They hadn't forgotten him since the days he filled the after-school routine of so many kids and their parents. The response grew louder as we headed down the street. When we reached the VIP viewing stand, Mayor "Buck" Rinehart jumped out of his chair and rushed to the side of the street. "Flippo! We love you!"

Without missing a beat, Flippo said, "Hey, I get *paid* to look funny—what's *your* excuse?"

The mayor laughed, flattered to be insulted by the King of the Clowns.

"As long as I'm in that clown suit," Bob would confide later, "I can get away with saying anything."

Our relationship gained traction when we were both invited to perform at the Ohio Theatre for the Regional Emmy Awards, a gathering of television people from four states. The audience, in attendance for awards and not interested in being entertained, didn't much care for either of our acts. We both "laid an egg," as Bob said, calling the event "the biggest abortion" he'd ever been part of. From that night on, however, our friendship flourished. I hadn't met Vicki yet, and his girlfriend had just moved to California, so just about every day when I wasn't on the road, we were free for breakfast, lunch, and dinner. I learned quickly how Bob, a thin young stud, had grown into an older man with a ballooning belly, and that, out of costume, he was even funnier than Flippo. A trip to the hardware store or the doctor's office would elicit a five-minute monologue. If he had to leave a voicemail, it would be seven minutes. Complete with sound effects and perfect character dialects.

When he'd visit the proctologist, Bob would announce that he was "going to get my tonsils checked." He talked about his relatives, in particular "Uncle Howie," who owned a local shop. "I asked him how business was going today, and he said, 'Oh, it was slow till noon, then it died altogether.'" Uncle Howie also "introduced me to my ex-wife, but I still talk to him anyway."

I told Bob about the time I was introduced at the district track meet as "Eric Gadoza," and he laughed for the longest time. "Gadoza!" he said. "I love it!" He created the adaptation of "Gadoozie," and from that point on, that was my nickname.

He came from a Hungarian family. His father was a painting and paperhanging contractor who mentored Bob into being quite the handyman. "My father had a saying," Bob explained as he attacked a home repair job, "We're going to 'Fishmanize' this," a term adopted from his authentic last name, Fishman, and he'd fix something so it would never break again.

"Now," he'd say with the task completed, "that's more better."

His basement was full of enough power tools to fill an industrial arts classroom. Over the years, he fixed everything for me, from my keyboard stand, to a broken door knob, to a faulty shelf. The first time I asked him for help I explained, "I don't know much about tools."

"Oh, you're wrong about that, Gadoozie," he replied, "you don't know anything about tools."

Every time I borrowed a tool, he'd remind me, "It's not an orphan, Gadoozie, so don't adopt it."

One of his two religions was watching TV.

He'd call several times a night to give me the latest report on what was happening on television.

"So, I'm watching *Wheel of Fortune*," he explained, "and the puzzle says '_limb every mountain,' and the contestant yells, 'G!'"

"G!" Bob says, "G!" And he sings, "Glimb every mountain . . ."

He'd keep me up to speed with the latest episodes of *Law & Order*, which he called, *Law & Hors d'Oeuvres*. When a new local news reporter would mispronounce a name or a town, he was all over it. And he told me stories, stories, stories about his early days in television. Comedian Jonathan Winters got his start at Bob's TV station, and when his request for a $25-per-week raise was denied, he decided it was time to go. "I remember the night we got together after work and passed a hat so Johnny Winters could move to California," Bob said.

Nothing made him as mad as when he bought a huge TV and it went on the fritz the day after the warranty expired.

"Sorry," the salesperson said, "it's one day past warranty." Bob fought with him and got nowhere. So he decided to call the owner of the company, whom he'd known for years because he'd advertised on his famous TV show. Bob got no return calls.

Fed up, Bob called the owner again and talked to his secretary, "You tell him that unless I get a call by the end of the day I'm going to show up in front of his store in my clown suit holding a sign that says, 'I got screwed at Sun TV!'"

No sooner had Bob hung up than the owner called back. "Hey there, Bob, how have you been? What can I do for you?"

The TV was exchanged immediately, leaving Bob to ask me rhetorically, "So what do you think made him change his mind? Was it that he's committed to customer service? That the customer is always right? Or was it the bit about me showing up at his store in my clown suit holding a sign?"

Bob's other religion was food. "I've never met a pizza I didn't like," he was fond of saying, and each of our football bets, which were many, ended up with the loser buying the winner a pizza. "I can't stand it," he yelled after a game. "The Browns need a field goal to win and they hike the ball behind the holder! When do you see that? Only if I bet on them!"

One time after he won, I got a phone call from him, singing, "When the moon hits your eye like a big piiiiizzzzzaaa pie . . ."

Other phone calls brought common dining requests:

"Hey, Gadoozie, let's go to Stan's for a *feeeesh* sandwich!"

"Let's drive downtown, I'm jonesin' for a 'dawg.'"

After a popular Mexican restaurant had reopened following a fire, he suggested we revisit. "Two for lunch," he told the hostess. "Non-smoking section, please." To her credit, she laughed.

One time we were at lunch together and a man asked if I was Bob's son. We were both insulted.

Bob had a habit of shopping, finding something wrong with his purchase, and returning it. Several times I went to his "geezer lunch" with him and his retired workmates, and the question always came up, "So, Bob, what did you take back today?"

He was a good cook himself, often bringing me barley soup. He almost always had something on the stove. At a comedic roast in his honor the year before he died, I saved his phone messages and edited them to illustrate his love of food.

First message: "And the French fries are really great!"
Next message: "And I'm thawing out a porterhouse steak."
Next message: "So the roast I'm making for future reference . . . and the steak is for tonight."
Next message: "And I think I'll make some noooodles."

Another time, he drove me nearly two hours south to have dinner at The Golden Lamb, a historic restaurant and hotel built in 1803 that has hosted twelve presidents, Charles Dickens, Mark Twain, Harriet Beecher Stowe, and other notables. The whole way, to and from, he played tapes of the best sax musicians of his time.

"Ya hear that?" he said. "Listen to that tenor man swing!"

"To swing" was the highest compliment a musician from the Big Band era could get.

Bob was born on January 6, 1927, in Mount Sinai Hospital, Cleveland, and made his first radio appearance as a singer at five. He sang at all kinds of functions, including on radio, and, at ten, sang at the 1937 World's Fair in Cleveland. When he was still in elementary school, he picked up the drums. Too young to drive yet, he loaded them up and took them from gig to gig on a coaster wagon. In junior high, an uncle died and the family gave Bob his saxophone.

"I started fooling around with it, and I found how to make a noise. And I was playing it before I ever took a lesson."

At John Adams High School, he conducted the stage band, and during his days in Korea while he was in the Army, he organized the Kimpo Combo. When he came back to the States, he entered Ohio State as an optometry major, switching to journalism, then, finally, music education. Thirty-two hours short of a degree, he was playing tenor sax at the Neil House in Columbus when he was "discovered" by a television program director, who hired him.

Once the Flippo character caught on, the TV station bought him a BMW Isetta, an egg shaped "bubble" car whose front door opened on the front of the vehicle. With a canvas roof, the Izetta was a one-cylinder car that was only 7.5 feet long and weighed less than 800 pounds.

"HERE COMES FLIPPO ON CHANNEL 10" was printed on the side. Wherever he went, he was mobbed.

Long after the Isetta days were gone and his TV stardom had vanished, Bob hung on to the memories and, understandably, found it hard to let them go. Still loved by his fans, he did a commercial from time to time and made a few personal appearances.

A local recording studio owner ribbed him about coming in to record with his "client."

Bob had a Cadillac with FLIPPO on the license plate, and apparently, in an attempt to rekindle the star of his former Izetta days, bought a white Geo Storm with aftermarket red and blue stripes outlining the doors and hood, musical notes, and a Flippo portrait with SEND IN DA CLOWN written on the rear window. Across the front hood was THE CLOWN DOES THE SNAPPERS, another Flippo portrait, and drawings of a couple of bundles of balloons and candy. On the side, he promoted his business: FLIPPO ENTERPRISES.

When he bought the car, he drove it over to my house and showed me the saying he had printed on the back bumper: "Do You Believe In Love At First Sight . . . Or Should I Go Around The Block Again!!!???"

Over the years he tried his hand at owning a couple of restaurants, but late in life his dreams to grow rich centered on winning the lottery. In his living room was his lottery ticket in which all his numbers matched the winners, with the exception of the final digit. He'd played a forty and the winner was a forty-one. He framed it, with a circle around the forty. After the sting of such a close defeat had passed, I'd tease him about it.

"I wish I could afford a new car," he'd say.

"You should have played a forty-one."

One of Bob's inner contradictions was that, for a man who had trouble trusting anyone, he sometimes trusted the wrong people. He kept his house locked with the curtains closed. When cell phones first came out, he bought a fake one so he could pretend he was calling authorities if he were threatened by someone while he was driving. He kept a stick—and a gun, I'm pretty sure—in his car. He told me, "Gadoozie, if you're ever going to commit a crime, do it by yourself. You can't trust anyone else to keep their mouth shut."

On the other hand, he entrusted thousands of dollars to a friend of twenty years, who, unbeknownst to Bob, used it in a Ponzi scheme. When we learned about his friend's fraud in the lead story of the Saturday newspaper, he called and asked, "Hey, wanna invest?!" Despite the joke, Bob was deeply hurt that his once-abiding "friend" gave him no acknowledgment when he said "hello" to him at the courthouse during his trial.

Bob was also a hypochondriac. He once had his entire wall-to-wall carpet taken out of his house because he thought the smell of it was causing him breathing problems. He wore masks on airplanes long before Covid, and always wore a Western bandana around his neck "on-account-of-because I want to keep the germs away."

On the eve of his seventy-ninth birthday, January 5, 2006, Bob was honored by the Ohio History Connection. "My folks always said I belonged in an institution," he quipped. He donated his clown suit to the museum, and they hosted a tribute to him that night.

I was one of the speakers.

"It's been said that Flippo's show was for kids but that was appreciated more by adults," I said, "because behind every gag, every comedic bit, every sarcastic aside, there was a deeper meaning for those who could see it. His comedy, simple on the surface, had substance underneath . . . Behind his wisecracks are, well, wisdom. And a humble heart. And, believe it or not, a sentimental man."

The day of my wedding he showed up, even going to the trouble of putting on a suit, a serious departure from his normal blue jumpsuit with the scarf around his neck. Arriving a few moments before ceremonies began, he sought me out as I paced the back of the church.

"Wow!" he said, surveying my tuxedo and shiny shoes. "Don't you feel weird?"

"I feel like I got a job."

Bob's laugh roared through the church. "You do! You do!" he said. "And it's forever! It's the longest job you'll ever have. And it doesn't pay real good either. It's a funny thing. You got a helluva job and you pay *her*! What an agent! She gets fifty percent of everything. And sometimes more!"

When my daughters were born, he was the first to stop by with toys. When my first one came home from the hospital, he wasn't far behind.

"Wait till you see this!" he said, handing over a gift-wrapped package. Inside was a mobile for her crib. Four soft clowns flying through the air in felt innertubes, circling a miniature beach ball to the tune of "Lullaby and Goodnight."

"I looked all over," he continued, "and finally found this! Can you believe it! Far out!"

In every subsequent conversation, there wasn't one in which he didn't ask about my daughters, sometimes with his eyes welling up.

"You know, don't you, these are the happiest days of your life."

If only I'd been able to embrace his wisdom at the time. Now that Caroline and Meredith are grown up and out of the house, I look back and see his words couldn't be more on target. Nothing lit up his face like a child, and nothing lit up a child's face like Flippo.

As his health declined, he received letters from his fans. Typical was from a viewer who had since moved out of town. "We will never forget those great afternoons with you—for a lonely kid it meant everything!"

Following the ceremony at the Ohio History Connection, his fans, most of whom were of retirement age, stood in line for an hour to express their appreciation. Fatigued and his voice weakened by age, he sat and listened to each one, and signed autographs.

"I could have moved to Florida or someplace warm," he told me, "but where else would I get this?"

Five months later, while at home, where he lived alone, he fell and laid helpless for days. When he was found, he was taken to the hospital, then the hospice facility. Following a second major stroke, he died on June 10, the eight-year anniversary of Gary's death.

I feel bad about not being at his home when he needed help, but I had a family by then, and our daily outings had become a thing of the past. The day of his funeral I spoke with his longtime next-door neighbor, Mrs. Gabor, whom Bob loved and talked about from time to time on his TV show—"My neighbors, the Gabors," he'd rhyme. She understood Bob, good and bad, and said, "When God made him, he broke the mold," a phrase that might be overused but was invented for Bob.

Bob sometimes tried my patience. "I can take The Clown in small doses," a friend told me, echoing the sentiments of many. But I stuck by him for more than two decades and don't regret a day. Not only was I entertained, I learned a lot about home repair, television, and good food. I also witnessed the dangers in holding on too long after your star has faded. When I was with him, I had to be content to stay in the background and "let the clown do the snappers," endure the embarrassment of him telling his out-of-fashion jokes to waitstaff, and persevere through his aversion to dealing with his deepest feelings. But he was a friend. A faithful one. Rarely does a day go by when I don't recount a story from Bob. And it's most always funny.

He said in an interview shortly before he died, "I just want to be remembered as a nice guy, who did some funny stuff, amused the kids."

But he was really more than that. Especially to me.

On a spring day we were driving down Lane Avenue. We'd just had lunch. He was unusually free and easy.

"You know, Gadoozie," he said, "you're about the best buddy I ever had."

Running in Cottonwood

FOR the longest time, I never let anyone pass me on the Olentangy Trail. I wasn't looking to race strangers, but I'd stay aware of what was going on behind me, and I'd simply pick up the pace until they, or I, took a turn. That policy fell apart in my late forties. I was running and I heard two guys behind me. I stepped up the pace, but was overtaken by a duo having quite a good time, laughing, completely unaware of me as they brushed by. To be passed was one thing, but to be overtaken by a pair of guys who had enough wind to laugh in conversation while running sent a chill through my bones. The message was unmistakable: "You are officially a Masters athlete."

From that point on, I realized I was heading down the backside of life, and I had an assignment similar to all aging people: Learn to deal with loss. All kinds. We have to accept and integrate loss into our lives. Like the diminishing list of people to call on a long drive. Or a rug with a hole in it, never to grow back. We learn to work around the losses. Cover the rug with a piece of furniture. A floor lamp. Or just let it remain for all the world to see. I've never felt that I'm good at dealing with loss, although I've had my share. Thus far, I've made it through with help from friends, family, work.

And mostly time.

When I was in college, I heard the late playwright Neil Simon interviewed about the death of his first wife. He was so distraught, he went to the top of a bridge to jump off. But then he realized that the motion we make to let go—extending our arms forward—is the same one we make to receive something new into our lives. That changed him, and I've never forgotten it.

Today, the cottonwood fluff settles on the edges of the Olentangy Trail, where I once led my eldest daughter, Caroline, on some training runs to prepare her for ninth-grade soccer. It seems like yesterday. It seems like many lifetimes ago. The longest, least-expected loss I've experienced is my daughters' leaving childhood behind. Even though I've made it through the worst of it, the longing is still there. It just came out of nowhere one day and hit me. Caroline was in eleventh grade, and my other daughter, Meredith, in ninth. I was looking over Delaware Run, pausing a couple of minutes before I started teaching my speech class at Ohio Wesleyan. Compared to the standards of our culture, I spent a lot of time with them. Yet, looking back, it feels like it wasn't enough.

"Daddy, do you teach tonight?" Meredith would often ask when I'd drop her off at Evening Street Elementary School. Funny thing is that now I'm the one who's asking if she'll be around tonight—or even anytime this year. I thought I was doing all the right things, being involved, avoiding Harry Chapin's "Cat's in the Cradle" syndrome. Even with such vigilance, however, I find myself with the sorrow that life slips through our fingers.

When Meredith left preschool, I sat in my office and cried, knowing that neither of my daughters would ever be as close to me during the day, because my office was just across the street from their preschool. My heart melts every time I think about Meredith's response to my apology for yelling at her once during those years. As I was putting her to bed, I said, "I'm sorry, honey, I'm just a very sensitive person." She replied, "Yes, but Daddy, I'm just a puff more sensitiver than you."

Then I cried again one morning when I looked at the unused swing set in the backyard. When I woke up and realized I'd never again pick up my daughters and carry them off to bed. The questions began. When was the last time my daughters grabbed my hand because they needed me? The last time I put them in a car seat, or lugged them around playfully in my soft keyboard case? Carried them on my shoulders? Read them a bedtime story?

What I'd give for one more day at the swimming pool with my toddlers. Picking them up in the water and tossing them in the air. How I'd love to watch one more soccer game or a musical where I wasn't recording video but just enjoying them. Or hold their tiny hands as we slogged through the slushy Kroger parking lot on the way to my truck, realizing that life will never get any better than this moment.

"Daddy, can we hide tonight?" they'd ask when they were little. Then I'd let them run off to bed, cover themselves in the blanket, and I'd act like I couldn't find them. With feigned exhaustion, I'd give up and sit on one of their beds, right on top of them, and exclaim, "What's this! Oh, my goodness, it's Caroline (or Meredith)," depending upon whose bed I was on.

On her fourteenth birthday, Meredith had two parties. One for the family, then one for her friends. Our next-door neighbor at the time played his part in making the day special by lending us his fire pit and four Adirondack chairs. After the party, I sat by the waning fire, down to coals actually, knowing that Meredith would never turn fourteen a second time, and soon she and Caroline would be gone from the house. Returning only for college breaks or visits with their friends.

It's sad, but also full of promise.

In the sixth grade, Caroline asked if I'd help her prepare for her audition in *Annie*. She wanted the lead role. We worked for a week on the script and the music. I drove her to school the day the cast list was posted. I waited in my truck. It was the longest five minutes of my life. In that time, I imagined how I would console her in a meaningful way if she didn't get the role.

Oh, honey, there'll be other parts . . . Things will change in high school theater, you'll see.

Then a flash came around the corner of the school. It was Caroline with the script in her hand. "I got Annie! I got Annie!"

I was more thrilled than she was. She got into my truck and we hugged.

On opening night, we held a pre-show party for her. As we were leaving for the show, I saw Caroline help her ninety-one-year-old Great

Aunt Jessie get to her car. Even with all the nervousness and anticipation of opening night, Caroline was thinking of someone else.

How proud I was to see that.

What I didn't know in those early years is that however much my kids felt they needed me, I needed them more. The need for them just keeps growing. So, too, does the physical distance these days.

This is a feeling, a grief, I dealt with for four years. I Googled the topic and found I was not alone. Many parents grieve the loss of their children's childhoods, but it's something they, especially men, don't feel they have the right to talk about because, in most cases, their kids are thriving. But I can't shake it. It's more common than we admit.

The strange thing is that it doesn't seem I'm grieving over what we *didn't* do together, but, rather, missing the things we *did* do. All the times the girls stopped me when I was working, asking me to do something with them. I learned these interruptions were actually the things that mattered most in life. Bills can wait. Emails. Composing songs. And writing books. Growing up as a caregiver, I was granted the perspective that taking care of others doesn't slow you down, but is what ultimately brings joy and meaning. We can zip through life without questioning, living the values and lifestyle prescribed by commercials and cultural myths, but happiness comes from not merely pursuing our own dreams, but by putting others first.

Still, as a parent I had to fight against my reflex to say no every time my girls wanted to go sledding, play kickball, or make a cake. I'd have to remind myself to drop everything, get them dressed, grab the sled, and go. It takes longer to dress the kids for sledding than it does to actually sled. They have short attention spans.

Their childhoods vanished with one-by-one pulls on the threads of my heart. Each time I dropped them off at school, or a party, or a game, they tore away another strand and stepped toward independence until I was no longer needed in their life's primary passages.

My girls are gone from the house now, off in separate parts of the world pursuing their own lives. I grieve for days gone by. But what I receive in exchange is what almost any parent feels watching their kids find their way in the world. Immeasurable pride. For who they are, where they're going, and the young people they've become.

This past Christmas, we had our family gift exchange at my mother-in-law's house. My nephew gave me a flannel shirt and a pair of slippers. I laughed to myself that the family now views me in "grandpa mode." I put on the shirt and slippers, sat in a rocking chair with my feet propped up, and watched the young people carry on.

I was the happiest man in the room.

The Road Away

SOMETIMES when I run, I work on song lyrics. But only if the song is already underway. I'll search for a word or a phrase and go over and over and over it again and again until I'm sick of the line, the melody, and usually the song itself. This is what a songwriter calls "crafting," what happens after inspiration leaves, after enthusiasm wanes. It's the third lap of the process, when quitting is easy, but if I stick with it, perseverance might reward me with a song that has integrity.

I look at my creative process like this: I work for an extended period with nothing happening. I'm bone dry. Restless. Maybe I sleep a lot. Going through familiar patterns, the same hackneyed ideas. Then, after I've given up, often convinced that I've never been a writer in the first place and just got lucky in the past, inspiration comes. The initial burst, which can last from minutes to several hours, takes me partway up the mountain of completion. It's during this period I feel I've finally gotten out of my own way, I'm really flying, no doubt creating the Greatest Work Ever! Then suddenly, just as mysteriously, the Great Inspiration withdraws, leaving me a choice to traverse the rest of the way "alone" or to put off the journey, meaning I may never come back to it. If I choose to proceed, that's when the crafting begins, drawing on my knowledge, experience, skill—and perseverance—to finish the work. I guess that's why I've always considered running to be an ideal foundation for my life as a writer and creator.

Each step is a race to be won.

No matter how familiar I think I am with the process, however, it still remains mercurial. Over a decade ago I visited the Museum of Glass in Tacoma, Washington, where American glass sculptor Dale Chihuly was in residency. Seated at a table, he was overseeing the production of his creations. As one glassblower moved a cooled-down, nearly finished piece to the next station in the process, the would-be masterpiece slipped through his gloved hands and fell to the floor, shattering into shards. Looking on, Chihuly, the master himself, didn't even twitch, as he had no doubt seen this before. Perhaps his lack of reaction was due to his understanding that, as much as we deem our own work sacred, some art is not meant to survive, or, perhaps we can only find its value by breaking it apart.

Once in a while, I'll roll out a new song and find it leaves the audience flat, or it just doesn't ring true to me. That's when I have to let my sacred creation slip through my fingers and crash to the floor. Only then can I sift through the ruins and see if there's a gem in the song worth keeping. Maybe a line, a word, an image, an idea.

Maybe nothing.

But then I think of the Ford Edsel. A marketing disaster, but one that ultimately led to Ford creating America's best-selling sports car, the Mustang.

To have pursued a path that is uniquely my own has tested my perseverance, endurance, and courage, but over time, the peace that has come with having been true to myself is immeasurable. I've often felt I'm in a skiff in the middle of the ocean while others pass me by on yachts or cruise ships in self-satisfaction, thinking they've really accomplished something, unaware that if the name on their business cards weren't followed by the corporation they work for, they'd be no one. So in a sense, they've not even begun the real journey. Yet being out there on my own, I've gotten to know the rhythms of the sea and the very nature of the water, which I can only hope counts for something in the end.

My professional journey officially began at age twenty-two, when I graduated from college with a major in journalism. My intention in college was to study pre-law, but during my first semester, I sat in a journalism class and was enamored by the professor, Verne Edwards. He was smart, direct, and he had a BS detector just like my father. He was the strictest editor I ever had, and he also hammered ethics into our brains. He taught from the textbook he wrote, *Journalism in a Free Society*. He dressed conservatively yet up to date. His sense of humor was dry, and when he entered the room to start class, I expected to hear the theme song from *The Tonight Show*.

While I benefited from and continue to be an ardent supporter of liberal arts, my education was put in perspective, or perhaps balanced, by the many jobs and internships I took during breaks and in the school year. I worked a couple summers in an advertising agency, and in addition to being the first intern WBNS-TV ever had, I worked at the world's first "interactive" cable network, Warner QUBE. Just being in the environment and getting to know the people who worked in it saved me ten years of exploration. More than anything else, the experiences taught me what I liked about certain businesses—and what I wanted to avoid. That was worth more than its weight in gold.

My senior year, I took a job as a city reporter at the local newspaper. Day after day I would visit the clerical staff, most of whom were older, having worked behind the same desks forever. Some were younger than I and had children already. Totally different aspirations from mine. But these were "real people," and I became aware that my education would be useless unless I learned how to communicate with people of all backgrounds, ages, and values. I had to earn their trust before I could ever motivate, entertain, and inspire them.

Through my final three years of college, I wrote a humor column for our college newspaper, and so when I graduated, my professional goals consisted of being a columnist, a television producer, and a songwriter. The summer after college, I took some humor pieces I'd written to Kaye Kessler, a newspaper columnist and father of a high school friend of mine. He laughed like crazy and even asked his colleagues to listen to some of the lines while he was reading them. "This is great stuff," he said, "but what are you going to do until you make a living as a humorist?"

I was astounded. He believed in me. Without a doubt. *Of course you're going to be a humorist*, he seemed to be saying, *you just need to figure out what to do for a living until then.*

So much different than any other adult in my life, whose message was, "You'd better find something to put bread on the table, because you'll never earn a living being funny." Such comments, I later learned, were about their own limitations, not mine.

My first full-time job after college was in government relations at the American Motorcyclist Association, while I freelanced on the side. I screamed in profanity-laced joy when I received a letter from *The Columbus Dispatch* telling me they were going to publish my first submission in their Sunday magazine. Soon afterward, I took a "job" delivering spoken commentaries, with no pay, every Friday on Columbus's NPR station, WOSU. It didn't occur to me until years later that, in college, I'd been afraid even to walk into the radio station because, deep down, more than anything, I wanted to be on the air. It was a great lesson that we're most afraid of the things we want the most. About two months into my public radio job, I had an idea for a satirical song about the emerging "Moral Majority." A song, I thought, would be a different way to reach people.

"Oh, good Lordy, it's the Moral Majority . . ."

Even though my song was a departure from a spoken commentary, the radio station aired it, and listeners responded positively. Soon, my weekly comments more often became funny songs about local, national, and international events. In the midst of a period of artistic angst, I learned the nature of my inner voice when taking risks: What propels me over the fear is not, *Think how happy you'll be that you tried it*, but rather *Can I live with myself if I don't?*

Knowing I couldn't live with the regret if I didn't at least give it a shot, I entered an open mic at a comedy club on a Sunday night. We were allowed seven minutes each, but I got on a roll and the emcee let me go for more than twenty. I received a raucous standing ovation, and won the contest. I was so high from the experience I went home and, long after midnight, rode my bike miles down an empty High Street. My award from the comedy club, in addition to a small bit of cash, was to open for that week's touring comedian. I still cringe when I think that the man I respected so much, Professor Edwards, showed up to see me that week with his wife and another couple, and the headliner was billed as an XXX comedian. Embarrassed out of my mind, I called them the next day to apologize.

"Don't worry about it," his wife said, "your material is great. We'll still come out to see you."

My relief was extreme.

Within days of winning the open mic, I worked up the courage to take my funny songs to a commercial radio station, where I not only got paid, but one of my first efforts landed me on *Entertainment Tonight*.

Wow, this business is easy!

But the radio station's program director did nothing to promote the song and later said he could no longer afford to pay me, offering me free albums instead.

I went to talk to the general manager. "What do you want from us?" he asked, acting as though I owed *him* for the "favor" of being on his air once a week.

"Well, first of all, I'd like for you to resume payment," which he said he'd look into, "and I'd like you to promote a weekly gig done in conjunction with the station."

"You won't find a radio station in the United States of America who'll do that for you," he said.

By contrast, a year earlier, I had met with Perry Frey, the general manager of the radio station's chief rival, WTVN Radio, who told me, "I love what you do, but I've got to get the right program director in here. Give me some time." Almost on cue, after my meeting with the other station, I got a call from Perry. "I've hired my programmer and you'll be getting a call from him." Three days after he was hired, Jack FitzGerald, a fireball of a programmer, called me for a meeting. I went in that day. Jack was thirty-three, bald, and pertinacious. "I saw you on TV in Denver," he said as he welcomed me in the lobby. "I see you've brought some tapes."

When we reached his office, already messy from the workings of his creative mind, I handed him a paper Kroger bag full of a dozen three-inch reel-to-reel tapes, scrambled, tangled, and unmarked.

"So here they are!" he said as he separated my songs from one another. He listened to a couple of them.

Jack got serious. "Can you do one of these a week?"

"Yes," I said, hoping I could live up to my word.

"Well, here's what I'm thinking," Jack said, and he placed before me a proposal on WTVN letterhead and ran through it one-by-one.

"You'll be our house comedian. We'll play your songs daily. We'll promote the hell out of you. We'll set up a weekly after-work party for you that we will turn into a station promotion. You'll keep every dollar you make on personal appearances and much more as things develop."

Everything I had dreamed of was right there in front of me.

Perry entered. "What do you think, Jack? I thought Eric might have something. Or it might be nothing."

"I think it's great stuff," Jack said.

Perry turned to me. "Eric, what you need is a base, and we can provide that for you."

"We'll start you on Monday," Jack said.

It all sounded great, but I thought I owed the other station a chance to make a counteroffer.

"What matters," Jack said, "is how welcome they made you feel when you were there, not what they say they're going to do for you now."

Jack had the necessary ethos, working as a top disc jockey in major markets and more recently as a program director. I was new to the radio business, yet what he said made plenty of sense. I told him and Perry I'd talk to the other station but would begin with WTVN on Monday.

Jack and I spent the rest of the day together, then Perry offered to take us to dinner. On the way to meet Perry at the restaurant, the usual second-guesser showed up in my head, and I said, "Jack?"

"What?" He stopped pushing through the revolving door and stepped back toward me.

"Are you sure this is going to work?" I asked.

He returned to his march through the door and said, "Hell yes, it's going to work! We're late for dinner."

Jack had gone through flight training in the Navy. I was afraid of heights. We were a perfectly imperfect pair.

Through those years, there was plenty to satirize in the news on a weekly basis through parodies and original songs. When Ronald Reagan slept through a Libyan jet attack, I wrote a parody of "Hush, Little Baby":

> Hush, Mr. President, don't wake yet,
> We're shooting down a Libyan jet.
> If that Libyan jet don't fall,
> We'll put a B-1 bomber on call.
> If that B-1 don't strike clean,

> We'll launch a Trident submarine.
> If that submarine gets sank,
> We'll send an M1 Abrams tank.
> If that M1 tank gets blown,
> We'll send the Nimitz to the zone.
> If that Nimitz wrecks at sea,
> We'll send a C-5A Galaxy.
> If that Galaxy's destroyed,
> We'll get a neutron bomb deployed.
> If that neutron bomb's on line,
> We'll be asleep for a very long time.

Then there was Jim and Tammy Faye Bakker's PTL scandal... Pete Rose pushing umpire Dave Pallone... and an oddball local news story that went international: A guy was driving his Mercedes-Benz to work, the city sewer gave way, and his car dropped 26 feet to the bottom of a 30 x 40-foot hole on Broad Street. Luckily the driver wasn't hurt. By noon that day, Jack had T-shirts printed that said, "WTVN-Radio, Your Official Sink-Hole Station" that we handed out on the Ohio Statehouse lawn, and I'd come up with a funny song for the radio.

Jack had a motto: "Whoever has the most fun wins!"

Working with Jack was a masterclass in having fun. My job was to give people a great time. The station featured me at an after-work party every week for several years, which garnered an audience of tens of thousands and launched me as a live performer.

It also gave me more than my share of opportunities to make mistakes.

The problem with working in front of an audience is that we make our mistakes in public, particularly an issue early in our careers when we're learning. "Educating yourself in public is painful," wrote the late Peter Schjeldahl of his own development as an art critic, "but the lessons stick." For me it was even more pronounced because all my growing pains were committed with my hometown audience watching, including many of my teachers and the people I grew up with.

You said that onstage? I still think to myself at three in the morning. *You did that in front of an audience?*

A few times when I was struggling before an audience, I'd change my routine to get them on my side, which, of course, only made things worse. It took longer than perhaps it should have, but I learned that our greatest regrets often come when we're rejected not for who we are, but for who we thought we had to be to please someone else. At least when we've been ourselves and we're rejected, we have peace of mind. But when we've tried to be someone else, there's no way to go back and say, "Listen, that's not really me. Give me another chance!" A painful lesson, but one that has become a cornerstone of my life.

I'm still particularly self-loathing over the embarrassment I brought upon a woman I went to elementary school with when she came with some friends to see me perform in my mid-twenties. In an attempt to be funny, I made some public comments to her that were rude and insensitive, which is another way of saying I was an asshole. She and her companions walked out, which I long ago recognized was the only proper way for her to respond. Even after all the years, that mistake in judgment makes me wince, along with other errors. I meant no harm—I was learning. Yet like anything else, I may have knocked a hundred baseballs out of the park, but it's those few pitches that sucked me into strikeouts I can't get over. And funny thing, I usually find out that most people don't remember the offense. But for me, it plays on a giant replay monitor in my mind, on a never-ending video loop narrated by an Old Testament God reproaching my "bad" behavior.

Nevertheless, I was invited to play everywhere, from behind the tie rack in a men's store, to opening for Big Names in concert halls, to comedy clubs, where I discovered the longest moment known to human beings is the split second between your first joke . . . and the laugh. I even played a horse show, pulled out on a flatbed trailer to start things off. As usual in those days, my good sense often ignored my inner editor, and I opened by saying, "Well, I'm the first horse's ass you'll see tonight."

I thought it was funny, but the tuxedo-clad crowd wasn't amused.

Columbus Monthly nonetheless paid me a compliment by naming me "Best Satirist of the Year," saying I was "A skeptic without being too much of a cynic. Witty and caustic without being cruel. A clever man and a pretty good musician."

As a result of my radio success, I landed other jobs concurrently, as a columnist for *The Columbus Dispatch* and a personality on the syndicated

TV series, *PM Magazine*. By age twenty-seven, I was making a good living writing and singing songs for the radio and TV, and writing a weekly humor column for *The Columbus Dispatch*. Stories about me and my songs appeared in newspapers across the country, including several in *USA Today*.

My phone rang late on a Sunday night.

"Hello, may I speak with Eric?"

"Who's calling?"

"This is Steve Wulf with *Sports Illustrated* and I—"

"I'm sorry," I interrupted, "I'm not interested in renewing my subscription."

"No, no," the voice laughed, "I'm the managing editor and I'd like to speak with Eric about his Pete Rose song."

"Oh, I'm sorry," I was tempted to say, "let me get Mr. Gnezda on the phone."

A week later, the song was featured in an issue with Michael Jordan on the cover.

* * *

I worked non-stop throughout my twenties, giving others a good time, never asking myself if I was having fun, which is essential when your job is to make people enjoy themselves. Meanwhile, the natural order was changing. Jack was awarded *Billboard* magazine's "Large Market Program Director of the Year," left WTVN to buy a radio station in Michigan, and I was yearning for more. More of what, I couldn't say. But I felt typecast. I was twenty-five when WTVN hired me, and at that age, I was willing to be whoever the programmer wanted me to be.

But I was turning thirty, and while I've since celebrated other milestone birthdays without feeling that life was slipping away, that birthday hit me hard. My girlfriend at the time dumped me, my career was no longer fulfilling, and, to celebrate my birthday, a male friend took me to a movie theater for a surprise, which turned out to be a two-hour compilation of the original Rocky and Bullwinkle TV shows. Although my friend meant well, I felt anything but celebrated, and I certainly wasn't entertained. I sat in the dark, feeling more disconnected than ever. *Here I am, no longer in my twenties, no girl, no career, sitting with a guy watching Rocky and Bullwinkle. Fuck me.*

Something had to change.

I could feel a deeper pulse resonating within me. I was tired of being the jester, killing myself with weekly deadlines to provide a laugh and maybe a message for the few who took the time, or were even able, to see beneath the humor. I identified with actors who've had success in one type of role but wanted to express other aspects of themselves. Plus, our culture was changing. We were entering an era when truth was becoming more outrageous than any satire could ever be.

"The problem with being funny," a friend of mine said, "is that nobody takes you seriously." Truer words were never spoken. I was having trouble taking myself seriously. There was so much more I wanted to be and to express. I was aching to deepen my connection with myself and my audience. With no plan or direction, I chose to walk away from radio and the newspaper, keep my television gig for a while, and fulfill my performance schedule. For six months I spent my days watching old movies and napping on the sofa. I allowed myself to rest and disengage without guilt. Day after day, I envisioned myself rolling down a long hill, an exercise I still practice when I feel spent and need to recharge.

I thought about the songs that had first influenced me as a child, one of which was "Eve of Destruction," recorded by Barry McGuire in 1965. That song took hold of me and lodged inside my songwriting embryo, giving birth to many songs about social and political injustice. Yet, the popularity of the protest songs of the 1960s was short-lived, as the music industry, responding to nervous radio programmers, turned away from songs that reflected social ills in favor of those money magnets that focused more on personal issues. For me, however, the die had been cast, although I must confess that my eight-year-old mind got one word wrong as I sang along with Barry McGuire on the radio.

As he sang the line ending in, "contemplating," I belted out, "I'm sitting here just constipating." My dad laughed so hard he nearly rolled out of the car.

I always loved my dad's sense of humor, and I was proud to be his heir. One of the greatest compliments I received in young adulthood came from Mom's sister, Jo, who had asked me a question. When I gave her an off-the-wall response, she looked at me, laughed, and said, "You know, I didn't think there was anybody in the world like Walt until I met you. You're exactly like your dad."

Nonetheless, the limitations of humor were dawning on me. Dad was right. Sometimes humor is the only way to get through pain and obtuseness. But I realized that after the laughs faded, albeit with spirits often lifted, then what? Who's got a plan to solve the problem?

It all became clear to me when I entertained a group of students at an Ohio State orientation. They laughed, but I saw in their faces a longing, an expectation, for something more from me.

But what? Where do I look? How will I know when I find it?

I wasn't done being funny, but it was time to move on.

Songs at the Center

I WAS reading my daily devotional when I came upon the line, "For you, too, there must be songs on the way." The words shook me. I "asked" what they meant, and "Nashville" echoed with a boom. *Nashville.*

It was the last thing I wanted to hear from my inner voice. Years had passed since I'd been there, and Nashville had been only a faint reflection in my mind, playing no part in the career I had built. From time to time, I would visit Music City, even earning a few single-song publishing deals, but for the most part, the town played no role for me, my work, or my life. I once happened to mention to a member of the Nashville Songwriters Hall of Fame that "I gained experiences beyond this world, but lost out on credentials not afforded to someone who took my route" and wondered if I made the right decision to stay in Ohio.

"Absolutely," he said, "look at all the people you've touched."

But still . . . Nashville is Nashville.

My last memory of Nashville was being in a well-known demo studio that was being remodeled by its new owner. I was nosing around when I saw a vault of now-obsolete two-inch tapes. On the spine, each one had the name of the writer and two to three songs on it. The writers were well known, but the songs? Never heard of any of them.

I kept looking.

Nothing I recognized.

Whoa, even among well-known songwriters, a well-written song is just a lottery ticket.

As I drove home through the darkness that night, I wondered if I moved to Nashville, even if I could write a hit or two, would it be fulfilling in the long term? Or give me the meaning I was longing for?

I thought about a Hall of Fame songwriter who told me, "I feel empty." I couldn't believe it. With all of his success? As I thought about it, I realized emptiness is not something I've ever felt in my pursuits. I've felt ignored, undervalued, passed over, even ridiculed, but my deepest motivations were always to find meaning, even when, at times, it seemed to hold me back from worldly success.

Nashville is filled with brilliant minds that create poignant songs. Great artists, too. We all see them, the ones who have a knack for communicating to a large number of people, if only for a while. But, like all businesses, the music industry is based upon transactions, so Nashville is in large part a transaction town. And music can be so much more than that.

Actor Matt Damon said about winning an Academy Award at age twenty-seven, "It can't fill you up. If that's a hole you have, that won't fill it." Despite the millions of dollars these songwriters have made off of their talent, perhaps for some of them commercial success itself didn't bring meaning. Surely, they're aware of how their songs connected with people's deeper human needs. But maybe the pressure of the music business to constantly produce has jaded them and they've lost sight of the unique privilege we songwriters have to engage people's hearts, heal, inspire, and lift them up through our music. These are the elements that add meaning to any art form. The rest is just commerce.

A top artist of his time told me he was shocked that he was discarded when he lost his record deal. He couldn't understand where all his "friends" had gone and why no one in the business would return his calls.

I understood how he felt. I'd lived it myself, on a smaller scale. When I walked away from the media in my twenties, no one in the industry was interested in maintaining the relationship. I had to learn they hadn't really been my friends. They were only "transaction friends," pals while we were doing business but nowhere to be found when I needed them. Having figured that out so early in my life was a big step in becoming free to pursue my own path and finding meaning beyond finances.

However, now I was being "asked" to go back to Nashville.

Why? Where would I start? Who would I call? Where would I even stay?

I got in touch with my friend Ty, who'd recently attended a songwriting workshop in Columbus that featured a powerhouse Nashville writer. Ty and I talked about my return to Music City, how to go about it, and, now in my middle-aged years, what to expect. Ty agreed I should go. And off I went for a couple of days to explore what would turn out to be important to the next phase of my life.

Another friend knew a few people in Nashville and introduced me to a composer, Steve Bashaw. We sat at Starbucks on West End Avenue, down a few doors from the Vanderbilt University bookstore. Halfway into our discussion, he stopped me and asked a question:

"Where do you ultimately see yourself?"

"Well," I said, not really knowing what was coming from my mouth, "I can see myself on PBS."

He looked at me as seriously as anyone ever has. "Don't ever forget that."

How prophetic Steve's words were. How could I have known that some ten years later, I'd create a TV series for public television called *Songs at the Center*. Television, especially PBS, was the farthest thing from my mind. I was still focused on why I was "led" back to Nashville.

Within months, I auditioned at The Bluebird Cafe, among the most famous listening rooms in the world for singer-songwriters, and forever famous for having launched Garth Brooks, Taylor Swift, Kathy Mattea, Faith Hill, and Kenny Chesney, among others. The day of my audition, the club was jam-packed with songwriters, all hoping to get invited to perform at the legendary venue. Amy Kurland, the original owner and founder, welcomed us and gave us detailed instructions on how to introduce ourselves and our songs.

"From the time I can remember," she said, "when I'd listen to the radio, I could tell within the first minute whether I liked a song. That's all it takes. When it's your turn to come up here, state your name, where you're from, the name of your song, and then sing one verse and a chorus."

She added that only 10 percent of the artists would be selected to play their club.

My nerves flared.

When I took the stage, I introduced myself, sang a verse and chorus of a song of mine, and just like that my minute was up.

Not until two hours into the snowy drive home, when I was sufficiently separated from Nashville, did I explicate my audition.

I called Ty. "I think I blew it, Ty. You know that last line of the chorus? I should have doubled it."

Ty didn't say anything. He let me talk, knowing I always second-guess whatever is better left alone.

Two weeks later, I got a letter from the Bluebird congratulating me on being selected.

I was elated.

I played the Bluebird dozens of times over the years. The first few appearances, I was struck by how many educated eyes were upon me. The audience of approximately ninety consisted of people who knew songwriting, including the producers, managers, and other industry people who might drop in because they have a stake in the game. Whether songwriting gurus, or folks visiting what they considered the real celebrity, The Bluebird Cafe itself, the audiences always displayed respect and abided by the club's good-natured admonition, "Shhh!" I will forever be proud of and grateful for playing the room so many times. The performance, the musicianship, and the charisma of the artists may be important, but the sole reason the Bluebird exists is to showcase *The Song*.

It wasn't until my Bluebird years that I experienced the city from the viewpoint of the writers. My previous exposure to the city was through publishers and producers, but not the songwriters, who are the heart of the music business.

"It all begins with a song" is the motto of Nashville Songwriters Association International, which now owns and operates the Bluebird. And it is true. Without a song, there is no music business, no dreams to come true.

My trips to Nashville became monthly, but because my family and I wanted—and *needed*—each other, I'd limit my visits to only a few days in a row, meeting other writers, going to workshops, and listening, listening, listening. I'd play the Bluebird a few times a year and stop by the club each night I was in town to listen to whoever was performing. I'd play some of Nashville's other clubs and learn from watching the most celebrated songwriters, who taught me that a great song gives you something to take with you—a line, a hook, a lick—something you remember the next day after only hearing the song once. These songs, not always popular, are few and far between, but when you hear one, you know the writer has been touched by the Songwriting God.

I maintain that the most powerful, purest musical experience is to hear accomplished singer-songwriters perform their own creations. One voice, one instrument. Untethered to complex arrangements, unladen by heavy production. A great song can console, inspire, heal, challenge, enlighten, tickle, even transform. A human heart knows truth when it feels it, and it needs nothing more than a single voice to communicate it.

When performing in a listening room, songwriters take the risk of pouring out our hearts and souls, and the audience, in return, agrees to give us a chance. It's a contract, sometimes like a blind date. Two parties agreeing to meet each other with a wide range of hope and expectations. At best, the arrangement bestows a once-in-a-lifetime bond between songwriter and listener. At worst, the setup is a mismatch, two parties enduring each other for an uncomfortable period and parting ways with indifference.

I grew to love Nashville's "in-the-round" format, created at the Bluebird, in which fewer than a handful of songwriters form a circle in the middle of an audience and take turns playing their songs. The variety of songs is appealing for the audience, and as a performer, it preserves the simple sound of one voice and an instrument, while relieving the pressure to be the only source of entertainment onstage.

Serendipitously, back home in Ohio, The Peggy R. McConnell Arts Center of Worthington (MAC) opened less than a mile from my house. A community arts center, the building was renovated from the original Worthington school building, built in 1915. Throughout my high school years, it was known as "the Annex" and housed most of the classes no one wanted to take or teach, such as health and driver's ed. My sophomore year, I had behavioral science in an auditorium-style room, where, bored out of my skull during class, I would copy from memory song lyrics from Jackson Browne, Jim Croce, and other popular songwriters of the day.

Who could imagine that one day the room would be transformed into the 213-seat Bronwynn Theatre (named after the teacher who taught me the *Brigadoon* sword dance), where I would realize the venue was perfect for showcasing singer-songwriters? I began hosting songwriter rounds at the MAC, as well as at another local club, *Natalie's*. I was not only amazed at how popular the Nashville format became among the audiences, but I was pleasantly surprised to discover the personal joy of showcasing fellow songwriters from all over the country.

Within a couple of months of booking and hosting the shows, I got an idea for a television series. It scared the hell out of me, but I couldn't wait to get started.

As my late friend Wendy told me many times, "When one is extremely drawn to a prospect, yet at the same time scared to death of it, they are standing on Holy Ground."

I took my "Holy Ground" idea to the MAC, where Andy Herron, the then-director of operations, and Jon Cook, the then-executive director, liked the idea and offered me the opportunity to produce the show at their venue. Not wanting to admit to my first guests I was taping a TV pilot, I asked a handful of my songwriting friends to come to the MAC "because it's a great venue to get videotaped."

I came up with the name, *Songs at the Center*, which has three levels of meaning: The show is taped mostly at the McConnell Arts Center, the songwriters are in the center of a circle, and, as songwriters, songs are at the center of our lives.

The local NBC affiliate took a look at the pilot and put it on the air for five weeks. Later that summer, a producer from our local PBS station, WOSU, asked me for an interview about my hometown of Worthington, about which she was doing an hour special.

"Everyone in this town certainly knows the history," the producer said, "but what do you think is the future of Worthington?"

"Songwriting," I said.

"*Song*writing?" she replied.

"Yes, I've been putting together songwriter rounds all over this town. And then there's my TV show."

"TV show?" Her head raised. "What's that? Can you send me a demo?"

I took out my computer on the spot and showed her my seven-minute pilot.

She grew excited. "You know my program director is looking for an arts show for the weekend . . ."

Within weeks, WOSU's Chief Content Director for Television, Stacia Hentz, called me and said if we could get thirteen episodes produced, she would offer us a slot on Saturday nights. It was time to call in favors, so Andy, Alan Beavers, our chief videographer, and some other camera operators, including our hand-held photographer, Jim Miller, agreed to shoot and edit eight more shows. We had our thirteen shows and a station to air them.

On January 9, 2015, *Songs at the Center* premiered on WOSU. Within three weeks, Stacia called us into her office. "Your show's doing great. I think it has national potential. I'd like to send it to a syndicator. Do you have any objections?"

Andy, Alan, and I looked at each other dumbfounded. "No!" one of us, or all of us, blurted out. And thus began a national show on PBS, and soon the re-emergence of Jack FitzGerald in my life.

Over the years, Jack called me every Christmas Eve and kept in touch from time to time, asking what I was up to. Insecure about the fate of *Songs at the Center*, I downplayed it as a little project. But now it was getting serious, so we talked for real.

As I explained to him, most people can name the singer who sang a popular song, but not many know the writers. But that's where the magic is. Whether the songwriters are famous or unknown, their stories can be powerful. I wanted to give the songwriters an opportunity to share their feelings and experiences that led them to write their songs. Through my own years in the songwriting journey, I know the depths of fears, the highs of acceptance, the lows of rejection, the elements of a great song, how to deal with fallow periods, the conflicts wrestling in artists' minds, and the tangled mysteries that lurk within creative people. Plus, my background in teaching and my work with the disabled and sick has taught me how to get out of my own way so I can let the artists be the stars of the show.

Something inside said I was meant to do this.

Jack told me he liked the idea and visited our tapings, but added, "I'm not interested in working on it if it's a vanity project or hobby for you."

"Vanity project? Who's got time for *that*?" I said.

If I couldn't create something worthy of financial support, I explained, I didn't want to bother. I wanted to spotlight great artists, famous and those who weren't known yet but deserved the world's attention. I'd host and perform my own songs on the show occasionally, but I wanted the focus to be on other artists. Maybe there's a fifteen-year-old out there who's feeling alienated, and she hears the story from one of our songwriters of how music changed his life, and all of a sudden, she picks up a guitar and her world is changed, too. Or maybe there's a disabled person who's unable to get out and hear live music. I wanted to do a show for these people, and if the rest of the audience follows, all the better.

Jack signed on and stayed with me for ten years until he retired.

Today, having aired on more than four hundred public TV stations, with loyal viewers, a crew of nearly thirty people, and engaged sponsors, JobsOhio and The James Cancer Hospital, *Songs at the Center* is in its second decade.

During the first few seasons, the amount of heavy lifting was overwhelming. My journalism background prepared me for writing our newsletter, using social media, promoting, and emailing everyone relentlessly. I also served as an agent and "went to school" on grant writing, licensing, insurance, public television, fundraising, lighting, staging, the basics of TV production, plus other back-office tasks that still dominate every minute of every day.

Wait a minute, I got into this for the music!

I knew when the project started that there were tons of things I would have to learn, but despite my apprehensions, I was looking forward to it. My internship at WBNS-TV years ago had taught me something I'd carried with me ever since: that for every person on stage or on camera, there are scores of people in the background working their tails off to make you look good. Their jobs are largely invisible, but nothing would be happening were it not for those dedicated people. With *Songs at the Center*, I led a small team with limited contacts and a growing national product. I could only do my best, and I'd have to be at peace with that.

Nevertheless, despite periodic reminders from our videographer, Alan, that, "it's not worth dying for," the show became my obsession. In the early years, the day after Christmas, I jumped out of bed, put on my boots, and scooted off to the bank, my mind crazy with many end-of-the-year chores for *Songs at the Center*. I ran into somebody I knew, carried on a ten-minute conversation, and took care of my banking business. It wasn't until I was returning to my car that I noticed my walk was out of whack. I looked down at my feet and saw that I was wearing two different boots, a brown L.L. Bean "duck" boot on my right foot, and a black Ecco Track 25, an inch higher, on my left. I didn't know then that I was launching a fashion movement.

A few months later, life demonstrated that extraordinary things can happen on the most ordinary days. My Aunt Jessie had died and left me her fifteen-year-old Dodge Neon. Primarily for safety reasons, I let my girls drive my "good" car, so I took over the wheel of the Neon. On the way to my college teaching job, I kept thinking, *Nothing says success like being in your fifties and driving a hand-me-down Neon to an adjunct professorship*!

My phone rang. It was a number I didn't recognize, so I let it go. Moments later, I listened to the message.

"Hi, I'm calling for Eric. This is John Oates..."

The John Oates, of Hall and Oates fame, calling to tell me that an agent, Steve Cover, was bringing him to Columbus, and he was curious about appearing on my show.

When I called him back, he was natural, normal, and respectful. "You know, I've had my day in the sun. A couple of days, actually," the Rock & Roll Hall of Fame member laughed. "But now it's enough to be a good person and a good father."

Weeks later, I picked him up and drove him to the studio. Once on the TV set, we covered the Hall and Oates years, the difference in playing stadiums versus small venues like The Bluebird Cafe, and songwriting. Among other subjects, he explained how the megahit "Maneater" was created.

John had gone to Jamaica on a holiday, and the chorus of "Maneater" showed up in his mind in reggae style.

"... And Daryl and I got together, and I played it for him and, this is his exact words, which I thought was great and funny. He said, 'Hall and Oates don't do reggae,' as if he and I weren't sitting in the same room together. And I said, what do you got in mind, and he goes, 'Let's make it like a Motown song.' And obviously I'm really glad I listened to him because it became a huge hit. That just shows you how a song can morph in the songwriting process."

Then he played "Maneater" in yet another style, Delta blues, as he sang it on *Songs at the Center*.

John remained kind and approachable. A couple years later, he released his book, *A Change of Seasons: A Memoir*, and I contacted him to see if he would agree to provide signed copies to sell at a local bookstore in conjunction with the release.

"I love the idea," he responded. The signed books arrived within a couple of days.

John was the first of many guests who were exceptions to the rule "Never meet your heroes, or you'll be disappointed." I learned that, as the saying goes, they are "just people."

The quintessential "just people" person was Peter Asher of the famous sixties duo Peter and Gordon. He later produced Linda Ronstadt and the Grammy Award-winning comedy album *Robin Williams: Live on Broadway*, and signed James Taylor to Apple Records. Appearing with the congenial rock legend Albert Lee, he was patient, kind, and seemed genuinely grateful to be sharing his music and stories on *Songs at the Center*.

Peter recounted how in his early days he had shared the top floor of his family home with Paul McCartney, and, as a result, happened to witness one of the most important moments in rock and roll history:

". . . and one day John Lennon came over, and the two of them were down there for a couple of hours . . . they called upstairs . . . invited me down to come sit there and hear this song they'd just finished. So, yeah, they sat side by side on the piano bench—no guitars, interestingly, though you think of it now as a guitar song but it wasn't initially—and they played me this brand-new song called 'I Want to Hold Your Hand,' and asked me what I thought."

That wasn't the only Beatles story I heard from a guest of *Songs at the Center*. We took our crew to Michigan for an interview with actor Jeff Daniels, who the world is just finding out is also a songwriter. Before Jeff landed famous roles in *Dumb and Dumber*, *Heartburn*, and *Gettysburg*—and won Emmy, Golden Globe, and Tony awards—he was an aspiring actor in New York.

"I was twenty-one, 1976, bought a Guild D-40, threw it in the back of the car," he said. "I knew five chords. I'm sure that while I'm sitting by myself in New York City, I'll probably have the time to learn how to play the guitar."

After our show recording, he took me upstairs to see his collection of guitars, including his Guild D-40, which became his constant companion as he traveled to his acting gigs through the years. George Harrison was a producer of one of his early films. During a break, Jeff was sitting with his guitar. George approached him, chatted, then asked Jeff if he could see his guitar.

"Then he played 'Here Comes the Sun.'"

Mind-blowing memory.

While cameras were recording, Jeff shared a story that resonated personally with me, for my life was changed, too, when I saw the late Steve Goodman in concert. I was a sophomore at Ohio Wesleyan when he stepped onto the Gray Chapel stage with nothing but a guitar that looked bigger than he was.

Steve sang his iconic song, "City of New Orleans," and a bunch of others. But from the first note, he had me in his pocket. I was amazed that one man could captivate an audience like he did—from his story about the song he wrote with his friend, the late John Prine, "You Never Even Called Me By My Name," to "My Old Man," a masterful song that takes the listener from laughter to tears.

I brought this up with Jeff Daniels.

"I go down to the Bottom Line 'cause that's a famous place where people play, and there's Steve Goodman, whom I'd always loved," he said about his early acting days in New York. "I go to see him. He didn't have a band, he didn't have a light show. He had him and that guitar. And his musicianship, his sense of humor, his writing, his stage presence. He owned the room. And I remember going—That! What's That?! How do I do that?

"But he was very inspiring to me. He could write funny, smart."

Another songwriter who's known for writing "funny and smart" is Country Music Hall of Fame and Museum inductee Ray Stevens, whose catalog includes the inspiring and inclusive "Everything is Beautiful," which won him his first of two Grammys, and the chart-topping novelty single, "The Streak."

"I've had many letters that said that this or that song had influenced some action that was, so far, positive," he said. "So, you know, you've got to be aware that people are out there listening, and music is so important in all our lives. I feel blessed that some of my songs have influenced things in a good way."

Rodney Crowell, a two-time Grammy winner credited for planting the seeds of Americana music with Emmylou Harris, John Prine, Guy Clark, Townes Van Zandt, Jerry Jeff Walker, Gram Parsons, and others, has also influenced music for decades. When he was a guest on *Songs at the Center*, he talked about his musical career and shared memories of Johnny Cash, who was his father-in-law for a number of years.

"He was Mount Rushmore," Rodney said. "His presence is like Mount Rushmore walks into the room, you know? . . . And John had great body language. His moves, it was watery. I mean, I've actually been behind a camera filming him in a hammock when stuff was going on around and it was time to go from being grandfather to Johnny Cash, and just"—Rodney snapped his fingers to signal an instantaneous shift—"and it goes from this sweet grandfatherly dude to this Mount Rushmore guy. With me even trying to describe that it's sort of poetic, you know. So the man was a poet and I think I remember when his passing Bob Dylan said, 'he was the true North Star.'"

A few years before I began the TV series, I had gotten to know Don Henry, a highly versatile artist, whose best-known song is, "Where've You Been?" a Grammy winner co-written with Jon Vezner and recorded by Kathy Mattea. Among his other hits is "All Kinds of Kinds," written with Phillip Coleman and recorded by Miranda Lambert. Don is the songwriter's songwriter.

Don paid me the ultimate compliment about a song I played at the Bluebird. "I loved it," he said. "Over the years, I've learned how to tell if a song is good. If I wished I'd written it, it's a good song. And I wished I'd written that one."

What a nice thing to hear from a Grammy winner. All I could do was give him a spontaneous hug. Right there in the tiny hall in front of the men's room at The Bluebird Cafe.

It was in large part to introduce the world to writers like Don Henry that motivated me to start our show. Having appeared on *Songs at the*

Center five times, Don is well known to the Nashville songwriting community, but less so to the general public. On our series, he talked about how, as an eight-year-old, he was a baseball fan and had a book report due. Knowing he didn't like to read, a teacher gave him a book on Jackie Robinson, which exposed him to racial issues and Martin Luther King Jr.

"I read this little tiny book about Jackie Robinson and it changed my life, and it turned me on to who Martin Luther King was, so I wrote this song, 'Beautiful Fool,' many years later. I'd always been inspired by Martin Luther King, but didn't know how to put it in words. And then it occurred to me I could do it from the point of view of that eight-year-old kid who didn't know what the hell was going on."

And he sang "Beautiful Fool," a sensitive tribute to the slain civil rights leader.

One of Don's frequent co-writers is Craig Carothers, an imposing man physically, and a witty guy. Craig was on *Songs at the Center* with Don and explained how their poignant song "Schenectady" was written. The two of them were teaching at a songwriting workshop in the Bay Area with fellow hit songwriter Steve Seskin. At the time Steve had a song called "New Orleans" on the radio, recorded by the late Toby Keith.

A woman attending the class asked him why it was called "New Orleans" since it wasn't about the city. Steve said part of the reason was that the city has some mystique, so it provided a colorful setting, but also because it sings well.

She seemed satisfied with this answer, so they went on.

About twenty minutes later, she raised her hand again and asked if Steve could give her any advice about choosing the name of a city for a song. Were there any rules or guidelines?

"Well," Steve said, "I guess if you're from Schenectady, you probably wouldn't want to use that!"

"And Don and I were in the back of the room," Craig said, taking Steve's offhand remark about Schenectady as the ultimate songwriting challenge. Over the lunch break, Craig and Don started playing with words that rhyme with Schenectady: "respected me, protected me, connect to me," and cobbled together a rough approximation of a chorus. Once back in the workshop, they played the fragment of their fledgling song, which was meant to be funny at the time.

The workshoppers loved it.

Weeks later, when Craig and Don got together to write, their minds drifted back to the workshop and the early version of "Schenectady." It wasn't until they looked up the meaning of the word that they, and the song, turned serious. Schenectady derives its name from the Mohawk word meaning "the far side of the pines," which is where the Mohawk believe we go when we die.

"We both got a shiver," Craig said.

Their idea evolved into the story of a young soldier coming home to Schenectady, who, not until late in the song, do we discover why—he's being laid to rest.

A second shiver came when they were able to invoke the title of Walt Whitman's famous work, *Leaves of Grass*, along with the meaning of Schenectady into the final verse.

I have seen both of them sing the song at various venues, including on *Songs at the Center*, and have yet to witness an audience that does not go stone-cold quiet.

While Don and Craig traveled to Schenectady in their minds to create a song, another writer, Grammy Award-winner Marc Cohn, actually found inspiration for his iconic song by taking a road trip to Memphis. Marc, who wrote and recorded "Walking in Memphis," talked about doing a "geographic," which he explained on *Songs at the Center*, "was to get the hell out of your hometown for a few days. Go somewhere you've never been. Take a bus, take a train, put your guitar or your keyboard in the trunk of your car. Whatever. And just go somewhere new."

It was an idea he got from James Taylor, a songwriter Marc hadn't met at the time of his trip and wouldn't meet until after his own success. "It had worked for him many times, and when he really felt like he was having writer's block, that's how he would open up his sensibilities, to just put himself in an unfamiliar place or situation. And I thought, 'Well, I might as well give that a try.'"

Consequently, Marc went to Memphis, where he visited Elvis Presley's estate, Graceland, listened to Grammy Lifetime Achievement Award-winner Al Green preach at his home church, and met a woman named Muriel, who became a central figure at the end of his famous song, an example of how a great song often has at least one "special moment" in addition to a memorable hook.

Marc also talked about an experience on the road that wasn't so special—when he got shot during an attempted carjacking as he drove with his band from a gig in Denver. The bullet, shot through the windshield, lodged in the soft tissue of Marc's left temple.

"I was one of the unlucky lucky ones that night," Marc said on *Songs at the Center*. "That's when things changed for me, and I just started to write. I needed some healing personally. And as always has been the case, and this was the same, it got me back to needing to express myself. So, I wrote a whole record called *Join the Parade*, with songs about faith and chance, and it had to do with [Hurricane] Katrina, had to do with my shooting. Lots of songs about life and death."

Marc's life was not the only one changed by random circumstance. Grammy nominee Tony Arata saw his dreams eventually realized by a chance meeting with a then-unknown songwriter at the now-closed Douglas Corner Cafe in Nashville.

"It was a really cold night," Tony, who would one day be a member of the Nashville Songwriters Hall of Fame, said on *Songs at the Center*. "I couldn't afford the cover charge, so I snuck in the back door. And sitting on a stool on the stage was this—he looked like a cowboy. He had a cowboy shirt on and cowboy hat, boots. I mean, he didn't look like Urban Cowboy, he looked like he really knew how to ride a horse . . . and it was a young man from Oklahoma named Garth Brooks."

The two of them struck up a friendship that night and began playing gigs together around town. Garth promised him that when he got a record deal, he'd record Tony's song, "The Dance."

Three years later, Garth asked Tony to listen to his new album in his truck. When the last song came up, it started with a piano track that Tony didn't recognize, so he thought, "Oh, no, 'The Dance' didn't make the record." But as the song continued into the guitar intro, Tony realized it was "The Dance," and over the next few months, Garth's promise was more than fulfilled. "The Dance" was *Billboard*'s Number One song for three weeks, named the 1991 Song of the Year and Video of the Year by the Academy of Country Music, and the Country Music Association named it the 1991 Music Video of the Year.

Quite a chance meeting.

Holding back tears, Tony explained how touched he and his wife were when Garth pointed them out at a concert in Dallas.

"Toward the end of the night he asked everybody to sit down. Except me and Jaymi. And he sang 'The Dance' and, you know, dedicated it to us. You don't get to share moments like that many times, you know, in your life. It meant the world to me, it truly did. And I'll never forget it as long as I live.

"The other thing I remember about the night," he said with a chuckle, "is it took us about three hours to get out of the place because when they found me in the lobby, a line formed, and then I had to go through what Garth goes through every night, which was greet and, you know, shake hands with everybody."

All these years later, Garth still claims "The Dance" is his favorite song.

Though not as famous as Garth Brooks among the public, yet well loved and respected in the music world, especially among songwriters, is the Country Music Hall of Fame and Grand Ole Opry member Don Schlitz. He has written twenty-four Number One songs, including "The Gambler" for the late Kenny Rogers, who said, "Don doesn't just write songs, he writes careers." Don also has over fifty Top Ten hits, and co-created the Bluebird's "in-the-round" format. When I was in Nashville for a Bluebird gig, I emailed Don and asked if he'd be willing to meet with me. He got right back to me and agreed to visit.

"You're in my town," he said when I attempted to buy a muffin and a cup of coffee and he insisted he pay for it.

Thanks to his good-natured personality ("I'm an introvert who can't shut up"), we got along like "two old pals," in Don's words, connecting on a variety of topics, from songwriting, to our love of college basketball, his team being the Duke Blue Devils.

A few weeks later, we taped the interview for *Songs at the Center* at his home. He took me through his house and, at my urging, showed me his two Grammys, three CMA Song of the Year awards, and four ASCAP Song of the Year awards, among others. But one of the things he was most proud of was a napkin he'd framed with the handwritten phone number of songwriting icon Mike Stoller, who gave it to him during a chat at a Songwriters Hall of Fame meeting.

"He's a hero," Don said.

Don was generous, humble, and grateful, as was his wife Stacey, who also happens to be his attorney, and, like most everyone else in Nashville, is also a singer.

"I'd like to call my attorney to the stage," Don is fond of saying at gigs, and on our show, the two of them sang "Not Too Much to Ask," a song he'd written with Mary Chapin Carpenter.

On Don's wall hangs a letter he'd received from his long-ago boss, when he'd worked as an overnight computer operator for Vanderbilt University, scolding him for sleeping on the job. Six months later, "The Gambler" was released.

"I'm living the weirdest life ever," he said.

I attended Don's official induction into the Grand Ole Opry by Vince Gill, an Opry member himself. As Don stood in the famous six-foot circle of the stage, he spoke about driving home with Vince the first night Vince had invited him to play the Opry.

"And I say, 'Vince, does it ever get old?' and he said, 'Nope.' And it never has and it never will. And the friends that I've made since you dragged me out here, the crew, the band, everybody involved in the Opry, and the fans. And it's like you guys always said, 'You just go out there and they'll love you.'"

Not that I ever doubted Don's words, but six months later, a band from Akron, The Shootouts, fronted by Ryan Humbert, made their debut at the Opry. I've gigged with Ryan a few times and had him as a guest on *Songs at the Center*. Sometime before The Shootouts's tenth appearance at the Opry, I told him how happy I was for him, and asked, "How does it feel to stand there in the center of that circle and sing?"

"It's funny," he said. "The band and I were so nervous when we arrived at the Opry, but once we got in there, everyone was so nice. It's like you can feel the spirits of all the great artists who played there. They embrace you, and from that point on, we were so relaxed. We had found our home."

I told him about Don's comment that playing the Opry never gets old.

"Let me put it this way," Ryan said. "If it were the only gig we did every year, it would be all we'd ever need."

In my conversation with Don Schlitz, I said I'd seen him at the Bluebird years ago and still remembered a song I'd never heard before or since, "My Heart May Be Broken."

"It's a great example of how a great hook, with one listen, stays with you for ten years. *That's* what a great song does for the listener," I said, restating my private thesis to him.

He glanced past my shoulder like he was trying to recall a question from a high school quiz. "You sure I wrote that?" he asked.

I chuckled. "You've written so many wonderful songs you don't even remember all of them."

The next day, having returned to Ohio, I got an email from Don:

> *I woke up at 4 a.m. and wandered to the coffee maker to find some peace of mind. Nearby was a stack of CDs with songs that I'd been wanting to make sure I had somehow magically saved into some catalog. This song was on top of the stack.*
>
> *I hope it holds up on the second listen.*

Attached was "My Heart May Be Broken," which he'd written with Gary Burr, who later became a guest on our TV series, along with his songwriting wife, Georgia Middleman. Don, Gary, and Georgia all spoke of how the first thing that must be done with a song idea is to "make it smaller."

"My heroes, they tell stories in three minutes, and that's so hard to do," Georgia said. "The more economical you are with lyrics, the harder it is to tell a story. And I just found that mesmerizing, and it became my life's mission."

"I always liken the opening of a song to the curtain opening. What is the first thing I see?" Georgia continued. "What's the second thing? What's the third thing? And as you see more details, the story starts evolving quickly. Within four lines of a lyric. And you know exactly where you are, who you're looking at, what's going on. It's very important as a writer to start like that."

Don, Georgia, and Gary were also authentic, which I have found to be the case among the most truly gifted people across the industry. They are conscientious and want things "right," but they are grateful for their successes, humble, and the easiest people to work with. While they hold themselves to standards higher than anyone else, they typically don't see themselves that way.

I brought up this subject on a show with top-selling singer-songwriter and pianist Jim Brickman, a Cleveland native.

"Definitely," he concurred. "When I work with iconic singers, which is partly to benefit the audience, but also selfish 'cause I want to. The idea of Johnny Mathis singing my song, or Carly Simon, or Kenny Loggins, or Olivia Newton-John, or Donny Osmond, any of these iconic singers—Kenny Rogers—every one of them is exactly as you say.

"And I think it's a combination, in my view, of knowing that a fifty-year career is always going to do this, you've been high, you've been low, you understand what it feels like when it's not your turn, and the swoop back up to iconic.

"Yes, the nicest, the most humble—you know, Kenny Rogers in the studio saying, 'Did you like that take? Or do you want me to do another one?' like I'm producing some twenty-five-year-old kid. Same with Johnny Mathis—'Were you happy with that?'—I don't know what to say. I'm like, 'Me?' What do I have to say about it?"

Grammy Award-winning songwriter Mike Reid demonstrated the same unassuming personality.

"Have you always been this humble?" I asked him at dinner the night before a *Songs at the Center* taping. He laughed, and said, "I can't wait to tell my wife you asked me that question."

Mike has every reason to be puffed up, yet he is real. A former football player, he won the Outland Trophy and Maxwell Award as a defensive lineman at Penn State, was selected seventh in the first round of the 1970 draft by the Cincinnati Bengals, and was named twice to the All-Pro team.

After his football career, Mike moved to Nashville and over the years wrote twelve Number One country songs, many for Ronnie Milsap, and was inducted into the Nashville Songwriters Hall of Fame. He won a Grammy for writing Milsap's "Stranger in My House," which was "a unique record for country because, you know, you do not hear songs in minor keys in country music," he said. "You just don't hear them." Then, accompanying himself on the piano, he played "a little more of a personal version" of the song.

He's perhaps best known for co-writing, with Allen Shamblin, "I Can't Make You Love Me," recorded by Bonnie Raitt.

I told Mike before the taping that "I Can't Make You Love Me" is a perfect example of what I wanted to bring to our television audiences. "I think Bonnie's rendition of your song is spectacular, one of the greatest records of the twentieth century. The perfect artist singing the perfect song. But when I heard your original demo—the one you sent to Bonnie—with just your voice, piano, and string pad on it, I have to tell you, it blew me away even more than Bonnie's version because I heard your heart, the heart of the songwriter, in every note. There's simply nothing like the song coming from the person who wrote it."

Successful by anyone's measure, Mike, like all other true writers, talked about being dogged by doubt almost every time he sits at the piano. He constantly has to fight off his inner voices that say, "Oh, look, you're an ex-defensive tackle. What do you think you're doing?"

Mike's colleague and friend, Tom Douglas, author of the Academy of Country Music's Song of the Decade "The House that Built Me," recorded by Miranda Lambert and also co-written with Allen Shamblin, defined his own internal doubts as "a rat that gets in your head that starts whispering all these lies."

"He sits on the edge of my piano with a long tail, gnarly teeth, and the only way that I can get through to even start the song is pick the rat up by the tail, put him in a Mason jar, screw down a brass lid, walk it out to the driveway, load up a 12-gauge, and blow it into smithereens. Then I can get started writing. But, man, the rat is—you never kill the rat, you just learn to deal with him over and over again. You face him every day."

Tom, a member of the Nashville Songwriters Hall of Fame, also talked about another regular obstacle: Rejection.

"It can drive you insane unless you just go back to, 'Wait a second, I got a gift, I create, and I share with anybody and everybody who'll listen,' and then I go back and create again. And that helps lessen the sting of rejection. But the rejection is real painful."

Then I brought up how songwriting and poetry are not brothers and sisters, as some say, but that the process of writing a song is actually more like screenwriting, creating scenes to build a story.

"That is the way that I have approached my process over time," he replied, "but I've never been able to connect those dots. I really am writing a script. I'm writing a movie. I have a scene. I'm trying to tell a very small story."

Multiple Grammy Award-winner Janis Ian is a master of scenic writing, as she demonstrated in her famous song, "At Seventeen." In our interview, I told her how I would select a few lyrics from her song and ask my college classes or songwriters in a workshop, "Can you tell me what you know about this girl from just a phrase?"

Janis also talked about the benefit of having lots of early success. "All it means is that when you're older, you'll still have a career." And she proceeded to sing the heart out of "At Seventeen" and "Jesse," giving me the most meaningful experiences I've ever had as an interviewer and listener. I sat onstage watching her and told her it was in that very room where, dreaming of being a songwriter in high school nearly fifty years ago, I would copy her lyrics instead of taking notes in behavioral sciences class, and that we were two hundred yards from where, my senior year, I sat in my car alone, coming home from a football game, feeling invisible, finding her version of "Jesse" to be the comfort I needed as it came on the radio.

And now, here she was, singing those immortal songs six feet away.

Janis's first hit, written when she was fourteen, was "Society's Child," a song about an interracial relationship that was so controversial in the mid-sixties that some radio stations banned it from airplay. Marshall Chapman, a songwriter and actress raised in South Carolina, had her own take on racism in those days when she told us about seeing the King of Rock and Roll at an early age in the Jim Crow South.

"We had this Black cook, and my parents were gone a lot; in fact, I thought the cook was my parent, and in most ways she was. And I remember going down to the kitchen, she said, 'Marshall, c'mon we're going to hear this man sing.' And then she told me his name. Elvis Presley. She just laughed. She thought that was the funniest name she'd ever heard.

"But we took a city bus, and she took me to hear Elvis. I was seven years old. And it was really like that scene of Scout in the courtroom in *To Kill a Mockingbird*. I mean, back then, it was the color of the band's skin that would determine who sat in the balcony.

"Because Elvis was white, the Blacks sat in the balcony and the white people were downstairs. Later, I went to hear Ray Charles, and the whites had to sit in the balcony and the Blacks were downstairs dancing. And that's sort of the way segregation worked for coming through Southern towns back in the fifties."

Many songwriters discover their passion as a way of dealing with brokenness and pain. Grammy Award-winning songwriter Jerry Salley was more than comfortable with it when he told us about writing "The Broken Ones" with Carl Vipperman and JB Rudd.

"I thought about my baby girl, Maggie, when we were writing the song. And I said, 'Boys, I think we need to name the girl in the song Maggie.' Unlike her two older sisters, who, every time a toy would break, they would come crying to Daddy that their toy broke, they needed a new one. Anytime one of Maggie's toys broke, she'd ask me to fix it."

He sang "The Broken Ones," which went to Number One on the Gospel charts.

Whether it be loss, addiction, gender identity, stuttering, race, or loneliness, songwriter Travis Meadows, who's written for many major Nashville artists, said, "I think the secret to finding happiness is knowing that you're broken and being okay with it."

Grammy nominee Mary Gauthier got to the core of songwriting when she said it's about making personal experience universal. "The personal is universal," she said before playing her well-known song, "Mercy Now," which begins with verses about her father and brother and then expands the camera lens to explore our country, the church, and, finally, all of us needing mercy. "That is what connects us. The deeply personal. Not our diaries, but what's underneath that. Not navel gazing, but what's underneath that. The experiences of being human in this world is quite universal."

Writing music serves us in many ways, and when Grammy Lifetime Achievement Award winner Tom Paxton, writer of "The Last Thing on My Mind," was on *Songs at the Center*, he said, "You get two people together and make some music and all of a sudden you've got friends."

Yes, friends who understand each other and why we have to create.

"Why do we do this?" Tom asked rhetorically. "And the bottom line is we do this because doing it keeps us sane. Not doing this would drive us nuts."

Indeed.

The Road Home

RUNNING down High Street just shy of two miles, I pass St. Michael Church as I reach Selby Boulevard, which leads me up a long hill into my old neighborhood, Colonial Hills. Across from the church is a strip center called Sharon Square, which has hardly changed over the years. The tenants are different, but the square looks almost exactly like it did when my mother used to bring my preschool self to pick up a pizza at Paul's, grab some groceries at Dawson's, or order pills and sometimes a milkshake at Nicklaus Drugs, which was owned by the family of Jack Nicklaus. Even the vintage steel sign still hangs from the strip center soffit, as it's done since the 1960s.

NO BICYCLES
ON SIDEWALK
OR IN ARCADE
Police Order

When I first attended St. Michael Church as a little boy, the structure was a Quonset hut. After a massive fundraising campaign, a new church was built, beautiful in its Romanesque architecture, cavernous, and to this day, resolute in its conservative roots. The inside of St. Michael is indeed stunning, however, and I am grateful that it has been open over the years for days of reflection, prayer, and meditation. I've worked many things out during the weekdays, sitting alone in the wooden pews. At turning points in my life, especially periods of doubt, fear, or depression, I would sit for hours in silence, trying to calm the voices of the world ricocheting through my head like pinballs. There have been times I visited so frequently I called St. Michael Church "my office."

After I had given up weekly deadlines for radio and the newspaper in my late twenties, I had time to think and, more importantly, to feel. I had a lot to consider, and no one, really, I could turn to for guidance, or even anyone whose life example I could follow. Looking at my past, particularly my dad's illness, I realized how different my life and my background were from anyone else I knew. Few times have I felt more alone.

Unaware I was on the threshold of diving into richer seas of creativity, I returned to the piano. With no expectations, I just played, easing into the more reflexive styles of my early years of songwriting. I became aware of how my feelings had been repressed. Hidden for a lifetime, the tears began to flow, along with the melodies . . . and the songs. They were raw emotions, anything but funny.

I started a song titled "Daddy," written from the hurting child inside me. I had everything done but the second verse. I was out walking one day when I passed a movie theater, and out of nowhere, the lyrics hit me. I cried uncontrollably. A concerned passerby asked if I needed help.

"No," I said through tears, "I'm just writing a song."

He moved on as if I'd come from a different world, which for most people, I do.

Once the song was finished, I kept it to myself for a long time.

When I finally got the courage to sing it for my friend Nelson, he challenged me to perform it at an upcoming gig for The National Speakers Association Ohio.

"I can't do that." I shuddered. "It's a private song. It's not meant for an audience. It's too personal. Plus, I've made my reputation on being funny. I can't just throw in a tearjerker."

"Let me ask you something," Nelson said. "Are your funny songs an honest representation of who you are?"

"Yes," I said.

"And how about this one?"

"Well, yes, I guess it is, too."

"As long as you're expressing an honest representation of who you are, your audience will accept you," he said.

I thought about his comments for days. I couldn't argue with them, so I made him a deal.

"If you come to my gig," I said, "I'll play 'Daddy' as my closing song."

He showed up, and I ended my show by saying, "I was very lucky to know a man who taught me something important. Early in adulthood, he was diagnosed with multiple sclerosis and, as a result, he wasn't able to pursue his dreams. But he showed me that a man's worth is not measured by his muscles, his money, or his job title, but by the size of his heart, the quality of his mind, and the radiance of his spirit."

Then I sang the song.

> You'd lie there in your bedroom, a too familiar place.
> Morning brought another day, a day you'd have to face.
> I'd be in the living room watching TV
> cause if you needed something you'd have to call for me.
>
> Daddy—
> Daddy—
> I can hear you just as clearly as can be
> call for me . . .

To my shock, the audience thundered to their feet, applauding, and the walls of the room were lined with people waiting to meet me. It was a turning point, for I realized that once you show your audience you have a heart, they trust you even more, and you can take them anywhere.

"Daddy" was the first song in which, as songwriters say, I dug deep. Although I've since written other songs about him, at that point I was abjectly terrified of my emotions, my past, myself, and I was afraid to face them, absolutely believing that I would discover a "bad" person on the other side. But after years of committing myself to the arduous but rewarding steps of self-awareness, I was amazed to find that the opposite is true. When we truly look in the mirror, we usually find a good, although flawed, person. During that period, I had a vision that I was standing by a still pond in a forest at night. Everything was black. A mysterious voice urged me to jump in. Afraid, it took me a while. But then I did and found, to my amazement, that the dark pond is where all the "good" stuff is.

I also discovered, through facing my own pain, that I could help other people, almost always by accident. "Daddy" proved to bring meaning to people dealing with various losses. A woman called to tell me that she and her father had become estranged. But now, approaching middle age, she was getting married and, as a way of bringing the two of them back together, she wanted to play "Daddy" for him at her wedding.

In a story that rips me to the core, Bernice Wilson, the former director of the Ohio Hospice Organization, came up to me following a performance at the Ohio Statehouse and told me about a father who was walking his toddler daughter across the street. "She dropped her juice box and went back to get it and was hit by a car and killed."

I gasped.

"He listened to your song, 'Daddy,' over and over and over," she continued, "and I'm here to tell you that song healed that man's soul."

A man I never knew.

I wrote more serious songs and merged them with my funny ones. I released an album with my inspirational songs on one side and live comedy on the other, titled *Two Sides of the Clown*. I added stories to my performances. In time, I became a keynote presenter who mixed songwriting with speaking, and a whole new industry opened for me. From that day on, I kept moving forward, not knowing exactly where I was being led. But I remained open, receptive. The answers came slowly. One gig at a time, often out of nowhere, from around the country. I was unknown to audiences, not a celebrity with a story everybody was waiting to hear. Only a guy with a willingness to share. I had to learn how to capture an audience, which gave me only three to seven minutes to get them on my side. Then I had to keep them, through laughter, stories, songs, and moments of common reflection.

I used to say during those days that if you can't be Elvis, the next best thing is to be a speaker who tells your own stories and sings your own songs. You are shown more respect than bands, get paid better, and if you can earn their attention, you have a captive audience.

I had learned during my radio years that audiences love to laugh, but it took me some time to adjust to their stillness and silence when they were moved. To hear laughter is instant validation, which is why meeting planners love humorists, but to hear nothing while people reflect on what is being said or sung can be frightening, especially if it's a new experience, as it was for me. Plus, there are often a few people who don't like to be moved emotionally and, when they are, they resent it. I paid the price for that a few times, and ultimately accepted it as an occupational hazard for any inspirational performer and speaker. Most adults, though, were fine with being moved, even hungered for it and demonstrated their appreciation.

While there have been many successful performances, the ones that taught me the most about life actually showed me every sign of failure. One of them happened at a school.

It all started with a call from my dear late friend E. Larry Moles, a humorist. Like most funny people, his humor was derived from pain. He told me he was a teenage alcoholic and found himself drunk in a jail cell overnight, his only companion was an older man he didn't know. The next morning his cellmate looked at him and said, "Hey, kid, how old are you?"

"Fifteen," Larry responded.

"What are *you* doing here?" he said. "I'm an old man, I've had my chance in life, and I blew it. But you're only fifteen."

At that moment Larry dedicated himself to recovery. And recover he did. Larry eventually moved to Lima, Ohio, where, among other honors, he introduced President Reagan to an overjoyed home crowd. He spoke all over the country. He billed himself as The Man from Pinch, and delighted his audiences with his many stories from his native town of Pinch, West Virginia.

On this occasion, Larry had a school gig he couldn't make, so he asked me to fill in. It was a few hours away, where he had spoken many times. "They're gonna love you," he promised.

When I arrived to set up, the principal told me that there had been a leadership change, and he had no idea I was coming. I offered to reschedule, but he said he'd rearrange the afternoon so they could do the show.

A spring day, close to graduation, students from sixth through twelfth grade sat in gymnasium bleachers. I was set up in the center circle of the basketball court. It was hot and humid.

I knew I was a dead man.

Even as I scanned for one face that was with me during my performance, I saw no signs of encouragement among students or faculty.

I left the school to the voices of kids hanging out the windows, mocking my song lyrics, making fun of me. I couldn't get out of town fast enough, but my car needed gas, so I stopped at a station just behind the school. No sooner was I there than the school bell rang, releasing everyone for the day.

Little did I know this gas station was the after-school hangout.

As I pressed the gas pump, hoping to make it work a little faster, a car came shooting into the lot and parked hastily. A kid jumped out of the car and walked toward me.

How much jail time if I spray him with this gas hose?

"Hey," he said, "my name's Heath." He stuck out his hand.

Apprehensive, I said nothing, but I shook his hand.

"Listen, I don't know what's wrong with my friends, but I got to tell you it was a great show."

"What?"

"Yeah," he said, cutting to the chase, "I want to tell you something. Two weeks ago, I lost my cousin. He committed suicide. No one knows why."

"Oh my goodness."

"But today was the first day I laughed and saw there was reason for hope."

This young man was beyond his years. Even most older people don't have the courage to be this forthright. I was taken aback.

Now that I knew he was serious, we talked for several more minutes, he invited me to his house to meet his parents, and we've stayed in touch over the years. I even sang at his wedding and his dad's funeral.

I think about this conversation once in a while and realize that sometimes when we think we've failed, we've actually done our most important work. We're the last to know, if we ever find out at all.

What I hadn't anticipated during those years was that by opening myself up to others, how many people would share their lives and stories with me. I was on the road to forming deeper connections with my audience and to discovering my "purpose." While I was gathering major corporate clients, ranging from IBM, General Electric, and Nationwide Insurance, my most gratifying gigs were for the hundreds of service groups—teachers, health care workers, hospice professionals, and others. I also performed for cancer and AIDS survivors. Special Olympians. Children with special needs. People dealing with grief. Veterans. The disabled. First responders and survivors of 9/11.

I was commissioned to write songs for many of these groups. I had reached a point where the songs I relished writing the most were for people who didn't have a voice, who faced challenges of a different kind, or who didn't feel understood because their lives were outside the mainstream of our culture. Populations often overlooked by the conventional music business and other industries.

One of my songs, "Everyone Wins," was commissioned by a man named Jimmie Young of The F.A.M.E. Games in Fostoria, Ohio, then adopted by Special Olympics Ohio, where I was asked to perform it yearly at their Opening Ceremony. Though I sang it for more than twenty-five years, the first time was the most vivid. A crowd of about fifteen thousand Special Olympians, their families, and supporters filed into the lower deck of Ohio Stadium. I was a nervous wreck. Storm clouds were coming in, and it began to drizzle as I went to grab the mic. Scanning the sky, the producer said, "You want to do this?"

Talking myself into it, I said, "Yes."

> . . . And so we move along, not sure just where it ends.
> We take a fall, then get up once again.
> We just never know when something we might do
> will knock somebody down, or maybe pull them through.
>
>> Everyone wins—when we're holding on together.
>> Everyone wins—when we reach with all we have.
>> When we give ourselves to something that comes from deep
>>> within,
>> Everyone wins . . .

I got halfway through the anthem, and, God as my witness, the rain stopped, the clouds cleared, and the sun was shining. The audience's wild enthusiasm was the second surprise of the evening. As I walked off the stage, a man came up to me, told me he loved the song and wanted a copy. I gave him one. It wasn't until later in the ceremony, when he was called up to speak, I realized he was Sargent Shriver, Chairman of Special Olympics International and husband of its founder, Eunice Kennedy. Not long afterward, I unexpectedly received a letter from him.

> You have captured the spirit of Special Olympics in your music and lyrics, the true meaning of competition and participation in sports.
>
> I was especially touched by two of the messages your song conveys: we never know whose life we are touching by what we say or do; and, the true joy we feel when giving ourselves to others.

His letter meant the world to me. A man as busy as Sargent Shriver taking the time to write to me from his heart, to let me know that he had heard the song at its deepest level. What also struck me was that, however unknowingly, he had also described where I happened to be in my personal journey. I couldn't get a higher compliment than that. For so many reasons, his letter, long since framed, still hangs in my office.

For another group, cancer survivors, I wrote "Blossoms of Hope," the title of an annual event conceived by hematologist Dr. Leslie Laufman, which I composed as a vehicle for the voices of survivors to inspire others. The first verse and chorus came fairly easily in the summertime, but I stalled when I reached "second verse hell," as it's known. Meanwhile, in the midst of writing the song, we got an unexpected dose of bad news. My sister Terry was diagnosed with cancer. Vicki and I canceled a trip to Europe and went to help her and her family just outside Washington, D.C. After witnessing her trauma, we returned home, and, in the middle of the night on New Year's Eve, I woke up to the lyrics. While I was happy to have finished the song, the best news of the whole experience continues to be that Terry recovered after "being at death's door," as her surgeon said.

With the song done, I attended a cancer survivors' meeting, led by an oncology nurse, Susan Werlinich, to recruit singers to perform on my recording. I found so much personal value in the survivor meetings, I ended up attending regularly for several years. I said little, listened a lot. I grew into understanding what Herman Hesse meant when he wrote in *Siddhartha*, "The river has taught me to listen; you will learn from it, too. The river knows everything; one can learn everything from it." For years I watched "the river" of cancer survivors come and go, and, through them, I learned. To hear people who are on the edge of life and death talk is, in the words of Bernice Wilson, "to learn at the feet of the masters." Everything said and done in that environment is real. The laughter is real. The tears are real. The fear is real. People don't have time to pretend or put on airs. If they are able to, they often quit their jobs and do what they've always wanted to do, whether it's art, writing, helping others, or resolving conflicts with their friends and family.

I made many friends in the survivor group, including Jake, a lung cancer patient about my age. He'd had an interesting life. At one time, in an attempt to battle his depression, he had moved into a monastery, thinking the solitude would do him good. He found no answers. "The people there had their problems, too," he realized, and after talking with the Abbot, Jake decided to leave. He then took a circuitous route to becoming a master chef.

When Jake was later diagnosed with cancer, he bought an old house in rural Morgan County that needed restoration, a metaphor for his life. "I like to make old things new," he told me, and while digging through the basement he happened upon an original newspaper article about President Lincoln. He was proud to show it to me.

Jake's property was five acres and, on one visit, he handed me a shotgun and taught me how to shoot. The recoil nearly knocked my shoulder out of its socket. On an entirely different note, Jake asked me to tape him delivering a "farewell" to his young daughter.

"There are some things you can't understand until you're older," he said to her, "but I won't be around then, so I'm telling you now." His advice ranged from practical to reflective. "Never buy a new car, find one with a few thousand miles on it." And this bit of universal wisdom: "You'll make some mistakes in love. Forgive yourself."

Although I deeply appreciated Jake's thoughtfulness, I also really enjoyed his sense of humor. In a survivor meeting one night, the conversation turned to whether we believed in psychics, and I said, "I think they're full of shit. I talked to one and she told me that I'd be living a life riding around in limousines. Yeah, like that's happened."

"Well," Jake replied with a grin, "maybe she meant you should've been a chauffeur."

The entire room broke up in laughter.

A few months later, Jake's health declined, and I visited him at Kobacker House. After chatting for a while, we moved outside to the private patio attached to his room. We were in a long conversation when he suddenly stopped talking, as if listening to the world take a breath. He finally spoke. "You know, I've spent my whole life living for everybody else." It was an epiphany for him. He was released from hospice that week, bought a motorcycle, married a woman, and the two of them took off across the country, finally settling in Florida. He was now living the life he'd always wanted. It wasn't until three years later that cancer finally claimed him.

Another young man I got to know in the survivor group, Ken, had advanced lung cancer. He and his wife, Laura, had originally come up to tell me they enjoyed hearing "Blossoms of Hope" over the summer at the survivor event at the Columbus Zoo.

Unfortunately, within a month or two, Ken's health gave way, and I visited him. When I arrived at their house, Ken was in a hospital bed that had been placed in the dining room. Nearby, his son Zac, who had just turned two, played on a massive train table Ken had made for him over the summer, knowing that he might not live until Christmas. As I sat with Ken and watched Zac playing with his trains, I thought about my one-year-old daughter. I couldn't begin to imagine Ken's heartache over leaving his son, whom he had tried to carry up the half-flight staircase a few weeks earlier, only to fall due to his lack of strength.

As I drove home from Ken's, I sat at the traffic light at Martin and Sawmill roads. It was one of the saddest moments of my life. The sorrow Ken and his family were facing was in stark contrast to the hordes of Christmas shoppers zooming by on autopilot.

Are these people even in touch with what matters this season?

Ken died a week later, and Laura asked me to sing at his funeral, two days before Christmas.

"Blossoms of Hope" is simple, easy to sing along with, perfect to be sung in groups. On the recording, we added a children's choir as a reminder that cancer touches everyone. I put together the Voices of Hope Chorus, which welcomed individuals with cancer, their caregivers, and whoever else wanted to join. We'd invite the audience to sing with us. There is simply nothing more inspiring than to see survivors singing about hope in the midst of their cancer journeys. We sang at survivor events all over the country, and I'm still amazed, but grateful that cancer and hospice groups throughout the United States and Canada are using the song to provide inspiration.

A survivor who'd lost a leg to cancer told me in tears she wanted to be a singer, but now with only one leg, that dream was gone. I told her she was wrong, and did what I could for her. I visited her in her apartment and asked her to sing the lead on "Blossoms of Hope" at the annual citywide survivorship event. As I got in my car to leave her home, I was overcome by spontaneous tears.

What if just one time someone had visited my father in all those years and asked him to fulfill a dream of his? How much that would have meant to him.

Another member of the chorus, Keith Brooks, was a lung cancer patient whom I drove to radiation appointments. He gave me a photo of a butterfly, a universal symbol of hope, that had been painted on his head, bald from chemo, at the Blossoms of Hope event. When he died, his widow asked me for permission to have the lyrics to "Blossoms of Hope" chiseled on Keith's gravestone. Her request took my breath away.

"There's your Grammy in heaven, dude," a friend said with a grin.

Two decades later, Keith's widow, Nancy, was diagnosed with cancer herself. In her final days, I visited her in hospice. With her family by her side, we grabbed hands around her bed and all sang "Blossoms of Hope." I leaned over and asked Nancy if she was afraid.

"No."

A few days later, I sang at her funeral.

> Surrounded by the darkness with nowhere else to turn
> and left alone to be a victim of the night.
> Then from out of nowhere someone comes along
> and with a loving hand they lead us to the light.

> Blossoms of hope grow side by side,
> friends help us cope till fears run and hide.
> Energy flows with the love that's inside
> those blossoms of hope . . .

So many of the funerals I was asked to sing at left me with special memories, but the first one, especially. I was sitting in St. Michael Church for a couple hours on a weekday, seeking guidance. I had written a new song I was scheduled to play on the main stage of Columbus's Fourth of July ceremony, *Red, White, and Boom*. The entertainment was running five minutes behind, and the Elvis impersonator refused to give up the stage time for one song, even though I was scheduled for it.

"Oh, man . . ." he indulged himself as his arm swept the massive crowd, "look at all these people here!"

So typical, I thought, and I turned around and walked against the current, blocks and blocks back to my car, into the faces of four hundred thousand people going the other way. The symbolism wasn't lost on me. Despondent, the next day I went to St. Michael Church looking for an answer.

I noticed a man had come into the church and didn't leave after a short while, which I found unusual. When I got up about an hour later, he followed me.

"Excuse me," he said, stopping me after I lit a votive candle, "but aren't you Eric Gnezda?"

I told him I was and he said, "I was just thinking of you today." And with that he explained he was a local funeral director. Curious but uneasy, I resisted joking that I hoped his thoughts hadn't been about measuring my body.

"A couple years ago," he said, "I heard you sing a song at a horse show."

Oh my God. Not that fiasco.

"You sang a song called 'The Gold.' I loved it. I bought a copy and now can't find it. Anyway, I thought it would be perfect for a guy whose service I'm planning now. Is there any way you could send me another copy? I'd like to have your permission to play it at his service this week."

He continued that the young man had some tough breaks in life as he tried to make his way as an entertainer. The funeral director felt the song would be a fitting tribute, especially meaningful to the deceased's family.

I was floored, and I have to say I don't know what got into me, but I told him I'd check my schedule and I'd play it live if I were able. Only later did it sink in that I'd just offered to play at a funeral. A stranger's, nonetheless. Looking back, I see that my prayer had been answered immediately that day. I was being shown there were people who needed my music. Maybe not the ones I had been reaching for, nor the buyers the music industry "targets," but a segment of people who needed comfort and healing.

Being brand new to the "funeral circuit," a shiver went through me when I arrived and was told to set up my keyboard right next to the body, of which, at that point in my life, I had only seen a few. An hour later, everybody walked in and was seated, his parents and family in the middle of the front row. As I sat next to the minister, I caught a glimpse of the death certificate and saw that the deceased was four days older than I.

Chilling.

Finally, it was time to sing. I was expecting the funeral director to explain why he had asked me to be there, but all he said was, "Our soloist today is Eric Gnezda." I suddenly wasn't sure why I had volunteered to attend, other than the funeral director had heard my song a while back and found it inspiring. The family and other mourners sat mere feet from me and my keyboard, making me feel all the more uncomfortable. My biggest fear was that the family might, understandably, see me as an uninvited guest, if not an outright intruder, and they might find the song all wrong for the occasion. I wondered if I would provide the comfort the family needed, and if I would speak the truth of a life taken too soon.

I stepped up to play as an outsider in this all-too-intimate environment.

I finished the song to dead silence, so to speak, which, of course, is expected at a funeral, yet it didn't quell my concern that the funeral director, with his best intentions in mind, may have made a mistake in judgment. After the preacher gave the eulogy, the funeral director rose to excuse everyone. The mother of the deceased interrupted and called him over. A brief whisper between the two, a pause, and then he said, "Eric, she'd like to hear your song again."

Surprised, I rose to sing "The Gold" a second time. I was deeply touched but also had to ward off the irreverent voice inside that said, *Holy shit! You're singing an encore at a funeral!*

Days later, to my amazement, the mother bought copies of the song for everyone who attended the funeral.

By sheer coincidence, after a couple years had passed, I performed at an assisted living facility, and the mother of the deceased came up to me afterward and reintroduced herself. It was wonderful to see her enjoy herself with the veil of grief partially lifted.

Funny how a song, written for a different purpose, can ignite awareness in someone else, even be a source of healing. I wrote "The Gold" during a Summer Olympics, feeling empathy for those who missed a gold medal by a fraction of a second, or who were tripped up during a race, or who, for some unknown reason, weren't themselves that day. I understood their pain and the disappointment in falling short of a lifetime goal.

Later, I was asked to sing at a veterans hospital. There had been no promotion for the concert. What was I to do? Only one patient came and sat alone in the vast auditorium. In my mind, I filled all of the empty seats with the spirits of people I'd known who had left this Earthly plane and played the concert for them and their mystical guests.

At the end of the show, the one man in attendance came up to me in tears.

"You know, my whole life, my family told me I wasn't worth a shit. But that one song you played about not winning the gold made me realize they were wrong. I am worth a shit. Thank you."

My eyes filled too. With gratitude. With empathy. With a strange feeling of brotherhood. We hugged and I thanked him.

I learned a lot that day, not the least of which is that no matter how few people come to a performance, you've always got an audience, even if most of it is in the Unseen.

> ... When you stop and think about it, you see that life has shown
> when you win the world is with you, when you lose, you lose
> alone.

If you wonder if it's worth it under such a circumstance,
just think of those who never take the chance.

> What do you do when you don't win the gold?
> When no one's there to hear you tell the tale you wanted told?
> What do you do with the only dream you knew?
> Well, the record may not show it,
> but you know that there's a champion in you.

Another memorable experience occurred a few years later. I received a call from an organization with an eleventh-hour challenge. They were planning a fundraiser with a major country star who had agreed to sing a song of their choice, if they let her know what it was in plenty of time. So, at the last minute, they contacted me about writing a theme song. "I'll give it my best, but no promises," I said, and I worked on it for several days straight, only to come up with music, but no words. I contacted the organization and apologized to them, saying that writing a song just wasn't in the cards.

Hours afterward, I heard that my friend Pat Hughes had died of cancer. I was heartbroken. Pat had been an unwavering friend, full of wisdom, light, and inspiration to me and many others. She had been sick for a number of years, although the abruptness of her decline was a shock. I sat at the piano to work out my grief, and serendipitously, words fell out about Pat, written to the music I'd come up with for the charity just a day before. I sang it at her funeral, and as her final gift to me, the song continues to provide comfort to people at many other funerals, including my dear friend Jacquie, who lost her nineteen-year-old son to a brainstem tumor. I was also invited to sing "Only God Knows the Reason" at the World Gathering of Bereavement.

More often than not, as a performer and songwriter I became a student, getting unexpected lessons in life. At a holiday vigil for Mothers Against Drunk Driving, my amplifier blew out forty-five minutes before I was to play, leaving me with no sound system. Ty, my sound engineer, called several people he knew for a replacement amp, but had no luck. I was distraught because these people in the audience were suffering, and

I wanted to give them the best music I could provide. It all was put into perspective, however, when the program opened with an address from a gentleman named Bob Kent.

"On Christmas morning at about ten o'clock," he said, "five police officers came to our door. One of them asked, 'Are you Bob Kent?'"

"'Yes, I am.'"

"'Do you have a son named Brandon?'"

"Yes, I do."

"The officer looked away for a moment then looked back at me and said, 'I'm sorry to tell you your son was killed by a drunk driver last night.'"

"My wife immediately collapsed. We just went numb. It didn't seem real then, and it still doesn't seem real even now."

As it turned out, Brandon and two of his friends were hit head-on by a full-size SUV going the wrong way on I-71. Brandon's Jeep flipped and caught on fire, "turning three young men, just beginning the prime of lives, into ashes," Bob said.

The driver of the SUV had three previous DUI arrests. He survived the crash and was sentenced to twenty years in prison.

"I truly believe," Bob said, "that everything you experience, everyone you meet, there's a purpose. We might not know what it is, but there's a purpose to it."

His story devastated me. I looked around the room, at the faces and the walls of photographs they'd put up honoring their lost loved ones. A sad assemblage. Of unspeakable injustice.

When it came time for me to play my songs with no sound, however, I didn't know what to do. Strictly on impulse, I stood up and spoke.

"I came here tonight wanting to play for you all, to give you my best because I can't even begin to imagine what you've been through. My amp went out a few minutes ago and there's no sound. I don't understand why, but as we just heard from Mr. Kent, there's a purpose to everything."

Without my sound system, I had no choice so I simply recited the lyrics to my songs. Afterward, a woman named Corinne LaMarka approached me and said, "Your lyrics are beautiful."

The heartbreak she was about to explain, however, was not.

Her daughter, Jennifer, who'd just graduated from college with honors, was working her first job as district manager at a large grocery chain. Twenty minutes after midnight, she got a call from one of her store managers alerting her to an alarm that was going off. Jennifer rose, got dressed, and took off to the store. Minutes later, at 12:32 a.m., as she was driving, her brand-new silver Camry was T-boned by a brand-new red Camaro that ran a light at 82 mph and sent her car careening into the front of a Lube Stop, which came crashing down on her.

She died at the scene. The other driver was unhurt.

"She was doing everything right," Corinne said, "but was hit by an impaired driver with previous convictions for DUI. She was all of my hopes and dreams. Every year since, I prayed we wouldn't have a Christmas. Christmas carols were Jennifer's favorite songs. Everywhere I went they were in my face. And I threw out my Christmas decorations. Every time I put them up, it killed me. Just killed me."

A musician herself, Corinne could no longer bear to play or listen to music after Jennifer's accident, each note a painful pulse reminding her of her daughter.

Corinne planted a blue spruce in Jennifer's memory outside of her bedroom window. "Now it's probably fifteen feet tall, and all I can think of is how much that tree is growing, and it's a symbol of all those things she's missed out on. The biggest thing I've learned from this is that I'm stronger than I thought I was. Helping other people is my saving grace."

Another mother, Marsha, approached me after a gig and told me the tragic story of how her middle school son was killed by a train. Whether it was an accident or a suicide was undetermined, but his class was graduating from high school in the coming month, and she wanted to make sure he was remembered. "I just can't bring myself to write anything," she said. "Would you?"

How can anyone turn down a request like that? I wrote a letter to the editor, in her name, and it ran the week of commencement.

One gig that made another large impression on me was when I was asked to perform at an awards ceremony for people who had served the community. I was expecting to see the usual faces: CEOs, sports celebrities, and local news personalities. Instead, there were scores of people I'd never even heard of but who had done extraordinary things. They'd contributed countless hours of driving the old and disabled, delivered meals to the homeless, and volunteered childcare. They preferred to remain anonymous and seemed embarrassed at being honored. I was struck by how much important work they'd been doing for no external validation.

These are the people doing the real work.

They taught me that the truest givers work for others with no expectation of anything in return. In time, they, along with a reading of *Let the Trumpet Sound: A Life of Martin Luther King, Jr.*, inspired me to write the anthem, "True Heroes."

> ". . . True heroes are remembered for how they live each day.
> True heroes are measured by what they give away . . ."

Months later, I was commissioned to write a song for a fundraiser to help the homeless. Perhaps I took homelessness more seriously than the event planners, for, as I arrived, they were fretting over the catering layout.

We're talking about homelessness, and you're worried about how the food looks?

Later that night, I sang the song to the standing A-list guests. I finished and walked off stage right. Every last attendee marched to the left. Talk about alienating a crowd. A few minutes later, a woman approached me. "I just came to observe," she said. "I was curious what this event was about. But after hearing your song, I want to contribute a little something." And she handed me a check for $10,000. I thanked her profusely and walked it over to the catering-concerned event planners. I said nothing. The check spoke for me.

I've written many songs since, humorous and inspirational, even had a hit with a Bluegrass song I co-wrote with my buddy Mark Brinkman. But with each step along my journey, I question my motivations. Why am I writing? To become known? To make money? To be a hit songwriter? What if I compose a song that nobody hears or that means something to only one person? Like every artist, I want a big audience to affirm my work is making a difference. After all, isn't success measured by the number of songs you have on the charts? The size of the crowds you play for? The number of books you sell? The paintings exhibited? The dances performed?

Our culture says, "Yes, that's success!" But my experiences gave me a different perspective, one that's confirmed in nature. The Cereus cactus produces a flower that blooms one night a year in the desert. By morning, the wide white flower has withered, along with its exquisite fragrance. No audience to speak of, except for the sphinx moths and nectar-feeding bats that come to pollinate. Apparently, nature provides beauty for beauty's sake, to serve any audience, large, small, or invisible.

Early in my career I performed in a desert of sorts. A nursing home, actually. Having never done it before, I had no idea what to expect. The audience ambled in, with some, sadly enough, immobile, brought in by staff. Throughout my forty-five-minute show, no response. Embarrassed, on my way out, I approached the activities manager to apologize when she grabbed me and said, "I can't remember when this group howled so much!"

I thought she was kidding.

"We'd love to have you back for Mother's Day when all the families will be here!"

Who'd ever kid about Mother's Day? So, I returned in a few weeks, with an expanded definition of a "howling" audience.

On another night, before a morning gig, I was too anxious to sleep, but drifted off just before dawn, only to be jolted awake by a realization:

Your job isn't to be liked. Your job is to serve your audience.

Suddenly, instead of worrying whether an audience was going to like me, my focus became giving the audience what they needed. I became a much more relaxed performer and looked at each job as though I were there for one person who needed something I could give. If every day I could make a difference to one person, then, over a lifetime, I'd reach multitudes. From that point on, validation came not from the size of an audience or their response but from a single individual who might approach me afterward wanting to tell me their story, heartfelt words from a grieving parent, or the guy who told me he'd gone through a divorce and it was the first time he'd laughed in a year. I recognized that I wasn't exclusively in the music business, or the entertainment business, or even the speaking business.

But what business am I in? What's the value of my work? Where do I fit in? Who am I?

I asked those questions for years, receiving no answers in return, wondering if I'd put more faith and belief in the world than it deserved.

I'd often think of the Rumi poem, "Love Dogs," which tells the story of a believer who prays often. When he is challenged by a cynic, he realizes his prayers have never been answered. So he falls asleep, where he meets the guide of souls. The believer tells the guide that all he's ever received from his prayers is a longing. The guide replies that the longing is the answer to his prayers.

Considering that much of today's art, especially many popular songs, provides escapism, I sometimes felt I was unwelcome in the industry because my music invites the listener to work *through* problems rather than avoid them.

In time, I drew encouragement from those who understood me, who took me seriously, and I tried to bring myself to wish the best for those who didn't. Living in a culture that puts so much effort into images, appearances, and credentials, paying less attention to developing virtues underneath, I found that being authentic was the best I could do. While I've never had it in me to play games to be successful, I also accepted in time that if I'm not willing to play the game, I can't expect to receive the world's accolades. I have a need to be honest. My heart needs to be honest. I cannot trust, and find no meaning in, a world that's largely transactional.

Through my years of struggle, people would encourage me to be patient.

"You're planting seeds!" I was told a million times.

But maybe my job was even more humble. Maybe it was to first soften the soil so that seeds, once planted, could germinate. Tilling inch by inch, I unearthed my own truths. Whether I was composing a song, writing a column, telling a funny story, teaching a class, giving a speech, emceeing an event, or sitting bedside listening to the sick or dying, I found my greatest fulfillment came in serving others, whatever form that might take.

Dad's Death

AT dusk, I stood looking out an upper-floor window of Riverside Methodist Hospital. Throughout his many stays in this hospital over the years, Dad had always joked about this particular view, for just over the highway you could see Union Cemetery.

"Just what you want to see when you're in the hospital," he'd say.

As I turned from the window, Mom clicked off the fluorescent lights on the wall above his head, in favor of a pair of table lamps. The lamps, along with the vinyl-cushioned bench that doubled as an undersized bed, were the hospital's way of making this private single room feel more like home. Outside the room, reserved at the farthest end of the hall for the terminally ill, a sign had been posted on the wall to the right of the door: "Family Only."

Mom, Terry, and I were in the room day and night. Niki was home with Gary and their young children. Mom placed her palm on Dad's forehead, clammy from the sweat seeping from his brown hair. We gathered newspapers and magazines that had been strewn about the room over the past few days and began to fan him. His eyes opened partially. The jaundiced whites surrounding his green irises had deepened to yellowish-beige, approaching the color of the brown sediment collecting in the urine bag clamped to his bed. He tried to speak, something he hadn't done in days. We leaned over the bed railing, holding our breaths, poised for a profound statement of wisdom and farewell from a dying man.

With our whole beings, we listened to each halting, barely audible word, anticipating the Secret to Life.

"I feel . . ." he sighed, "like . . . the Shah."

Mom laughed.

It was the first week of June 1980, and because he was so sick with his advanced MS, symptoms of other illnesses were hard to identify, but on Memorial Day, Mom took him to the hospital.

"We can't be sure," the doctor told us in the hospital's private conference room, "but it looks like liver cancer. He's too sick to do a biopsy. I don't think he's going to survive this."

The hospice movement was barely underway in the U.S., so by today's standards, "end of life" treatment was crude, bordering on torture. Every few hours, a respiration "therapist" would show up with his machine. Upon sight of him, Dad would resist, shaking his head and murmuring in terror, "no, no, no." The therapist—a machine himself—showed no emotion as he jammed the green tubes down Dad's nostrils into his lungs to clear fluid, leaving Dad gasping in a gurgling moan.

Hour by hour, Dad's stomach swelled, his already limited movements diminished. The doctor commented on how strong he was. "He wouldn't be hanging on if he weren't such a strong man," the doctor said. Although I had heard the word "strong" in relation to my dad throughout my life, this was the first time it began to register. I filed away his statement.

Dad kept asking, "What's wrong? What's wrong?"

In truth, we didn't know for sure. Mom, never hiding anything, said she didn't know. Nonetheless, Dad requested that he be buried in his blue suit, which he hadn't worn for years.

Tuesday afternoon, the Italian priest whom Grandpa Fort had once cussed out, arrived to administer the Last Rites. Dad was genuinely grateful, and managed to mumble a "thank you." For as long as I could remember, the priest had visited our house regularly to see Dad, always arriving with a smile and a box of Perugina Baci truffles with hazelnuts. A gift we all loved.

"He's a nice guy and a good priest," Dad said one time, "but he's also a fascist."

I chalked up Dad's assessment to his common use of hyperbole to make a point or to evoke a chuckle. But in less than a week I would discover what he meant.

Later that day, Mom took a call for Dad from the familiar voice of Stan "just-too-calm-cool-and-collected" Zalar. Mom put the phone to Dad's ear, and Stan told him the astonishing news that he, himself, was dying of cancer.

By Wednesday night, Dad couldn't talk. "Blink your eyes for yes, Walt," Mom directed. As the week wore on, the parade of characters grew more bizarre, capped off by the dingbat overnight private nurse who failed to recognize Dad had lapsed into a coma. Our patience with her ran out, but she wasn't aware enough to pick up on it.

"I want that woman out of here!" Mom commanded.

"May God bless you all," the dingbat replied as she left with a vapid smile.

The adept hospital nurses, one of whom I went to high school with, took over just past dawn, arriving with Dad's death rattle, each guttural breath slowing like a clock during a countdown. He seemed to be rallying, so we took a momentary leave and sneaked away to the hospital cafeteria for breakfast.

"You know," Mom said, "mornings are the hardest. There's so much hope on the outside, but so little in here."

We returned to Dad's room after 9 a.m. I asked the nurse to step out, and I spent time alone with him. Didn't say much, I just wanted him to know I was with him. Shortly afterward, Mom came in, and as we stood by his bedside just before ten, his eyes widened, cast a golden glow for a second or two, then closed as he drew his last breath.

"Walt! Walt!" Mom cried.

A wind swept through the room to the windows, even though they were fastened shut. With spiritual smugness, I looked to the ceiling to say goodbye and to acknowledge I knew where Dad went. Immediately a voice admonished me to drop my eyes and refocus on the world.

"You've got work to do down here."

It was June 6, D-Day, aptly enough. Dad was just fifty-three, the same age as Gary, eighteen years and four days before cancer took him, too.

On our way home from the hospital, Mom talked about an appropriate way to honor Dad. "I want to give him the recognition he never received in life," she said, "like maybe through a scholarship at Ohio State or something like that. Let's think about it."

I mulled over the options while I showered. At the moment the OSU scholarship entered my mind, the lights went out. "That's it!"

I told the family about the signal I had received.

"Oh, were you in there?" Terry laughed. "I didn't know. I turned the light off."

So much for my second misinterpretation of Divine Intervention that day.

We went to the funeral home, where we chose his casket, and I dropped off his blue suit. Then we went to dinner. I pledged I'd never leave a crumb uneaten after watching the prolonged pain of Dad's last days. In the morning, the train of neighbors began, each delivering plates and plates of food, all kinds. When Ted dropped by to see how I was doing, he asked what he could do.

"Eat some of this food!" I said.

We arrived at Dad's visitation an hour before visitors. Upon seeing him in the casket, Mom cried, "That's not him. He's gone."

"There's got to be more than this life," she said, "or none of this makes any sense."

Conventional wisdom is right about the value of having so much to do after a death—funeral arrangements, writing obits, contacting people—because you can't deal with the grief immediately. The first step of my grief occurred during visitation at the funeral home. Someone said something stupid and I told myself, "I can't wait to go home and tell Dad!"

It hit me. There would never be another chance to go home and tell Dad. Anything. Or hear his funny responses. The waves of grief set in. Washing me away. Out of nowhere. With no warning. Immediately. Unexpectedly. On a car ride. At dinner. In dreams. During a conversation. Walking. Running. Reading. On the phone. I never knew when they would hit. Or how long they would last.

For a man who didn't live a life in the world, Dad sure had a lot of people come to his funeral. My family learned through the years another awful reality surrounding sickness and disability. As Dad's condition worsened, many of his friends from the past, whom we once assumed to be lifelong, grew uncomfortable with his demise and drifted away. In contrast, a few people, some we didn't even know well, stood by Dad every step of the way.

"You learn who your friends are when you're sick," Mom had said many times.

When the funeral came around, it seemed everybody, some perhaps looking to relieve their guilt, came to pay their respects. People told me how much they admired Dad—and my mom. How funny he was. How much I was like him. How he inspired them to endure their own struggles. And yes, some mouthed the tired condolence, "He's in a better place now."

A couple days before the funeral Mass, Mom asked the priest if I could say a few words about Dad during the service.

"Only a priest can speak from the altar," he replied.

Mom, masterful at getting her way through tact, finally talked him into it.

I was told to keep it short, which I did, talking about how Dad would cheer up others, how even in his own four walls he kept up with world events, and how resilient he was in accepting what life had handed him.

A few days later, a cassette tape of the funeral Mass arrived in the mail from the priest. I snapped it into the player, grateful to have an audio monument to my dad, which would include, of course, my tribute to him. Mom and I listened, teary-eyed, in anticipation of my words. When it came time for me to speak, however, there was a click, and the audio cut directly to the priest resuming the service.

The priest had paused the record button while I was speaking.

"See, I told you he was a fascist," I could hear Dad say with a twist in his voice.

"That was the only part of the service I really wanted," Mom said, heartsick.

As the years pass, I continue to discover new depths and dimensions to Dad—and to the stories, images, and memories that still flow from him. No, I still don't know *how* Dad kept going all those years. But as a husband and father myself now, I have some understanding of *what* kept him going—the love he had for his family and friends, the love we had for him, and a deep faith that he never specifically alluded to, yet demonstrated through the quiet acceptance of his illness.

On my bedroom wall hangs a black-and-white photograph of him that Niki took when he was in his mid-forties. He is just as I had seen him thousands of times during his life—lying on his back, arms folded behind his head, his eyes fixed pensively on the ceiling of his bedroom.

Where did his mind travel during all those hours, days, weeks, months, and years when he was left to his own thoughts?

As a college student pondering my own future, I sat in his wheelchair, next to his bed.

"Dad? What did you used to dream about when you were my age?" I asked.

"All the money I'd have," he replied in a tone, not of bitterness at what fate had handed him, but of a wiser man now amused at the irony of what he once considered important.

"And how do you accept things you can't change?"

"You just do."

Words so pure and simple, but demonstrating such strength.

The doctor's words come back to me: "He wouldn't be hanging on if he weren't such a strong man."

My dad *was* strong.

I had witnessed it firsthand throughout my life, but it didn't register until he was in the hospital for the last time. He held on so bravely and for so long because it was the only way he could show me his strength, inside and out. Life gave him no other way. How sad. How remarkable. A life with disability was his endurance race, and he showed me how to run it with faith, one step at a time, giving it every last breath he had.

When I was home from college on summer break, one night I was particularly aware of how alone he must have felt. I gathered my courage and went into his darkened bedroom.

"I love you, Dad."

"I love you, too, Eric."

And I walked out.

Words I will never regret.

Unlike Mom and me, Dad and I never got to enjoy each other as two adults. How I'd love to sit in his wheelchair again, by his bedside, and talk. And listen. And laugh. I might even tell him how sorry I am that it took his dying for me to fully see who he truly was.

"That's the way it goes," I can hear him respond.

Yes, that *is* the way it goes, I've learned. But how lucky I am to have been his son. Every day he still shows me so much about life. More than if he'd been healthy. How I miss him. He was a living testimony to the value of any life. As long as we can breathe, we can give. We can grow. We can love.

* * * * * * * * * * * *

DADDY'S WHEELS

Daddy's first set of wheels was a hand-me-down Schwinn.
Leather seat and a canvas bag to carry newspapers in.
It was an uphill demon and a downhill flash.
The fastest bike a boy had ever owned.
    When he finished up his route, he'd buy himself a double scoop.
    Then Daddy's set of wheels took him home.

Daddy's next set of wheels was the one he called "the Bomb."
Polished chrome and a red rose for his first date with Mom.
He took it slow and steady, but they both fell fast.
The only love their hearts had ever known.
    Before the end of spring, he surprised her with a ring.
    Then Daddy's set of wheels took them home.

        Thirty years of happiness, good health, good home, and thankfulness.
    Then out of the blue one day, he lost the feeling in his legs.

Daddy's last set of wheels were on the side of a chair.
Padded seat and two handles so we could push him everywhere.
He fought an uphill battle, he went downhill fast.
The bravest man I swear I've ever known.
    I sat there at his side, he squeezed my hand "Goodbye."
    Then Daddy's set of wheels took him home.

Daddy's first set of wheels was a hand-me-down Schwinn . . .

ABOUT THE AUTHOR

ERIC GNEZDA is an award-winning singer-songwriter and the creator and host of *Songs at the Center*, a TV series that airs on PBS stations throughout the country. On his TV shows, he features and interviews well-known songwriters, such as Janis Ian, John Oates, Ray Stevens, and emerging talent.

Based in Ohio, Eric entertains throughout the country, performing his own material that ranges from serious to humorous, at such notable venues as Nashville's Bluebird Cafe and concert halls.

His songs have been featured on ESPN, *Entertainment Tonight*, *Car Talk*, and NPR's *All Things Considered*. Also a keynote speaker, Eric inspires audiences at countless events for corporations, service, and trade associations. His anthem, "Everyone Wins," has been used nationally to promote the Special Olympics, while "Blossoms of Hope" has been a favorite song among cancer survivors throughout the U.S. and Canada.

Detroit-area DJ Phil Maq deemed his ballads, "Daddy's Wheels," about his disabled father, and "Separation," commenting on a fractured America, two "of the best songs ever recorded."

Eric is a recipient of the Ohioana Citation for Music Composition, and was named "Best Satirist of the Year" by *Columbus Monthly* magazine, which described him as "witty and caustic without being cruel." He was also a humor columnist for the *Columbus Dispatch* and an Emmy-nominated TV journalist.

Eric taught public speaking for twelve years at his alma mater, Ohio Wesleyan University, and earned his MFA from the Rainer Writing Workshop at Pacific Lutheran University.

For more information on Eric, see his website, **gnezda.com**.

www.ingramcontent.com/pod-product-compliance
Lightning Source LLC
Chambersburg PA
CBHW010929180426
43194CB00045B/2840